Public Pages

Joe R. and Teresa Lozano Long Series in Latin American and Latino Art and Culture

Public Pages

Reading along the
Latin American Streetscape

MARCY SCHWARTZ

University of Texas Press *Austin*

Copyright © 2018 by the University of Texas Press
All rights reserved

Requests for permission to reproduce material from this work should be sent to:
Permissions
University of Texas Press
P.O. Box 7819
Austin, TX 78713-7819
utpress.utexas.edu/rp-form

♾ The paper used in this book meets the minimum requirements of ANSI/NISO Z39.48-1992 (R1997) (Permanence of Paper).

Library of Congress Cataloging Data
Names: Schwartz, Marcy E., 1958– author.
Title: Public pages : reading along the Latin American streetscape / Marcy Schwartz.
Description: First edition. | Austin : University of Texas Press, 2018. | Includes bibliographical references and index.
Identifiers: LCCN 2017036470| ISBN 978-1-4773-1517-0 (cloth : alk. paper) | ISBN 978-1-4773-1518-7 (pbk. : alk. paper) | ISBN 978-1-4773-1519-4 (library e-book) | ISBN 978-1-4773-1520-0 (nonlibrary e-book)
Subjects: LCSH: Literacy programs—Latin America. | Literacy—Latin America. | Reading—Social aspects—Latin America. | Literature and society—Latin America. | City and town life—Latin America. | Public spaces—Latin America.
Classification: LCC LC155.L3 S37 2018 | DDC 374/.0124098—dc23
LC record available at https://lccn.loc.gov/2017036470

doi:10.7560/315170

In memory of Sarah Hirschman, mentor and friend, who empowered thousands across the Americas to read and enjoy literature.

For Rick, Ab, and Sam, my family of readers.

"Necesidad"
Entrar a los baños públicos únicamente para leer lo que escriben en las puertas.
["Necessity"
Going into public bathrooms only to read what people write on the doors.]
IRMA VALDÉS TRUJILLO, *SANTIAGO EN 100 PALABRAS*, VOL. 10

Culture is conversation, and writing, reading, translating, publishing can be the spark that lights the fire of that conversation. Publishing a book means placing it in the middle of a conversation; organizing a publishing house, a bookstore, or a library is organizing a conversation. A conversation that begins as a local tertulia *but that embraces all times and places.*
GABRIEL ZAID, *LEER*

Contents

List of Illustrations **ix**

Acknowledgments **xiii**

Introduction: City Reading: Public Space and Cultural Citizenship in Latin America **1**

1. Campaigning for the Capital: Bogotá and Buenos Aires as UNESCO World Book Capitals **39**

2. Reading on Wheels: Stories of *Convivencia* in Bogotá and Santiago **84**

3. *Cacerolazos y bibliotecas*: Solidarity, Reading, and Public Space after the Argentine Economic Crisis (2001–2002) **122**

4. Recycled Reading and the Cartonera Collectives: Publishing from the Ground Up **149**

5. Books That Bite: Libraries of Banned Books in Argentina **191**

Conclusion: Stories at the Intersection **227**

Notes **239**

Works Cited **263**

Index **283**

Illustrations

Figures 0.1a and b. Pedro Nel mural and detail **6**
Figure 0.2. Biblioteca José Vasconcelos, Mexico City **10**
Figure 0.3. *Literatura de cordel* **11**
Figure 0.4. "Cuento contigo" banner, Montevideo **17**
Figures 1.1a and b. Marta Minujín's *Torre de Babel de Libros* **40**
Figure 1.2. Bogotá World Book Capital logo **47**
Figure 1.3. Bogotá, an Open Book, call for proposals **54**
Figures 1.4a and b. Gente y Cuentos folder **60**
Figure 1.5. Biblioestación **62**
Figure 1.6. Banner with Bogotá campaign logo **63**
Figure 1.7. Feria Internacional del Libro, Buenos Aires **67**
Figure 1.8. Buenos Aires World Book Capital logo **68**
Figure 1.9. Books published under the Buenos Aires World Book Capital campaign **69**
Figure 1.10. Oliverio Girondo book offered to tram passengers in Buenos Aires **71**
Figure 1.11. Cover of *La ciudad contada* **74**
Figure 2.1 Libro al Viento logo **95**
Figure 2.2. Books at TransMilenio stations **95**
Figure 2.3. Libro al Viento books **97**
Figure 2.4. *Bogotá contada* cover **103**
Figure 2.5. Santiago en 100 Palabras books **105**

Figure 2.6. Winning story displayed on bus billboard   **106**

Figures 3.1a and b. Pots and pans, symbols of the street protests   **125**

Figure 3.2. "Out with them all!" flyer   **126**

Figure 3.3. Centro Azucena Villaflor flyer   **130**

Figure 3.4. Newsletter cover   **132**

Figure 3.5. Balvanera newsletter cover   **134**

Figure 3.6. Brukman Factory newsletter   **134**

Figure 3.7. Newsletter cover   **137**

Figure 3.8. Questionnaire, Belgrano-Nuñez newsletter   **138**

Figure 3.9. Questionnaire results, Belgrano-Nuñez newsletter   **139**

Figure 3.10. Newsletter cover   **142**

Figure 3.11. Newsletter cover   **142**

Figure 3.12. Newsletter cover   **147**

Figure 4.1. Cartonera archival materials, University of Wisconsin–Madison   **150**

Figure 4.2. Selection of Eloísa Cartonera books   **151**

Figure 4.3. Painted storefront window of Eloísa Cartonera, Buenos Aires   **152**

Figure 4.4. Lúcia Rosa of Dulcinéia Catadora working with a stencil   **156**

Figure 4.5. Bookmaking at the Eloísa Cartonera studio   **156**

Figure 4.6. Cartonera publishers' binding and decoration   **157**

Figure 4.7. Dulcinéia Catadora books   **157**

Figure 4.8. Encuentro Cartoneras, Santiago, Chile, 2015   **159**

Figure 4.9. House on Eloísa Cartonera's rural property in Buenos Aires province   **160**

Figure 4.10. Eloísa Cartonera stand at the Twenty-Seventh São Paulo art biennial   **165**

Figure 4.11. Photograph by Paiva and poem by Barbosa in *SigniCidade*   **167**

Figure 4.12. Sandwich board urban writing intervention   **169**

Figure 4.13. Eloísa Cartonera kiosk, Buenos Aires   **175**

Figure 4.14. Eloísa Cartonera kiosk, Buenos Aires   **175**

Figure 4.15. Mural painted on Eloísa Cartonera kiosk, Buenos Aires **176**

Figure 4.16. Map in Amapola Cartonera's *El regateo, la ñapa y la vaca* **182**

Figure 4.17. Amapola Cartonera's *El regateo, la ñapa y la vaca* **183**

Figure 4.18. Amapola Cartonera's *Libro contable* **183**

Figure 4.19. Collage in *Libro contable* **186**

Figure 5.1. *Los condenados de la tierra*, Marcelo Brodsky **192**

Figure 5.2. Censorship decree, Museo del Libro y de la Lengua, Buenos Aires **195**

Figure 5.3. Mural at the Archivo Provincial de la Memoria, Córdoba **195**

Figure 5.4. Archivo Provincial de la Memoria: broken wall **197**

Figure 5.5. Archivo Provincial de la Memoria: facade **199**

Figure 5.6. Sign for Olimpo library **204**

Figures 5.7a and b. Shelves of banned books at Olimpo **205**

Figure 5.8. "Life albums" in memory of Olimpo victims **207**

Figure 5.9. Olimpo's banned books at the 2010 Frankfurt book fair **210**

Figure 5.10. La Grieta logo **213**

Figure 5.11. Shelf at La Grieta **216**

Figure 5.12. Poster for Libros que Muerden event **217**

Figure 5.13. Walrus role-playing activity **217**

Figure 5.14. Pages from *Libros que muerden* **220**

Figure 5.15. Display of banners at the Archivo, Córdoba **224**

Figure 5.16. Rayuela from the video *Los condenados de la tierra*, Marcelo Brodsky **225**

Figure 6.1. *Juanito Laguna aprende a leer*, Antonio Berni **228**

Acknowledgments

When a graduate student gave me a little book of short stories about Santiago, Chile, written by ordinary citizens and distributed free in the subway, I had no idea that it would send me on a ten-year exploration of public literary reading programs throughout Latin America. My first thank you goes to Macarena Urzúa, now a valued colleague and dear friend, whose gift launched the following pages.

The urban public campus of Rutgers, the State University of New Jersey, has been my professional home since the beginning of my career. Our fascinatingly diverse student population, including many first-generation college students, and our location in the middle of a gritty river town with dynamic Spanish-speaking immigrant communities have shaped my teaching, community service, and research. I have welcomed the challenge of rethinking how cities work, read, speak, move, and change in dialogue with students and colleagues.

I am especially grateful to the American Council of Learned Societies and the National Endowment for the Humanities for yearlong research fellowships that offered me the time for research, travel, and writing. I gratefully recognize Liliana Sánchez, who was the chair of my department at that time, for her unfailing support for my research. I thank the Rutgers School of Arts and Sciences Dean's office for supporting me during these two years of fellowship leave, for a sabbatical, and for research funds provided for this project. My thanks also to the Rutgers Office of Research and Sponsored Programs for a Research Council grant to cover the cost of images.

Rutgers has offered me a number of stimulating opportunities for research and interaction with scholars outside my department. In particular, I benefited from a year as a faculty fellow at the Center for

Cultural Analysis from 2011 to 2012. My colleagues who coordinated the seminar on public knowledge, Henry Turner and Meredith McGill, encouraged a productive and supportive intellectual exchange that propelled this project. The Aresty Undergraduate Research Center at Rutgers facilitated my research through the undergraduate research assistance program. Working with students who were new to humanistic research was a happy experience, and I especially want to thank Harold Mesa, Julia Bordelon, and Imani Reed for providing not only key technical support but also enlightening dialogue and lasting friendship.

I owe a debt to Melissa Gasparotto, the Rutgers University librarian for Spanish and Latin American studies, who assisted me every step of the way. My immense gratitude for her keen eye in identifying books for my project on her acquisition trips, for her bibliographic guidance, for her dogged attempts—always successful!—to resolve my RefWorks challenges, and for reading drafts of chapters. Always an inquisitive and engaged interlocutor, she has become a beloved friend.

Libraries have understandably been key sites in my research for this book. They are not only essential repositories of knowledge, but also sites for public reading where I've been privileged to observe programs during my fieldwork. Each one of them, from the modest San Gabriel community library in Sopó, Colombia, to the Princeton University Library, to the huge public Biblioteca José Vasconcelos in Mexico City, has given me a wealth of resources and hands-on experience with what the institution of a library can accomplish.

I am immensely grateful for the guidance of and conversations with librarians who have generously shared their resources, expertise, technical know-how, and kind encouragement. Fernando Acosta from the Princeton University Library has been a generous interlocutor and has offered me privileged access to materials even before they've been catalogued. In particular, Princeton's unique Latin American Ephemera Collection has been an invaluable resource. I am very grateful for the help of Paloma Celis Carbajal, Latin Americanist librarian at the University of Wisconsin–Madison, who generously has extended herself to me for interviews, read drafts of chapters, and shared documentation. She hosted me at the library, where I spent a marvelous week reading and photographing *cartonera* books and benefiting from the internationally renowned collection established through her tireless efforts. Thanks to Ksenija Bilbija and Paola Hernández, as well, for inviting me to speak on campus, for logistical help, and for their excellent company during my Madison visits. Patricia Vélez, currently the director of the library at the Universidad del Externado in Bogotá, has helped me learn and appreciate how libraries in Latin America function, are maintained, are sustained (or not), and serve the public. We spent an unforgettable marathon week together visiting libraries in Medellín, complete with the International Poetry Festival, which would have been instructive but not nearly as much fun without her master planning, good nature, and *camaradería*.

During the course of researching public reading, I have been invited to lecture at academic institutions, libraries, and nonprofits in the United States and in Latin America. Along the way I received essential feedback and much encouragement. Rossana Nofal invited me to participate in a fascinating symposium on literature and social action at the Universidad Nacional de Tucumán, where I learned about many inspiring reading programs, such as those conducted in prisons and rural communities. I was honored to speak at the Congreso de Bibliotecarios hosted by Colombia's Biblioteca Nacional, where I met dedicated librarians from all over the country working in some of the most difficult and tragic circumstances imaginable. Each one of these occasions offered me privileged opportunities to interact with readers, colleagues, and students, and to learn directly from the institutions, organizations, and individuals on the front lines of reading promotion in Latin America—often against all odds.

This project has required extensive travel to Latin America, and on-the-ground assistance made each visit productive and thoroughly enjoyable. Without this help, I would have returned with lots of books and intriguing urban itineraries but might have bypassed the real action in public reading. The logistical support, hospitality, and extended conversations turned interviewing and fieldwork into a source of lifelong friends. My appreciation is truly heartfelt for Julio Paredes Castro, Ana Roda, Patricia Vélez, Erika Ávila, Roberto Gutiérrez, Carrie Bancroft, and Juan Villegas in Colombia; Rossana Nofal, Gabriela Pesclevi, Josefina Delgado, Washington Cucurto, and María Gómez in Argentina; Carmen García, Antonia Viu, Claudia Darrigrandi, Macarena Urzúa, Viviana Pinochet-Cobos, and Juan José Adriasola in Chile; Dan Russek and Pamela Scheinman in Mexico; and Lúcia Rosa and Jorge Schwartz in Brazil.

I have been active for twenty years in the nonprofit organization People and Stories/Gente y Cuentos, through which I lead short story reading and discussion groups at prisons and adult education centers in New Jersey. Thanks to Sarah Hirschman's vision and leadership, this group that began in Colombia and became established as a nonprofit in New Jersey has returned to Latin America. The training workshops and follow-up mentoring I have been part of in Colombia, Argentina, and Chile have been most rewarding experiences that have greatly informed this book.

I am fortunate to have dedicated mentors with seemingly infinite patience and generosity. For this project in particular, Vicky Unruh, Alejandro Herrera-Olaizola, and Diana Sorensen have been steadfast supporters. I offer them my deepest gratitude and the commitment to pay it forward with my own students and colleagues on the basis of their example.

I am very grateful to those who read drafts of chapters along the way and offered valuable feedback: Pamela Scheinman, Paola Hernández, Georg Leidenberger, Carla Giaudrone, Antonia Viu, Nancy Sorkin, Dan Russek, and my own family: Rick, Sam, and Abbie. I hope they will see their hand in the pages that follow.

Selma Cohen—faithful research assistant, editor extraordinaire, and devoted friend—performed more essential functions than I can enumerate. Her keen eye, expert fact-checking, bibliographical mastery, and intelligent interventions throughout the process have contributed enormously to this project. My appreciation is boundless for her dedication, patience, sense of humor, hand-holding, and ever-present companionship and affection. In this unusual relationship, in which we have taken turns as teacher and student, I am certain I have benefited more than she has.

Many thanks to the University of Texas Press acquiring editor Kerry Webb and her assistant, Angelica Lopez-Torres, for their enthusiastic response to this project from the start and for their expert shepherding of the book to publication. I also gratefully acknowledge Craig Epplin and an anonymous reader for their pertinent suggestions.

The biggest thanks of all goes to my family for believing in this project, putting up with my absences while traveling, and always encouraging me. Our daughters, Abbie and Sam, as teenagers convinced me that these public urban literary findings from my trips to Latin America should become a book. Urban adventurers themselves, they have guided us on wondrous city rambles where they have introduced me to some of my favorite bookstores and public culture. Their own writing—poetry, zines, illustrations—tops my private reading canon. I am grateful to my husband, Rick, whose intellectual brilliance and tough questions keep me on my toes (especially when we dance salsa!). His love, understanding, and ever vibrant conversation weave through everything that I do.

A shorter version of chapter 2 first appeared as "Reading on Wheels: Stories of *Convivencia* in the Latin American City," in *Latin American Research Review* 51, no. 3 (2016): 181–201. A shorter version of chapter 3 was published in Spanish as "Cacerolazos y bibliotecas: Lectura, solidaridad y espacio público después de la crisis argentina de 2001–2002," *Revista de Humanidades* 35 (2017): 15–43. I gratefully acknowledge both journals' permission to reprint parts of these articles in this book.

INTRODUCTION

City Reading: Public Space and Cultural Citizenship in Latin America

First, some numbers. Chilean citizens submitted more than 50,000 stories to the short story contest Santiago en 100 Palabras in 2007. UNESCO named two Latin American cities, Bogotá and Buenos Aires, World Book Capitals in the first ten years of this annual award. Nearly one hundred cardboard-book publishers have been founded all over Latin America and abroad to make and sell inexpensive handmade books since Eloísa Cartonera started binding books in reused cardboard in 2003. Two of Argentina's public memory centers, former secret centers of detention and torture, collect and display hundreds of books banned during the country's last dictatorship. The Mexican nonprofit Brigada para Leer en Libertad, established in 2010, has given away 500,000 books, all of them literary and historical titles that the group publishes to accompany free reading events held in public spaces. Libro al Viento, a municipally sponsored series that circulates literary books on buses in Bogotá, Colombia, has published more than one hundred titles since it began in 2004.

These initiatives, all examples of public reading in Latin America in the past fifteen years, demonstrate how cities have harnessed reading literature as a collective activity for social and political results. For this book I have studied recent and ongoing public reading programs in cities in Argentina, Chile, Mexico, Brazil, and Colombia that defy the conception of reading as solitary and private by taking literature to the streets and creating new communities of readers. These programs have in common a cluster of characteristics: they all use public space, distribute creative writing to a mass public, foster collective rather than individual reading, and provide access to literature in unconventional arenas. From institutional and official to informal and spontaneous, these programs invest in reading for both social and literary value.

Evident in these programs is a shift in emphasis in urban cultural policy since 2000 that responded to economic and political change. Public reading demonstrates how, after decades of neoliberal economic policies following (or sometimes working hand in hand with) dictatorship and political violence, literary works are put to the service of rebuilding civic trust and urban belonging. In order to do this, the programs coalesce around three broad goals: first, reclaiming of public space after years of neoliberal privatization; second, reinvestment in urban citizenship amid the transition to democracy and struggles for peace; and third, a questioning and reconfiguration of the lettered city in attempts to expand access to books, particularly literary works, beyond the urban elite. In order to lay the groundwork for appreciating the contribution of literature to contemporary urban public citizenship, this introductory chapter offers a historical overview of reading and book culture and reviews definitions and debates around ideas of the public sphere in Latin America.

Rather than taking a completely novel turn, recent urban public reading programs in Latin America revise and reenact some historical strategies from the colonial and early national periods for forging a literate, or lettered, elite and for implementing expansive literacy and education policies. Although this book looks at programs that promote literary reading rather than functional literacy training, the extensive literacy campaigns in the mid to late twentieth century in Cuba and Nicaragua following those countries' revolutions offer more recent examples of politicized national initiatives akin to those in the region's emerging nations in the nineteenth century. The fact that nearly every Latin American country today has at least one and in some cases several national organizations for promoting books and reading also demonstrates a high level of institutional support and recognition for the importance of reading in public life.

The public literary programs I study here are linked to a historical panorama of policies and projects that reveal the long-standing presence of reading in Latin American culture, which Claudia Darrigrandi and Antonia Viu define as "a complex and multidimensional phenomenon that involves regulating institutions and structures, practices available through particular technologies, carried out within politically situated corporalities and within concrete sensorial frameworks, and that relies on specific material formats and modes of circulation, ... expanding the definitions of reading ... from an exclusively cognitive activity ... to examine reading as an experience, and not only as a means to other ends" (12).[1] This book contributes to the history of Latin America's culture of reading by exploring recent programs in cities, particularly those that exemplify what Viu and Darrigrandi identify as the spaces and types of sociability, as well as the materiality of printed books put in circulation in order to reach a wider range of readers.[2]

Literary texts are what these public reading programs print in books, on billboards, and in pamphlets; and literary sources are at the center of the performances and activities that public reading sites host. The works range from texts by classical and renowned writers to those by emerging writers and even ordinary citizens. In their own way and in concert with their objectives, the programs define literature and determine the kinds of works they are interested in promoting. Yet they all coincide in recognizing the category of literature as creative writing in any genre that circulates for aesthetic pleasure and imaginative experience. Literature as conceived, produced, and distributed by these programs has intrinsic poetic and humanistic value. Reading the texts and participating in activities around them does not help participants acquire skills; nor does it constitute completion of educational assignments or preparation for any concrete aim.[3] These programs invest in reading for enjoyment that prompts social interaction to construct new collective urban imaginaries.

Due to the complex nature of the texts in these programs, reading them presupposes a certain level of literacy. Therefore, the programs that I consider are less concerned with functional literacy—reading and writing competence as educational and practical skills—than with the social and political benefits of literary reading. Brian Street, one of the pioneers of New Literacy Studies, calls for an interdisciplinary approach to literacy that brings together ethnography, sociology, sociolinguistics, education, material culture, and literary studies "to explore the associations between cultural conventions, literacy practices, notions of self, person and identity and struggles over power" (*Social Literacies* 135). This approach insists that "reading and writing are always social and cultural events" (Sheridan, Street, and Bloome 4) and distinguishes between "autonomous" functional literacy and a more interconnected and fluid view of reading and writing practices: "rather than view literacy practices as a static set of situated ways of using written language, it may be more useful to think of literacy practices as an evolving and dynamic set of social practices that are always at a nexus of processes of social change, struggle and stability" (Sheridan, Street, and Bloome 5).[4] Contemporary urban public reading programs in Latin America emerge precisely to address the changes and struggles of their communities of readers. From the content to the material formats, these initiatives, which rely on urban infrastructure and emphasize circulation and accessibility, respond directly to each city's particular opportunities, needs, and crises.

While my consideration of public reading is anchored in contemporary Latin American urban contexts, David Henkin previously coined the phrase in *City Reading*, a study of reading in antebellum New York. Henkin describes public reading as "a set of practices that pervade everyday life" and that "take place in the bustling public space of New York, rather than in one of the domestic interiors in which we often set the modern reading experience" (17, 2). He examines an array of printed media—commercial signs, banners, newspapers, and broadsides, as well as books—as building blocks of urban space and experience. For Henkin, cities like New York "were built, in part, of words, words that took material form in public space, . . . rendering much of the city legible to strangers and facilitating forms of access and interaction" (5, 14).

Although most of the examples I elaborate in the following chapters involve printed books put into circulation in Latin American public urban space, they often rely on other printed visual forms, as Henkin shows for New York, such as banners, signs, billboards, newsletters, flyers, and posters that are extensions of those books. These various print formats not only publicize the books but also make them more publicly visible by inserting them into everyday urban experience. According to Susana Zanetti, an Argentine literary critic who devoted most of her scholarly work to reading in Latin America, "there has not been much research on reading, on the reading habits of different sectors of the reading public, or on the differences between these sectors in various parts of the Americas, or attention given to different historical periods" (27). This book aims to fill part of that gap by revealing the connection between literary reading and urban public space, and the impact of this connection on citizenship and urban belonging, through current municipal policies, institutional programs, and grassroots initiatives.

The Place of Reading in Latin America

Pedro Nel Gómez's (1889–1984) painted mural in 1979 titled "Homenaje a la Inteligencia Antioqueña" (Homage to Antioquian Intelligence), located at the entrance to the Pilot Public Library in Medellín, Colombia, depicts human development through reading (see figures 0.1a and b). This library, which opened in 1952, is the second UNESCO-sponsored pilot library (the first was in Delhi, India) and the first in Latin America. It is part of an international initiative to boost libraries and access to reading in developing countries.

Gómez's mural occupies the walls just inside the entrance, now a reading room, where the city's first bookmobile, the Bibliobus, parked in the 1970s and 1980s. The Bibliobus appears in the mural, as do numerous scenes of reading that illustrate the importance of books to people at every stage of life, from infants whose mothers read to them, to children and adolescents reading with their teachers, to adult professionals with shelves full of books. Gómez dedicated much of his work to large-scale public murals, whose social function, like that of libraries, is to reach a broad public. In his own writing about mural fresco painting, the artist calls the mural a poem and extends the metaphor to an open book: "A mural is an open book that people will read every day without even being aware of it. They'll live with it, and it will fill them with hope" (quoted in Bedoya de Flórez and Estrada Betancur 25–26). The mural invites *antioqueños* to embrace the emancipatory role of human intelligence that the library serves and supports.

The integration of reading and literature in public space and public policy is not new in Latin America; in fact, putting literature and reading to the service of social and political agendas was one of the strategies of colonization and Christianization, as well as a crucial tool for nation formation after independence. While the mural in the Medellín library presents reading and books as edifying tools for peace, education, culture, and cooperation, in Latin American history the book has also been a tool of subjugation, violence, and domination.

A pivotal episode of Francisco Pizarro's conquest of the Incan empire, for example, hinges on a book and marks reading as a dangerous scene for misunderstanding and destruction. In 1532 the Incan leader Atahualpa was to meet Pizarro in Cajamarca's main square. Pizarro and his soldiers hid in waiting while the Incan was carried in on an elaborate altar. The Dominican friar Vicente de Valverde approached him, handed him a book, and told him that it held God's truth. The Incan leader briefly leafed through the pages but found no truth in this "European object which had no counterpart in the prehispanic Andes" (MacCormack 163), and so he threw it to the ground. His rejection of the book and, by extension, of Christianity, was grounds for

Figures 0.1a and b. Pedro Nel mural and detail; author photo

attack by the Spaniards. They descended on the square, captured Atahualpa, and took over the empire. In the many versions of this story, including pictorial versions such as woodcuts and even drawings by Felipe Guaman Poma de Ayala, the role of the book is central. Peruvians still retell the story, treating it as a seminal scene in the contact zone, in which a book that held dubious untranslated knowledge wielded enormous destructive power.[5]

Another dimension of the colonial and postcolonial relationship between books and power is spatial. The intricate association between urban infrastructure and literate and literary culture has its roots in what Ángel Rama calls the lettered city, a concentration of legal, religious, and educational writing institutions established in colonial urban centers and perpetuated after independence. Rama's class-based analysis of the urban lettered elite points out how the persistent exclusion of the majority of people in Latin America from public access to information, education, and published work limited their active participation in civic culture. Both bureaucratic city administration and the geographical mapping of colonial urban design left lasting constraints on urban interaction and expression. Rama first reviews how imposing urban order was one of the European strategies for taming and controlling Latin American "New World" territory, a process that required both a map and a script so that urban space and writing became intertwined: "they required a writer of some sort (a scribe, a notary, a chronicler) to cast their foundational acts in the form of imperishable signs" (6). As cities consolidated literate culture, intellectuals became the "designers of cultural models raised up for public conformity" (22). Rama's suggestion that public ideologies are designed in and emanate from spatial practices in the city has particular relevance for this study of urban public reading.

Rama's *The Lettered City* is an unfinished work published posthumously one year after his tragic death in a plane crash. The last chapter, "The City Revolutionized," treats the dynamics of late-nineteenth- and early-twentieth-century urban life; it appears that Rama planned to continue to trace the Latin American urban lettered trajectory up to the present. Projecting forward from what does appear in *The Lettered City*, one can see Rama's work in dialogue with the "right to the city" theories of David Harvey and others. Harvey's *Rebel Cities* updates some of Rama's Marxist arguments about global social space in the city since 2008, with the cautiously hopeful valorization of urban popular culture "as produced through the common relationships of everyday life" (112).[6]

Juan Poblete traces some of the significant prescriptive strategies around reading during the colonial period, when the church controlled who read the Bible to protect it from individual interpretations, and in the nineteenth century, when serial novels revolutionized a wider reading public. Poblete distinguishes between the sacralization of the book for Christianizing indigenous peoples and the secularization of reading, particularly in urban centers, after independence, thanks to the proliferation of print periodicals. The increased circulation of and access to literary materials such as serial novels marks the "persistent shift from the scarce and elitist book to the newspaper and relatively large amount of mass-printed matter" that was able to reach a much wider reading public, including women ("Reading as a Historical Practice" 183). I question Poblete's stark differentiation between individual and collective reading; in the chapters that follow I describe how individual and collective reading practices often overlap and motivate one another. While Poblete concludes that reading during colonization and early nation building in Latin America offers "important technologies in the formation of submissive subjects, worshippers, and/or citizens" ("Reading as a Historical Practice" 190), I assert that contemporary public reading creates participatory citizens.

As William Acree demonstrates so convincingly in *Everyday Reading*, "the act of reading was one of national importance" in Latin America's new independent states (11). He distinguishes "everyday reading" from reading for personal aesthetic or specialized knowledge, which implies much more limited access. Acree's study reveals a productive meshing of written and oral everyday reading practices, and of individual and group reading. He concludes that for the historical period that he studies, "group reading was hands down the most frequently exercised reading practice," and he notes "the gradual progression from collective, group reading to individual silent reading on a large scale" into the twentieth century (191). I concur with Acree that print culture goes beyond the materiality of printed texts and written words; it encompasses "the relations between the practices of reading and writing, on the one hand, and social behaviors, individual and collective values, economic transactions, political decisions, state institutions, and ideologies, on the other" (3). Printed images, schoolbooks, postage stamps, and currency all constitute print culture, as do those who read them, distribute them, collect them, or listen to texts read aloud. These scenes of reading, then, include printed texts as well as the people who read or hear them and the places or circumstances in which they are consumed, enjoyed, or enacted.

The rapid urban growth in the River Plate region between the late nineteenth century and the first decades of the twentieth has been well documented.[7] This urban expansion went hand in hand with the proliferation of print journalism—Adolfo Prieto calls the growth in daily and weekly periodicals in Buenos Aires "explosive" (14). This proliferation accompanied significant technological innovations in transportation, architecture, and urban planning. New patterns of reading spurred by urban expansion also resulted in a burgeoning reading public of women who read serialized novels.[8]

While public education was championed all over Latin America following independence, Argentina and Uruguay developed the most successful programs. For Domingo Faustino Sarmiento (1811–1888, president of Argentina 1868–1874), public education was a top priority for national consolidation. He traveled the world to observe public education systems and based his plans for the country on the US system (see Sorensen 87–88). Solidifying public education boosted print culture through the publication of textbooks, the establishment of libraries, and the founding of teacher training centers. Chile and Mexico also promoted public education, and urban growth in these countries similarly was accompanied by an increase in print journalism and circulation.

An early-twentieth-century initiative that links literature, open public space, and urban inhabitants corresponds to post-revolutionary Mexico. José Vasconcelos (1882–1959), one of Latin America's statespeople and a crucial figure following the Revolution, emphasized books and reading as cornerstones of his official policies. This emphasis produced a lasting legacy. When Vasconcelos was rector of Mexico's Universidad Nacional Autónoma, one of his main contributions was an extensive series of classic texts translated into Spanish, published in beautiful editions, and distributed free in public parks and plazas. According to Enrique Krauze, Vasconcelos's program "jumpstarted for the first time, a massive publishing industry in Mexico" (63). His educational project for the masses led to literacy campaigns, and in 1921 Mexican president Álvaro Obregón appointed him secretary of education. In the process of establishing public education, Vasconcelos also tackled Mexico's lack of libraries and sent "missionary" teachers to remote areas with wooden crates full of books carted by mules (67). Mexico City's modern megalibrary, Biblioteca José Vasconcelos, opened in 2006, pays homage to his leadership in library development nationally (see figure 0.2).

Brazilian chapbooks called *literatura de cordel* offer another exam-

Figure 0.2. Biblioteca José Vasconcelos, Mexico City; author photo

ple of reading in public space. These printed books were simply made and brought together oral and written literature with woodcut prints for their covers (see figure 0.3). To attract readers, the books hang from a string in markets and plazas—thus the name *cordel*—and their authors sell them as they deliver oral poetry readings. The history of these inexpensive, often self-published booklets goes back to European oral poetic traditions such as medieval epics and early modern ballads; in both Portugal and Spain, pamphlet-like books circulated widely. These *folhetos de feira* (fair pamphlets), as they were originally named, circulated in Brazil in the mid-nineteenth century; the tradition of hanging them from string dates from the late 1870s (Muzart Fonseca dos Santos 614).

The most elaborate tradition of *cordel* literature is from Northeast Brazil and consists of rhymed six-line stanzas written in regional Portuguese to disseminate local news; retell historic episodes; or, using a didactic tone, serve the mission of literacy and basic education. While reading and performing these works aloud is the intention and preferred means of transmission of *cordel* literature, one of the chapbooks' important roles has been to bridge popular oral and

Figures 0.3. *Literatura de cordel* woodcut print cover; author photo; courtesy of Special Collections and University Archives, Rutgers University Libraries

lettered culture (Muzart Fonseca dos Santos 618). This largely rural and small-town public literary tradition has recently expanded to Rio de Janeiro and to the megalopolis of São Paulo, predominantly due to migration from the northeast to urban centers. Other changes are evident in cross-fertilization between *cordel* books and newer media such as comic books, graphic novels, and soap operas (Slater 40). Not surprisingly, these poetic ballads and stories, which previously resisted modern media, now appear on the internet (Mühlschlegel and Musser 156–158). Despite some fear of change or of disappearance of the chapbooks, many scholars of the genre and *cordel* poets themselves note these changes as signs of the form's remarkable flexibility. As Candace Slater concludes in her landmark study from the 1980s, *cordel* literature's "variety and often surprising freedom explains more than any other factor its continued survival in the midst of rapid change" (226).

The oral and performative function of *cordel* literature, together with its material printed form and rich visual tradition of woodcut prints, points out another dynamic feature of public reading: a blending of written, oral, and visual media. Many of the public reading programs explored in this book rely on performative strategies, oral public readings with groups, and visual installations or projections in public space.⁹ However, printed books remain at the center of these initiatives, with extramedial extensions. In the following pages, I explore print culture in recent Latin American urban public life, where books and other media continue the commitment to a lettered citizenry. Although one can consider digital publication a complement and not just an alternative to print initiatives, my research revealed a much more limited range of digital activities that incorporated the outreach and scope of the print projects.

Reading in Print and Online

The internet offers an enormous extension of the public sphere. However, despite its potential I found a number of limitations in the uses and practices of reading digitally in Latin America. The circulation and distribution in public space of printed books in the last fifteen years has covered more ground and reached a wider number and a broader sector of readers (in terms of social class, age, and level of education) than digital literature. A recent study by the Centro Regional para el Fomento del Libro en América Latina y el Caribe (Regional Center for Promoting the Book in Latin America and the Caribbean, hereafter CERLALC) notes the "still timid" approach to electronic books in the region (Jaramillo H. 43). The yearlong World Book Capital programs in Bogotá (2007–2008) and Buenos Aires (2011–2012), for example, hosted very few initiatives involving digital reading.¹⁰

Other examples from recent surveys, reports, and official announcements in Latin American cities confirm a preference for printed books. In a large-scale survey on national reading practices carried out by the Fundación Mempo Giardinelli in 2013, 31 percent responded that the internet interfered negatively with reading. In Didier Álvarez Zapata's review of seventeen Latin American national reading plans for 2013, he confirms that the plans favor print materials in promoting reading (213). All of the national reading programs that year underscored the social element of community reading with a particular focus on schools and libraries, as opposed to digital reading that is generally individual. Indeed, the plans encourage "social spaces of reading" beyond schools and libraries, and include in their goals the development of alternative or unconventional places for reading in a "vindication of the social" (Álvarez Zapata 196).

Latin American writers have a strong literary presence on the internet through blogs and other websites, but their work and their digital platforms for the most part do not emphasize the goals of public reading. Experimental digital literary works such as those by the Argentine Belén Gache, the Peruvian-Venezuelan Doménico Chiappe, the Peruvian Roxana Crisólogo, and the Mexican Cristina Rivera-Garza offer interactive reading experiences that push the boundaries of form and reception (see my "Beyond the Book"). Eduardo Ledesma studies digital literature that incorporates coding and electronic music, examples of experimental intermedial compositions that are not readily legible to the general public (see his *Radical Poetry*). Despite open access on the web, these writers' works remain rarified aesthetic experiences for a narrow intellectual audience. The authors do not participate overtly in the project of broad access across social class and generational lines; nor do they necessarily promote the values of local civic engagement and sociability so central to the programs that the following chapters explore. Furthermore, digital literature presupposes that "traditional literature is stripped of its intrinsic creative quality" (Gainza 6), but current urban public reading initiatives reaffirm, on the contrary, the imaginative potential of printed and physically circulating literature for the public good.

An article from the newspaper *El Tiempo* in Bogotá in 2015 reported that e-book sales were much lower than print book sales internationally (Motoa Franco). Because the programs I study make books available free or at very low cost, my research over the past ten years confirms this preference in Latin America for the physical book over electronic formats for reading. Publishers, editors, booksellers, librarians, critics, and municipal cultural managers with whom I have spoken over the past ten years support the view that print culture is still the preferred means of literary production and reception.

Print culture in Latin America relies on public libraries and book fairs, two urban institutions that anchor regional reading practices in Latin America and also support public reading in the region. Newly independent nations established libraries as significant symbolic and archival monuments for national identity, generally locating them in urban centers as part of the lettered city. More recent libraries, like the Vasconcelos in Mexico City, demonstrate a commitment to accessibility and outreach that defies the limits of the traditional lettered elite. Book fairs not only serve a commercial function for the publishing industry, but also provide a social function for the masses across class divisions. These facilities and events promote reading in a more institutional or corporate mode than the programs discussed in the following chapters; nevertheless, they provide key infrastructure and distribution mechanisms that support and intersect with public reading programs.

Libraries: Reading for the Public

The redesigned Biblioteca de México, renamed La Ciudad de los Libros y la Imagen (The City of Books and the Image), opened in 2012. This site, known as the citadel because of its military-like austerity, was built in 1807 as the Royal Tobacco Factory and was transformed over the years into a military base, a prison, an arms factory, and a warehouse. In 1931 it was declared a historic monument, and it became a major library in 1946. The renovated facility on this same site, coordinated by the Consejo Nacional para la Cultura y las Artes (National Council for Culture and the Arts, Conaculta), cost 540 million pesos. It now houses the personal libraries of five Mexican writers and thinkers: Antonio Castro Leal, Alí Chumacero, Jaime García Terrés, José Luis Martínez, and Carlos Monsiváis. Each wing was specially designed to best house and display a writer's collection, with comfortable furniture for reading and staff on hand throughout the day to assist visitors. This national effort to collect materials from five important figures, digitize them, and make them available to the public demonstrates more than recognition of lettered patrimony and a commitment to the preservation of knowledge. This monument to Mexican thought and writing is also an urban public institution whose accessibility to and integration of citizens as readers expands the public sphere. When I visited the library in 2015, the main patio was packed with people reading, studying, and researching. As I walked through the different wings devoted to each of the writers, the staff invited me to take books off the shelves and sit down and read.

Public libraries were founded early in the independence period in Latin American cities and contributed to national consolidation. Buenos Aires's first library was established in 1812, Montevideo's in 1816. Brazil's national library was founded in 1810 (although it was basically a relocation of the Royal Library of Portugal), and the Library of Bahia was opened in 1818. Brazil had 5,000 municipal and other public libraries in the early 2000s (Mindlin) and Mexico currently has 7,000 nationally (Argüelles, personal interview).

National, municipal, and specialized public libraries (libraries for the visually impaired, foreign language libraries, libraries sponsored by cultural organizations like the Alliance Française, for example) are not the only ones open to the public in Latin America. Sarmiento founded Argentina's first community (*popular*) library in 1866 in his native province of San Juan.[11] In 1870 he established the Comisión Nacional de Bibliotecas Populares (National Commission of Popular Libraries, CONABIP), which sponsored small community libraries all over Argentina, many of which still exist today. These libraries have emerged thanks to the initiative of neighbors and community members who have seen a need for a local neighborhood library, particularly where there is no public library in the vicinity. Currently there are 2,000 CONABIP community libraries across every region of Argentina, staffed by 30,000 volunteers.

The scale of libraries in Latin America spans grandiose structures with every imaginable amenity to small rooms of donated used books in a municipal office building or a church. Many public libraries throughout Latin America were housed in unattended, disorganized, musty spaces until recent decades, in part as a result of increased privatization, which left public facilities abandoned and unresponsive to the neighbors. A happy consequence of the return to public investment has been a movement to revitalize, modernize, and digitize existing libraries.

Newly designed libraries also have enhanced public interaction through their attractive, dynamic spaces. Perhaps the most dramatic is the Biblioteca España in Medellín, opened in 2007. This monumental project of three boulder-like structures sits atop one of the highest points in the city in the middle of one of the poorest and, in the 1990s, most violent neighborhoods in Latin America. One of a series of "library parks" in the city, each one a complex of buildings, auditoriums, and landscaped plazas designed by renowned architects, the Biblioteca España, together with other urban improvements in Medellín, like expanded public transportation access through the new cable car extension of the subway system, is credited with transforming this area of the city into a safer neighborhood with amenities that even attract tourists. Colombia had also opened a series of five megalibraries a few years before in Bogotá, as part of that city's facelift and reinvestment in public spaces. Bogotá's largest public library, the Biblioteca Luis Ángel Arango, founded in 1958 and managed by the cultural branch of the Banco de la República, is one of the busiest public libraries in the world. This "vast universe of knowledge" has space for 2,000 patrons (Guerrero 171) and receives 9,200 visitors a day (Silva, *Bogotá imaginada* 267).

Other large libraries, such as the Biblioteca de Santiago in Santiago, Chile (opened in 2005), and the Biblioteca José Vasconcelos in Mexico City (opened in 2006), contribute to this new wave of major urban public libraries in Latin America. Librarian Raúl Hernández, who helps direct the Biblioteca de Santiago, calls this a "new style" of library that is "more welcoming and friendly"; it does not just store books but promotes reading by hosting attractive events and reaching out to the community (Hernández, personal interview, my translation).[12] Hernández calls the Biblioteca de Santiago "a public plaza with books" (personal interview, my translation). This approach furthers the stated objectives of the UNESCO pilot libraries, of which the Medellín Pilot Public Library is an example: to serve as models for the local and regional library movement in each country where they were established. UNESCO aimed for each of these libraries to be "not merely a depository of books, but something dynamic, an institution aware of the problems of its social environment, . . . in constant touch with the citizens it claims to serve" (UNESCO, "The Pilot Public Library" 5).

Newer libraries have had the burden of reversing the public's attitudes, perceptions, and habits after years of institutional neglect and an unwelcoming ambience in most libraries throughout Latin America until this century. Juan Domingo Argüelles, who worked for nine years as an administrator in the Mexico City municipal library system, notes how important it has been to revise the perception of libraries as "places for completing assignments and homework" and insists on disassociating reading from formal education (in Spanish, *desescolarizar*) in order to restore it as a pleasurable experience (Argüelles, *Leer bajo su propio riesgo* 98–109). Hernández points out that in Chile during the dictatorship, schools staffed their libraries with teachers who had never been trained in library science and had no affinity for the profession or for the mission of a library. This resulted in unwelcoming school libraries and the need to undo people's expectations and reorient them in how to use a library. These newer public libraries put enormous effort into community outreach, and the results are evident in the numbers: Mexico City's Biblioteca José Vasconcelos welcomes four thousand visitors a day. The institution devotes staff, space, and programming to its very complicated and needy surrounding neighborhood, even making home visits to encourage participation. Librarian Carola Diez considers the facility a mix between a library and a cultural center (personal interview). Vasconcelos library director Daniel Goldín aims for the library to serve as a welcoming meeting space; "it doesn't matter how they come in, what matters is how they are when they leave" (personal interview, my translation).

Figure 0.4. "Cuento contigo" banner, Montevideo; author photo

Latin American cities have spearheaded efforts to promote the enjoyment of reading by reaching beyond schools, libraries, and other institutions. This is the story that I aim to tell here: how alternative sponsors, from city government ministries to grassroots cultural organizations, harness literary reading and insert it into public space for the social good. According to Argüelles, the future of reading all over Latin America lies in small-scale community initiatives that empower ordinary citizens (personal interview). He refers to programs that tap the public to distribute books and host reading activities in their homes and neighborhoods. He particularly praises the Mexican program Salas de Lectura (Reading Rooms), which since 1995 has provided a collection of books and training for ordinary citizens to be "reading mediators." They agree to set up a reading room in their house, garage, or office, in a park or church, even using the trunk of their car. There are more than three thousand Salas all over the country, and CERLALC recognized the program as a model to be replicated in other Latin American countries.

A similar program in Uruguay, called Cuento Contigo, para Vivir la Lectura (I Count on/Read to You, Bringing Reading to Life), a play on words since the verb *contar* means both "to tell a story" and "to count," began in Montevideo in 2013 (see figure 0.4). The program distributes an anthology of short pieces by Uruguayan writers to volunteers, who read from it to groups of all ages in a variety of settings. In 2015 the program had 6,500 volunteer readers throughout the country. The programs that the following chapters describe have stronger ties to the cities in which they are carried out, sometimes through official sponsorship, other times through urban infrastructure, and still others through local political and economic arrangements. They further the kind of work that these broad-based national programs, often originating in cities, continue to do in the recent wave of public engagement through reading.[13]

Book Fairs: Promoting Reading, from the Commercial to the Social

Book fairs in Latin America offer another venue for presenting and celebrating books. The director of CERLALC, Fernando Zapata López, calls book fairs "a true festival of reading" and considers them "a fundamental link in promoting the circulation of the rich editorial production in the region" (11–12). While many European book fairs are either events for book professionals for commercial and training purposes, or exhibits and sales open to the general public, the Latin American book fairs blend the two in an "integrated model" that offers an enormous range of activities for both professionals and the public (Zapata López 35). Beyond their commercial purpose, Latin American book fairs have become major cultural events, particularly in cities, as well as "spaces for public policy" (Dos Santos Piúba 54). Their goals include promoting broad access to books, training readers through workshops and other activities, promoting the symbolic cultural value of books and literature, and boosting the book trade (Dos Santos Piúba 48). One overview of book fairs throughout Latin America notes that since the early 2000s, organizers place much more emphasis on promoting reading and the social function of these fairs, including the link between reading and citizenship (Dos Santos Piúba 46–47). Attendance is massive, with busloads of schoolchildren, multigenerational family groups, and all kinds of book professionals (booksellers, librarians, teachers, writers, editors, and publishers) pouring through exhibition pavilions and fairgrounds. Interviews, readings, book signings, award ceremonies, and workshops are all features of the fairs, which sometimes span several weeks.

The largest book fairs in Latin America are those held in Guadalajara, Mexico, and Buenos Aires, Argentina. But every city seems to host several smaller book fairs each year, often outside in public squares or plazas, or in arcades, pavilions, or other covered spaces. Some fairs are general and broad, while others target a specific audience or focus on a particular genre, such as children's literature or religious books. A growing number of independent publishers have emerged as a response to the transnational conglomerates that consolidated book publishing under neoliberal economic policies, and these small presses often organize their own alternative book fairs, such as La Furia del Libro (The Fury of the Book, a play on words between *feria* and *furia*) and the annual exhibit and symposium of *cartonera* publishers, both in Santiago, Chile.

The Cuban book fair merits special attention for its distinct commercial, educational, and social parameters, which reflect the country's communist economy and cultural policies. The first book fair in Cuba took place in 1937 when a group of booksellers gathered in Havana, but the Havana book fair as a significant international event began in 1982. Cuban publishing did not recognize authors' copyright for a full decade after the Revolution, and book publishing is subsidized by the government; thus the Cuban book fair has not always had the commercial focus of the other major urban book fairs in Latin America.[14] Rather, the event is much more oriented toward accessibility of books for the public and literary visibility for writers. The book fair gives away many free books and sells others at very low prices; in the context of the Revolution's literary project, as José Quiroga points out, "the symbolic value of the book exceeded the specific value it materially represented" (116), and the dreadfully long lines to enter the book fair attest to the book's continuing symbolic value. The Havana fair had 130 exhibitors and 300,000 visitors for the ten-day event in the capital city, according to the CERLALC report; but these numbers do not include the traveling versions of the fair that occurred in smaller towns all over the country.[15]

Since 2000 the Cuban book fair has been a national traveling caravan: after the ten days in Havana, smaller exhibits and book events visit towns and cities all over the island. Recognizing that interest in reading had suffered as a consequence of the economic crisis of the 1990s Special Period, the fair shifted its "purpose, nature and scale" to become "more reader-focused" with a push for broader distribution, particularly of children's books (Kumaraswami and Kapcia 218).[16] In 2000 the main fair site in Havana was relocated to La Cabaña Fort but also expanded to host some events in bookstores all over the city. That same year, smaller traveling versions of the fair visited eighteen other municipalities. Every year the number of these provincial sites has increased; in 2007, thirty-nine cities and towns held book fair events. Thereafter, the global economic crisis in 2008 and several severe hurricanes took their toll on Cuba, and the number of provincial locations was reduced. Nevertheless, according to Kumaraswami and Kapcia, "it is the Feria's provincial iterations which are the real success story" (226). The fair's massive attendance goes beyond any correlation with sales, as many attend for the cultural festival atmosphere and not only to buy books or listen to readings. The main goal of the fair is not to push everyone to read more but to celebrate "the intrinsic value of the book, and of the act and process of reading itself" (Kumaraswami and Kapcia 228). The Cuban book fair's emphasis on distribution, inclusion, and national accessibility make it unique in the context of Latin American book fairs.

The strong commercial impetus notwithstanding, Latin American large urban book fairs increasingly emphasize social inclusion, democratic access to books and reading, and the connection between reading and citizenship. Other large but less official book fairs held in Latin American cities, such as massive book sales in parks organized under the banner of the UNESCO World Book Capital award in Bogotá and Buenos Aires and the Zócalo Plaza Book Fair in Mexico City, aim to attract "those people who would never go into a bookstore" (Sáiz, personal interview, my translation). Paloma Sáiz, who directed the Zócalo book fair for several years in her role as coordinator of promoting reading for Mexico City's Secretariat of Culture, considers these fairs "truly for the people" and calls the Zócalo fair "the biggest open air bookstore in the world" (personal interview, my translation).[17]

The role of book fairs in the landscape of urban reading in the region coincides with many of the national reading plans in their orientation toward "a more social and integrated vision of written culture and new modes of reading" (Álvarez Zapata 208–209). Each of the conclusions in the 2013 CERLALC study of national reading plans throughout Latin America, the Caribbean, Spain, and Portugal insists on the social elements of reading. The plans converge in recognizing reading as a tool for achieving a more informed and participatory citizenry, and in calling for improved social infrastructure and better public-private integration in promoting reading. The book fairs contribute to these goals, along with sales and distribution, through their programming for the public within a reading-centered festival atmosphere that attracts massive attendance.

The City or the Country? Rural Reading Programs

A young woman travels to small villages along the Pacific coast of Colombia as a state-sponsored *promotora de lectura* (reading promoter). It's the early 2000s, the height of the violent conflicts among leftist guerrillas, the military, the paramilitary, and drug traffickers, and she is greeted with suspicion or indifference. After perilous travel by boat or truck, and frequent interruptions at gunpoint by local militia, she arrives in each town to find libraries closed and local officials unavailable. When she inquires at each destination about the boxes of books sent from Bogotá, the librarians or elected officials, many of them illiterate, respond vaguely.

Despite the title of Mery Yolanda Sánchez's novel *El atajo* (The Short Cut), there seem to be no short cuts for the protagonist of this story; on each leg of her journey, she encounters obstacles and terrifying threats. The villages are filled with residents whose homemade, makeshift prosthetic limbs signal that they are victims of landmines, and severed limbs begin to appear in the protagonist's dreams. Despite the village residents' and officials' resistance to supporting their local libraries, reading in this novel becomes a crucial tactic and a matter of survival for the protagonist. Sánchez sprinkles the narration with various forms of *leer* and *lectura*, either literal references to alphabetic reading or metaphorical accounts of her struggle to semiotically decipher her new surroundings. The books and the protagonist come from the capital city, and the geographical, cultural, and linguistic gulf between the city and the rural villages is wide. When she returns to Bogotá her coworkers celebrate her homecoming as if she has been abroad: "Thank God, now you're back in Colombia!" (74).

Although I focus in this study on reading programs that rely on and interact with municipal public space, this is not to imply that reading happens only in cities or that reading is ignored as a strategy for community development and reconciliation in rural areas. There are many dynamic initiatives around reading in rural areas of Latin America, such as the one fictionalized in Sánchez's novel.

The literacy campaigns carried out in Cuba in 1961 and Nicaragua in the early 1980s, after those countries' respective revolutions, intervened primarily in rural areas where literacy rates were lowest.[18] Although these campaigns addressed functional literacy rather than literary reading, they were intricately linked to revolutionary state ideology and public policies. In both Cuba and Nicaragua, the revolutionary leaders identified literacy as one of their earliest and most urgent initiatives. In Olga Montalván Lamas's historical overview of the Cuban literacy campaign, she calls it a "fundamental aspect of the ideological development of the Revolution" (116). David Archer and Patrick Costello elaborate on the complexity of the goals in the Nicaraguan campaign that extended beyond functional literacy: "The aim of the crusade was not to dictate the aims of the revolution or to transfer the techniques of literacy. Rather, . . . the idea was to promote creative participation in the revolution via creative use of the written word. In adult literacy, mastering oral and written language constitutes one dimension of the process of being expressive. Another dimension involves enabling people to 'read' their reality and 'write' their own history" (25).

Both literacy education campaigns reached huge numbers of mostly rural citizens: over 700,000 people were trained to read and write in the span of one year in Cuba, raising the literacy rate to 96 percent; 400,000 learned to read and write in Nicaragua, whose literacy rate reached 86 percent (Archer and Costello 31). Although creating a readership for literature was not the campaigns' primary goal, it was one of the results: expanding the number of readers made lettered culture more accessible to the masses. Particularly in Cuba, literature and literacy "were already clearly linked in theory and practice, and would thus be related in cultural policy making. . . . The fact that a mass readership was quickly being constructed via the Campaign. . . suggests that the Campaign must have been fundamental to the future activity of literature" (Kumaraswami and Kapcia 44).[19]

Several examples of rural reading initiatives are located in Peru. The cartonera group Qinti Qartunira in Lamas, Peru, was formed to address the lack of teaching materials in the Quechua language. Although most of the cartonera groups coalesce in urban surroundings because these alternative publishers' principal raw material, cardboard, is abundant where greater concentrations of people produce garbage and recyclables, there are exceptions. This rural Peruvian group not only teaches language but also imparts elements of rural culture such as myths, legends, music, and arts. Alfredo Mires Ortiz, a Peruvian anthropologist, has been promoting reading in the country's Cajamarca region for years. He directs the Red de Bibliotecas Rurales (Network of Rural Libraries) and has compiled and published numerous volumes of oral literature and books on local Andean culture.

One of the most moving programs I discovered in researching public reading is Retomo la Palabra (I Reclaim the Word), a national program for rural communities in Colombia that have been affected by armed conflict. Sponsored by a presidential commission during Álvaro Uribe's term (2002–2010), the 2007–2009 program promoted reconciliation in communities that had suffered violent attacks from insurgents. Support for Retomo la Palabra fell under Uribe's commitment to programming efforts toward the reinsertion into civil society of former members of armed groups such as the FARC. The program provided fourteen rural towns or villages with a library for their community centers, which received some four hundred carefully selected books. Trained local individuals used these books as they led activities that brought together victims and perpetrators to create a climate for restoring trust. The books covered a wide range of disciplines (human development, psychology, art, literature, history), and extensive workshops helped facilitators make use of the resources for reconciliation in the community. The project prepared a resource guide called the "Caja de ideas" (Box of Ideas)—literally a box with large durable cards, color coded by discipline—which accompanied the library collection in each center. The facilitator training included aspects of the People and Stories/Gente y Cuentos methodology, and taught facilitators to read literature aloud and lead discussions that promoted community healing. Retomo la Palabra incorporated creative writing as well; it published two anthologies of ex-combatants' writings (see Schmidt Quintero; Montt).

Examples abound of literary activities in rural areas all over Latin America, particularly benefiting children: poetry and theater workshops presented in schools and churches, libraries housed in community centers, and schools being remodeled and repurposed as cultural and literary centers after being burned by rebels.[20] All of these programs promote reading as an active, engaged, strategic endeavor that not only provides personal satisfaction and imaginative enrichment, but also encourages community empowerment, collective mourning, and reconciliation. These collective reading experiences do not rely on urban physical space, administration, or institutions; nor do they function in resistance to those structures. Although their missions often overlap with those of public reading programs in cities, they work within and address a series of geographic and demographic concerns that differ markedly from those of urban reading programs. Therefore, in the following chapters I mention rural reading programs only in passing from the perspective of their intersection with city initiatives.

Reclaiming the Public Sphere: New Definitions, New Everyday Practices

On Corrientes Avenue in downtown Buenos Aires, renowned for its concentration of bookstores, a newsstand on a heavily traveled corner draws attention for its alternative merchandise. Instead of the usual offering of newspapers and magazines, the kiosk sells inexpensive cardboard-bound, hand-painted books. Eloísa Cartonera, the first cartonera book publisher, decided to expand beyond a studio in the neighborhood of La Boca in order to reach more readers and to better interact with the public. This example of the intersection of literary reading and public space is also a response to the cultural consequences of the region's neoliberal economic policies over the last few decades. Renewed attention to the public sphere has encouraged cultural expression in urban open spaces—in this case, artisanal bookmaking and literary reading on a busy street corner. Some of these activities in public space count on official municipal sponsorship, and others, like the cartonera kiosk, are independent grassroots initiatives, often referred to in Spanish as *autogestionados* (self-managed efforts). The chapters that follow explore examples of both kinds of programming, institutional and municipal, and independent grassroots, all of them reactions to decades of neoliberal privatization and to an ongoing transition to democracy from a violent, authoritarian past, which has prompted a return to investing in the public.

Among the most vibrant recent discussions in cultural studies has been a reconsideration of ideas of the public. From the theoretical to the experiential, from the philosophical to concrete applications in policy and planning, from the environmental to the aesthetic, the public is recognized as a key factor in multiple issues, including literacy, the economy, and citizenship. The public has become a central concern in Latin American studies as well, particularly in urban contexts, as part of the continuing assessment of the repercussions of neoliberalism and increasing privatization in recent decades. Collaborative scholarship and debates at international conferences demonstrate the region-wide urgency to reclaim the public—conceptually, ideologically, and in planning and policy making.

Two academic programs in Latin America, the first in Mexico City and the second in Buenos Aires, frame this period of renewed interest in the public. In 2001 sociologist Néstor García Canclini organized an international conference in Mexico City titled Reabrir espacios públicos: Políticas culturales y ciudadanía (Reopening Public Spaces: Cultural Policy and Citizenship) and published an edited volume, with Lourdes Arizpe S., by that name. Spanish specialists, such as Catalonian Jordi Borja, and Mexican philosopher Roger Bartra presented cases and strategies for reclaiming public space. In 2016, the social sciences think tank Consejo Latinoamericano de Ciencias Sociales (Latin American Council of the Social Sciences, CLACSO), based in Buenos Aires, announced a call for research proposals that would address "The Struggles over the Public in Latin America and the Caribbean." The announcement encourages projects that explore the "achievements, limits, and challenges" of popular social movements' efforts to defend the public arena.[21] The urban reading initiatives examined in the following chapters document this trend of embracing the public in the first fifteen years after the turn of the century; this section reviews the political philosophies and conceptual genealogy that public reading programs put into practice.

A cluster of European and North American thinkers have indirectly contributed to Latin American ideas of public urban space. Jeff Weintraub identifies four structural distinctions between the public and the private found in classical philosophy and more recent thought: in the liberal economistic model (the state versus the market), in the republican model (community and citizenship versus the market and the state), in the concept of interactional sociability (as differentiated from the private individual), and in the private family (versus the larger public economic and political order). Most theorists acknowledge the primacy of the private in the modern West, where the rise of market capitalism has served to safeguard individual rights but also contributed to diminishing civic engagement. Ferdinand Tönnies's distinction between community and society in his landmark book *Community and Civil Society*, originally published in German in 1887 and reprinted in eight editions, is grounded in this sharp split. He shows how the rise of the market eroded communitarian arrangements, in which art and religion were inseparable from domestic and civic life, and bolstered the rational calculation and commodity-oriented production that he associates with society, in which art is relegated to the auction block and the museum. Tönnies's work has been translated into Spanish, and sociologists throughout Latin America consider his work foundational.

Jürgen Habermas's *The Structural Transformation of the Public Sphere*, from 1962, reprinted in eight editions and translated into Spanish in 1981, has also been a major contribution to rethinking the public. Habermas offers a more interrelational view of the public and private, whereby the public is made up of private individuals who intervene in rational-critical debate about public issues. He critically examines the ever more important category of the family in European bourgeois culture as a private domain with an essential role in forming the individuals who participate in public debate. Much of his argument rests on the essential role of reading: "private reading has always been the precondition for rational-critical debate" (158).

The "world of letters" (Calhoun 10) that lays at the foundation of the Habermasian public includes journals, newspapers, and even literary fiction, which are available to a continually expanding audience. Habermas's view of the public sphere grows out of his formation in the Frankfurt School and his acceptance of this group's critique of mass culture, leading to his insistence on quality and quantity—that is, broad participation—in rational public debate. Often this public sphere offers an arena for opposition to the state, yet the public might also include agents of the state. The undermining of the public sphere, which Habermas calls its transformation, is brought about by private organizations increasingly assuming public power while the state further penetrates the private realm. In the "world of letters" a wider reading public, together with mass media, increased access but paradoxically debilitated the quality and level of participation in rational-critical debate, a depoliticization that impoverished the public sphere. Critics of Habermas note the contradictions in his model of the public sphere, the limited role for women, and the limitations in his approach in terms of accounting for everyday practices and interpersonal interactions. While Habermas's idea of the public is theoretically inclusive, as Craig Calhoun points out, "it took that older, elite public as constitutive of the whole relevant citizenry" (16).

In Latin America the emergence of a bourgeois society occurred later and had a much more limited scope. Rather than a response to a monarchy or royal class as in Europe, it was an expansion of the lettered elite bureaucracy. Ángel Rama's Marxist, class-based critique of urban space in *The Lettered City* could be situated between Habermas's theory of the European public sphere and its transformation in bourgeois society, and Benedict Anderson's consideration of the role of print culture in modern nationalism. Where Rama departs from Habermas is in the role of social status. While Habermas presumes the ideal of an egalitarian disregard for status, a presupposition of equality among interlocutors (36), Rama points out how status excludes the majority of individuals in Latin America from public access to information, education, and published work, and therefore this majority is precluded from participating in the active interaction and debate that Habermas considers essential. More recent considerations of public space in Latin America benefit from Michel de Certeau's work on everyday practices, in which reading constitutes one of his frequently mentioned examples; Manuel Delgado's approach to urban social space; and García Canclini's theory of hybrid cultures and urban imaginaries.

Most theorists tackling publicness point out the false dichotomy between the categories of public and private (Weintraub; Wolfe). Hannah Arendt's work, for example, underscored the rise of the social as a mediating zone between the public and the private. More recent political theories stress publics (plural), intermediary groups, and associations with shared norms that are partially private (see Wolfe), prefiguring to some degree what Michael Warner elaborates in *Publics and Counterpublics*.

Other recent work questions the operative linguistic metaphors for the public, such as *sphere* and *network*, and suggests instead *modalities* in order to underscore the multiplicity of movement and activity that crafts the public (Brouwer and Asen 3). This mobile and elastic frame for examining the public better serves the Latin American urban context. Social scientists, urban planners, and social geographers in Latin America propose definitions and models that account for diversity and heterogeneity but still reveal a debt to Habermas, particularly the tension of rational-critical debate: "one of the challenges in redefining the public is recognizing the different forms of organization, communication, and identity formation that come together that cannot be resolved in a pure exaltation of differences or in a facile celebration of consensus" (Rabotnikof 329). Another recent definition of public space, from the Facultad Latinoamericana de Ciencias Sociales (FLACSO), a renowned Latin American interdisciplinary social sciences think tank, characterizes the public sphere as a social space "where the discourses from and about the city traffic are put in circulation, are recontextualized and reproduced" (Buendía Astudillo 258). This conception incorporates a less dichotomous, more dynamic approach, in which movement, process, circulation, and continual redefinition account for the heterogeneous social experience of the public in urban Latin America.

The problematic public/private dichotomy takes on a new dimension in the rise and fall—or current questioning and assessment—of neoliberal economic policies in Latin America since the 1980s. García Canclini, for example, recognizes the shifts and transformations in what he called hybrid cultures in the 1980s, and even admits to their "disintegration" under neoliberalism (*Imaginarios urbanos* 20). Alan Wolfe discusses the public and the private in US politics and culture, which reflect a similar tendency to that in Latin America, and predicts that "once the current flirtation with privatism runs its course, a counteremphasis on the importance of a public sector will emerge" (200). Calhoun concurs: "the recovery and extension of a strong normative idea of publicness is very much on the current agenda" (42). Although these comments do not refer to Latin America directly, this is precisely what has been happening in Latin American urban policy, where a resurgent commitment to the public, particularly in urban planning policies, is evident. A prime example is Bogotá's Cultura Ciudadana (culture of citizenship) under Antanas Mockus's two mayoral terms (1995–1997 and 2001–2003), during which sidewalks were repaired, parks were restored, and traffic congestion was addressed in order to improve sociability by combatting urban violence and alienation. From mimes in the street for calming road rage to creative firearm buybacks, Mockus's innovative projects not only had shock value but apparently worked: violence and traffic accidents decreased dramatically (see Cala Buendía).

Reclamation of public space in Latin America often highlights reading by including the mass public in literary experiences. These initiatives are reminiscent of Habermas's recognition that reading is a key preparation for engaging in public debate; on the other hand, Habermas contends that the expanded public for literary fiction, and mass media in general, is one of the sources of the bourgeois public sphere's political demise. Public reading programs aim to create a common conversation, to pull together the citizenry through a collective literary imagination, and to foster an inclusive discursive space for mutual understanding and *convivencia* (sociability, getting along with others).

The enormous success of the Chilean annual short story contest, Santiago en 100 Palabras, is evident in the massive number of participants. The Argentine public memory centers in former detention and torture sites represent a more sobering example of embracing and redefining public spaces. These complexes commemorate the disappeared and victims of torture, but also honor the restoration of democratic citizenship and freedom of the press. Here again, reading plays a meaningful role: two of these memory spaces designate areas for libraries of books once banned by the dictatorship. The culture of reading inscribes urban itineraries and moves toward collective rather than private individual reading. These initiatives demonstrate a reliance on symbolic content for reimagining urban public space. As Bartra notes, "political alternatives are finding little popular support in the economic realm and move more and more into symbolic and metaphorical domains, which are public spaces" (Bartra 335).

Critics of Habermas and other European theorists of the public question the extent to which Western theories and practices can account for the development and experience of the public in postcolonial and transnational contexts (Brouwer and Asen 15). In the case of Latin America, the ideals of the public, particularly with respect to urban public space, grow out of some European models at the same time as they challenge and reinvent them. Dialogues between European and Latin American thinkers emerge as well, such as in Henri Lefebvre's *The Production of Space*. This seminal study, which launches new philosophical and social geography, begins with an epigraph by the Mexican poet Octavio Paz. Lefebvre's insistence on the connection between urban practices and ideology comprehends the urban "as a complex social, political, economic, philosophical cultural system" where public space needs to be reclaimed for its cultural and social opportunities (Fraser 11).

The evolution of Lefebvre's theories on the right to the city are evident in the work of fellow Situationist Certeau, who developed the connection between urban space and people's ordinary daily activities in *The Practice of Everyday Life*. Certeau proposes that reading is not only a key metaphor for semiotic deciphering of urban experience, but also an everyday practice like walking, cooking, and shopping, which he identifies as human ways of marking the city. In Certeau's concern with power dynamics, walking and reading pertain to an individual's tactics for moving through the city, the deviations around the powerful forces from which the individual walker and reader is excluded. In his analogy between language and urban movement, the city requires semiotic deciphering not only of streets and signs, but also of the movements of vehicles and other walkers. Yet for Certeau reading is also an ordinary practice that urban inhabitants engage in regularly.

A Certeauian analysis of public reading in Latin American cities reveals reading as both strategic (employed by powerful institutions) and tactical (used by marginal individual others to maneuver around official institutions). I extend Certeau's theory of urban practices from individual maneuvering to the impact of group experiences; reading in Latin American urban public space exploits a personal tactic for survival and orientation to promote civic belonging.

An uneasy alliance between the strategic and the tactical in municipally sponsored reading initiatives that potentially empower the masses parallels the persistent blurring of the public/private distinction. On a broader level, Bartra calls this the "state-ification of the public" that occurs alongside the "re-publicanization of state management" for political organizing on the left and urban planning (338). Harvey, in *Rebel Cities*, also points to a new pattern of urban governance that "mixes together state powers (local, metropolitan, regional, national, or supranational) with a wide array of organizational forms in civil society (chambers of commerce, unions, churches, educational and research institutions, community groups, NGOs, and so on) and private interests (corporate and individual) to form coalitions to promote or manage urban or regional development" (100). The frequent mixing or blending of alliances between the public and the private emerges in the field of cultural management as well, an area under which public reading programs often fall. The brochure describing the academic program in cultural management at the Centro Latinoamericano de Economía Humana (Latin American Center of Human Economy) in Montevideo, Uruguay, alerts prospective students to the overlapping categories of public and private: the borders of these supposedly distinct domains are not always clearly delineated.

The interrelation of the public, the private, and the state presents a complex network of shifting positions, rather than a stable cluster of interests and approaches. Its variously configured intersections have a significant impact on policies that concern culture. Warner eschews any singular definition or function of the public in favor of plural publics that often bypass the state and whose operation always relies on discourse. For Warner, a public "is a space of discourse organized by nothing other than discourse itself. . . . A public organizes itself independently of state institutions, laws, formal frameworks of citizenship, or preexisting institutions" (67–68). In the discursive constitution of publics, circulation plays a key role; Warner gives examples of print journalism, public address, religious sermons, and other discursive genres, as well as literary texts. Like Certeau, he recognizes reading as a private and individual act that allows "participants in its discourse to understand themselves as directly and actively belonging to a social entity. . . . [that places] strangers on a shared footing, . . . making use of the vernaculars of its [language's] circulatory space" (105, 108).

However, Warner expands on Certeau's recognition of reading by clearly articulating how everyday reading practices create multiple publics by encompassing the poetic. He outlines how a public "is poetic world making" because the efficacy of public discourse "depends on the recognition of participants and their further circulatory activity. . . . Strangers are less strange if you can trust them to read as you read" (114–116). Warner's conception of publics as fellow readers and poetic interpreters of discourse in circulation illuminates the social and political dimensions of literary reading in public space that the Latin American programs covered here exploit.

The renewed attention to the public in Latin American urban theory and planning is a result of the impact on public space in Latin America of decades of neoliberal policies, in some cases implemented under dictatorial rule. The Chilean librarian Hernández, one of the directors of the Santiago Library, lamented that shopping malls had taken over the city's plazas in gathering people together in public space (personal interview, my translation). He happily praised the library as a new public urban plaza. In Chile the neoliberal economic model was implemented fervently and has come under fierce criticism from the cultural left. Norbert Lechner remarks on the repurposing of Chilean public spaces that "not only promotes structural fragmentation in society but also generates a new type of sociability. . . . New and continually changing signs of social distinction are superimposed on the traditional class schisms" (quoted in Ossa, Richard, and Téllez 111). Many Chilean cultural critics on the left have decried the impact of neoliberal policies for their effect on income inequality, culture, the arts, and social interactions.

Neoliberal economic policy took hold in most of Latin America in the 1980s when import-substituting industrialization in the region became increasingly unstable and inflation and foreign debt reached new highs. At that time, the United States, the International Monetary Fund, and the World Bank began to push structural changes that moved Latin America toward globalization and supported minimizing barriers to trade to liberalize the market.[22] Neoliberal policies diminish the state's role in managing the economy and social welfare in favor of privatization of public resources and suppression of labor unions. The goals of these policies included debt reduction with the promise of increased prosperity, but the results have been much greater economic inequality throughout the region. The neoliberal value of limited collectivism penetrates social interactions and "fundamentally deepens class divisions" (Braedley and Luxton 18). Mexican cultural anthropologist Amparo Sevilla laments the loss of public space as an arena for socialization, a direct consequence of a privatized consumerist mode of urban interaction. She fears that reclaiming public space "for the development of playful forms of sociability outside the logic of financial gain, appears to be out of our reach" (193).

A stellar exploration of the effects of neoliberal policies on consumer culture, public behavior, language, and literary production in late-twentieth-century Chile is Luis Cárcamo-Huechante's *Tramas del mercado* (Plotting the Market). He considers Chile an exceptional case of extreme neoliberal zeal and demonstrates how the structural economic adjustment also imposed a cultural and symbolic shift in the country (15–17). He features the work of Alberto Fuguet, a writer associated with the McOndo generation, whose fiction incorporates the rhetoric and imaginary of consumer society and commodity fetishism in such a way that "the free market acquires the status of literary fiction" (165). Scenes in shopping malls, globalized brand names, and a linguistic register that appropriates US popular youth culture make Fuguet's fiction an advertisement—or cautionary tale—for neoliberal urban angst. The public reading programs I discuss in the following chapters emerge from a different angle from Fuguet's literary project by taking a corrective stance. In their outreach, urban intervention, and even published materials they encourage a reengagement with the public, spatially and civically. Francine Masiello also contributes to the discussion of art, writing, and culture in the Southern Cone's neoliberal, postdictatorship period in *The Art of Transition*, where she explores how "intellectuals faced the task of rebuilding a public sphere: they asked how to recuperate memory, how to bridge connections to the past, how to make sense of democratization as a market-run global enterprise" (24).

Enter the Plaza, Get on the Bus, Open the Book

The following chapters group together reading programs that emerge out of analogous circumstances or that depend on similar urban infrastructure. They all exemplify the social, aesthetic, and political motivations of recent public reading programs. Each chapter focuses on sustained literary reading initiatives implemented at the local, municipal level (citywide as well as neighborhood-based), such as circulation of free books on public transportation, production of handmade books out of recycled materials, promotion of reading as a tool for battling economic and political crisis, and encouraging rediscovery of banned books. The book is structured thematically from the top down, beginning with high-level institutional programming and moving to more grassroots, spontaneous, and independent initiatives.

Chapter 1, "Campaigning for the Capital: Bogotá and Buenos Aires as UNESCO World Book Capitals," discusses campaigns in the two Latin American cities that UNESCO has honored as World Book Capitals: Bogotá in 2007 and Buenos Aires in 2011. Because programming was largely orchestrated through each city's municipal Ministry of Culture and other established institutions, the projects presented in this chapter are the most official examples of public reading. A close analysis of these two municipal campaigns uncovers how institutional cultural management promotes public reading. The professional field of *gestión cultural* (cultural management), a field that many of the reading initiatives rely on, is most institutionally evident in the World Book Capital programming. The Bogotá campaign oriented the year's activities around increasing access to books and literature by empowering ordinary citizens as active participants. The Buenos Aires campaign took as its point of departure the idea that the city has always been a literary city; most of the year's events connected with other local, national, and international institutions. The identification and branding of each city as both a literary capital and a lettered city proceeded quite differently in each setting. By tracing the divergent trajectories of reinforcing the traditional lettered city (Buenos Aires) versus embracing a more expansive and inclusive lettered city (Bogotá), this chapter begins to probe some of the central questions of public reading that the other chapters explore.

High-level urban institutional sponsorship comes into play as well in chapter 2, "Reading on Wheels: Stories of *Convivencia* in Bogotá and Santiago." Here I consider Santiago en 100 Palabras in Santiago, Chile, and Libro al Viento in Bogotá, Colombia, two municipal programs that circulate free books on buses and in subways to promote local belonging and civic values. These programs intersect with transportation administration, libraries, and mayoral campaigns for improving public space and combating violence. They emerge in the midst of major municipal projects to renovate public transportation by building bus rapid transit systems in both cities: TransMilenio in Bogotá and Transantiago in Santiago. Both systems aim not only to improve transit but also to enhance social connectivity (*convivencia*) and urban belonging through sponsoring reading and creative writing programs. The combination of public and private funding for Santiago en 100 Palabras and Libro al Viento introduces a complex relationship between aesthetic literary innovation and institutional and corporate sponsorship. In both programs, massive individual creativity and participation requires both public and private investment, particularly in the case of Santiago en 100 Palabras, whose authors are ordinary urban citizens.

The next three chapters veer away from programs that rely primarily on support from high-level municipal and corporate institutions to discuss initiatives generated by grassroots community efforts. Although the order of these chapters does not suggest a diminishing scale of institutional sponsorship, they all explore reading programs that have emerged from below in response to economic and political crisis, change, and transition. Chapter 3, "*Cacerolazos y bibliotecas*: Solidarity, Reading, and Public Space after the Argentine Economic Crisis (2001–2002)," demonstrates the role of reading as a key factor in responding to crisis. After Argentina's economic and political collapse in 2001–2002, neighborhood associations organized a solidarity economy that, along with *cacerolazo* protests, sponsored public literary readings and community libraries. The emphasis on books and reading appears in newsletters from every neighborhood association; each one had an active committee for cultural programming, revealing that cultural activities were deemed as essential as food, clothing, housing, and medical care for weathering the crisis. The associations' monthly newsletters announced literary readings and theater and writing workshops. The associations also collected books to establish public libraries in occupied buildings that had been turned into community centers, confirming the groups' dedication to making literary culture accessible to the public.

The Argentine crisis produced Eloísa Cartonera, an alternative publishing venture of binding books in reused and hand-painted cardboard. Since this group formed in 2003, it has inspired dozens of independent bookmaking collectives all over Latin America and in Europe and Africa. Chapter 4, "Recycled Reading and the Cartonera Collectives: Publishing from the Ground Up," reviews this burgeoning initiative and highlights Eloísa Cartonera's work and that of groups from Peru (Sarita Cartonera), Brazil (Dulcinéia Catadora), and Colombia (Amapola Cartonera). An analysis of their urban interventions as artistic and literary responses to economic and housing crises demonstrates how these cartonera collectives engage in outreach, activism, education, and advocacy in concert with their publishing programs. The chapter discusses their interventions and collaborations in the community and reveals the strong connections between the groups' social commitment and their literary production.

Collecting and performing rather than producing books is the topic of chapter 5, "Books That Bite: Libraries of Banned Books in Argentina." Recently established libraries of books banned during the last Argentine dictatorship (1976–1983) not only collect banned books but also program performances, workshops, and interactive events for visitors. Collections are ongoing at the Olimpo center in Buenos Aires, La Grieta in La Plata, and the Archivo Provincial de la Memoria in Córdoba, motivated and sponsored by their local communities. Two of these libraries—at Olimpo and the Archivo—occupy spaces formerly used for detention and torture during the military regime. Many of the neighbors and community members who helped establish these libraries are survivors of detention and torture or members of victims' families. This chapter elaborates on the performative strategies that commemorate repression while bringing these books back to life. Rather than being static memorials, these ongoing collections put material culture in motion through memory pedagogy, in which community members participate in reconstructing the books' stories and movements. The centers place these book collections at the service of a broad range of current human rights efforts while they recuperate the past.

The book concludes with "Stories at the Intersection," a brief overview that highlights convergences among these various reading programs to reveal their shared goals of public access, urban intervention, sociability, and citizen engagement. A transnational conversation among different public reading initiatives has emerged from these urban literary initiatives and confirms the broad regional trend of reasserting the social value of public space through the experience of collective literary reading. This concluding section also reviews the current political, economic, and social climate in Latin America and its impact on cultural policy and reading. After a decade or more of left-leaning and labor party presidential terms, recent presidential elections veering to the right indicate a potential return to neoliberal economics. The crises in political leadership in Brazil and Venezuela point to grave consequences for cultural policy. The ongoing peace negotiations in Colombia and efforts to support memory work in the Southern Cone hang in the balance as economic and political challenges take center stage. The question now is whether we will see a continuation of the emphasis on the public and on citizen participation that responded to disillusionment with neoliberal policies, or whether that emphasis will recede as new right-leaning leaders emerge.

"Read at Your Own Risk" in Latin American Urban Space

Wherever we go, we have music with us (sometimes our own humming) and it's a constant part of our daily existence. Reading could be like this too if people are able to discover its benefits, if we can appreciate its wonders and make carrying around something to read in the streets, on public transportation, in our free time, in waiting rooms, a normal, common, ordinary act, and not a surprising thing that makes us look at someone reading in the dentist's office as a strange creature.
JUAN DOMINGO ARGÜELLES

In a project that spans over a dozen cities in Spain and Latin America, Universidad del Externado (Bogotá) professor Armando Silva's Ciudades Imaginadas (Imagined Cities) recomposes the collective imaginaries of each city. Local teams of researchers for the project surveyed thousands of urban inhabitants about their fears, memories, personal itineraries, and aspirations for their city. They asked residents about the most dangerous neighborhoods, their favorite nightspots, where to spend free time, and where to go on a date. The project published their subjective responses in books devoted to each city (for example, *Bogotá imaginada*, *Montevideo imaginado*, *Santiago imaginado*). The responses present an array of city scenes that Silva calls "urban sketches" ("Identidades urbanas" 3), in which multiple voices and images, including those from historical newsreels and personal family interviews, provide a collage of impressions.

Among other questions, the researchers asked participants about their reading habits. Along with participants' reading of the cities they live in, their reading of printed materials contributes to the project's profiles of urban life—reading at home, on public transportation, and in the library; reading of novels, magazines, poetry, and newspapers; and reading for school, at work, and in participants' free time. According to Silva, the project aims to uncover "sites that produce a recognition of collective identity.... The research we have done in Latin America does not study maps but rather studies urban sketches, geographies without a place, but that take place in each citizen. Not a city of objects but rather a city of people who construct their own way to be urban" ("Identidades urbanas" 3–4). For these researchers, reading plays a significant role in defining the urban collective imaginary, a socially constructed and composite subjectivity of the city.

Ciudades Imaginadas gave reading a prominent role in the project's questionnaires and statistical data as well as in the essays in the published volumes. In the first volume, *Bogotá imaginada*, Silva invites *bogotanos* "who read and watch us, to make this a book-city to take on buses, ... and that pushes us to think about civic policies" (29). Some of the books devote sections to reading, such as "La alegría de querer leer" (The Happiness of Enjoying Reading) and "Quito busca quien lo lea..." (Quito in Search of Readers) (*Bogotá imaginada* 264–767; Aguirre, Carrión, and Kingman Garcés 68–72), where the essays report on book fairs, libraries, bookstores, and statistics on literacy and numbers of books read per year. The Bogotá volume prints graphs depicting the survey responses to questions about newspaper reading and library visits (245, 280) and reports that 33 percent of *bogotanos* across all social classes consider reading "a consistent habit" (265). One graph shows that in seven of the eleven cities surveyed, a majority of the respondents identified reading as their preferred leisure activity (Ossa, Richard, and Téllez 150).[23] To help draw mental maps of urban space, the project also tracked information about where respondents read, the media platforms they use, the sources of their reading material, and the contexts in which they read.

This book continues some of the conversations in the comparative Ciudades Imaginadas project, but instead of drawing from large data sets derived from answers to questionnaires and interviews, the following chapters examine urban public reading programs in their specific spatial and social contexts, through their publications, activities, and participants' experiences. A short story from Santiago en 100 Palabras leads us into the programs to which this study is devoted. One of the featured stories in the program's 2015 annual contest, "Reflection," presents a scene of reading on the subway as a gateway to an interpersonal encounter. Two flirtatious, imaginative passengers catch each other's gaze in the train car window and then retreat into their books:

"REFLEJO," BY MAXIMILIANO BOLADOS ARRATIA
Te miro por el espejo que forma el vidrio al pasar por el túnel, distraída lees un libro, de vez en cuando subes tu mirada y miras mis ojos calcados en el vidrio. Me asusto, me escondo y me tapo con mi libro; tú te cansas y vuelves a lo mismo. Así, el metro es un campo de batalla, el libro una trinchera y tu mirada un disparo que a ratos anuncia la bajada.

["REFLECTION"
I look at you in the mirror that the glass creates as we pass through the tunnel, you're distracted reading a book, from time to time you look up and catch my gaze traced on the glass pane. I'm frightened, I hide and cover my face with my book; you get tired and go back to yours. So, the metro is a battlefield, the book is a trench and your gaze is a shot that sometimes announces the next station.][24] (*Santiago en 100 Palabras* 9:88)

Meeting a stranger is risky and provokes fear, yet this is what *public* means: sharing space with strangers.[25] The sensuous attraction prompts a defensive shyness, and the protagonists' gazes alternate from the windowpane to the books they are each reading as they tentatively consider their options. The activity of reading provides a refuge, a trench in the battlefield of urban movement through public space. At the same time that reading protects them, it offers them a point of connection, a built-in conversation, a common shared experience of everyday life.

In 1936 the Mexican philosopher and diplomat Alfonso Reyes addressed a historic meeting of the PEN Club hosted in Buenos Aires. He argued that Latin American "intelligence," or thought, had acquired maturity and stature, had "come of age," and claimed that "la inteligencia americana está más avezada al aire de la calle; entre nosotros no hay, no puede haber, torres de marfil" (233) (the Latin American mind is more accustomed to the air of the street; we do not have among us, we couldn't possibly have, any ivory towers).[26] The renewed relevance of Reyes's claim in postneoliberal urban Latin America is evident in the contemporary urban reading programs explored in the following pages. As these programs occupy public space with collective literary reading, they make good use of the street; there is no other place they would rather be.

CHAPTER 1

Campaigning for the Capital: Bogotá and Buenos Aires as UNESCO World Book Capitals

Bogotá needs a new story.
MARTHA SENN, BOGOTÁ SECRETARY OF CULTURE

Rumor has it that in Buenos Aires you don't have to look for books, because books come to you.
BUENOS AIRES WORLD BOOK CAPITAL, STRATEGY AND BUSINESS PLAN

The *Torre de Babel de Libros* (*Tower of Babel of Books*), an installation by Argentine artist Marta Minujín, opened to the public in the Plaza San Martín in Buenos Aires in May 2011. Over twenty-six thousand visitors walked up the winding ramps to the top of the ephemeral seven-story sculpture. The wire mesh walls of the spiraling tower were covered inside and out with thirty thousand books donated by various embassies and international groups in as many languages as the organizers could find (see figures 1.1a and 1.1b). Banners printed with the word *book* in multiple languages surrounded the base of the structure, and a sound recording of the word repeated in different languages played as visitors walked along the ramps. While waiting in line to enter the Bruegel-inspired tower, visitors were handed gold-bound copies of Jorge Luis Borges's story "La biblioteca de Babel" (The Library of Babel).

The event was such a resounding success that demolition of the piece was delayed to keep the installation open for several extra weeks. All the books were subsequently donated to one of Buenos Aires's public libraries, creating the city's first officially multilingual collection.[1] Scheduled just after the annual Feria Internacional del Libro, the

Figures 1.1a and b.
Marta Minujín's *Torre de Babel de Libros*; author photos

Torre installation was among the inaugural events of the Buenos Aires Capital Mundial del Libro campaign, and the most high profile of the year's urban literary activities.

From major events like this installation to smaller-scale happenings, the municipal government's Ministry of Culture planned, publicized, and implemented twelve months of activities that promoted books and reading in Buenos Aires under the umbrella of the city's UNESCO award as World Book Capital from April 2007 to April 2008. UNESCO pronounced a city World Book Capital for the first time in 2001. The award recognizes cities that offer innovative programming and unusually open access to books and reading through collaboration among libraries, booksellers, publishers, and other institutions. The annual award begins on 23 April, International Book and Copyright Day, and continues for one year. Madrid was the first designee in 2001, and since then two Latin American cities have been named, Bogotá in 2007 and Buenos Aires in 2011.[2] This chapter reviews the two cities' campaigns and the results of their public reading programs.

In both cases, the coordination between the municipal government and other institutions, both private and public, reveals the intricate pathways to reading in public space. In both Bogotá and Buenos Aires, official programs promoted books and reading to expand the reading public from children to senior citizens, in schools and libraries, at home and on the streets. As the following examples will demonstrate, the two cities oriented the programming in different directions. Bogotá used the campaign to establish itself as a lettered city and extend reading opportunities to a wider public by supporting initiatives that relied on ordinary citizens and unconventional venues. Buenos Aires's campaign strove to connect the city's already celebrated literary culture with new modes of cultural expression through broad institutional alliances.

The World Book Capital reading campaigns, like many of the programs reviewed in the following chapters, rely on a combination of public and private institutions. Ministries of municipal governments—in the two cases discussed here, Bogotá's Ministry of Culture, Recreation, and Sports[3] and Buenos Aires's Ministry of Culture—submitted proposals to UNESCO and then, upon being awarded the honor, programmed and implemented the year's activities. While the lettered-city institutions (schools, libraries, urban civil service bureaucracies) initiated and carried out most of the programming, the stated purpose of both campaigns was to extend reading beyond the urban cultural elite to reach and include other populations whose access to books and reading had been more limited. At the same time, the activities of the banner year aimed to celebrate each city's tradition of literary culture and the established institutions that promote books and reading. These seemingly contradictory goals—underscoring established cultural institutions and reaching out to new publics— propose a causal link, the former inspiring and supporting the latter, in efforts to promote citizenship and sociability (*convivencia*) through reading.

All aspects of the public, as defined by Jeff Weintraub, are at work behind World Book Capital programming: the state (represented here in municipal government) initiates a campaign to affect the wider community (the classical idea of republican virtue and the polis) through programming around reading that encourages "more fluid and polymorphous sociability" (7). Reading as a private, individual experience is intercepted by the municipality and appropriated by these campaigns that simultaneously reward and dismantle the lettered city. Both Bogotá and Buenos Aires honored their established literary institutions but also strove to dilute their exclusivity through articulated efforts in expansion and inclusion. Literary experiences sponsored by public governmental agencies thus burst out of the private realm, spilled onto the street, and invited new readers and writers, spectators and actors, performers and audiences to partake. The Bogotá campaign directed much of its programming to targeting a broader readership, while the Buenos Aires campaign coordinated with local and international entities to affirm its lettered reputation.

The World Book Capital campaigns, more than any other public reading initiative reviewed in this book, bureaucratize reading and literary experience. They exemplify a relatively new field in Latin America, identified as cultural management (*gestión cultural*), that has emerged in the neoliberal period. Consciously and deliberately bridging culture and management, this field encompasses "the production of cultural goods and services, the ability to compete with other leisure time options, an impact on the preferences of the intended audience, and initiatives to minimize the impact of barriers and restrictions, with the aim of contributing to the quality of citizens' cultural experience and enjoyment" (Pérez 36). Cultural management emerged in Spain and Latin America during the political and cultural transition after years of dictatorship and censorship; the return to democracy "led to the need for a new approach to cultural policy and specifically to cultural management" (Martinell 100).

The professionalization of cultural management generally includes goods and services in the domains of the fine arts, patrimony, and cultural traditions, sometimes for profit but more often not for profit. Certificate, undergraduate, and graduate degree programs in cultural management have been established in Spain and Latin America, with the goal of training a new cadre of individuals who intervene in cultural programming at various levels of the society. Argentine anthropologist and sociologist Néstor García Canclini refers to this postdictatorship emergence of programs to train professionals in cultural management, which grew out of "a social view of culture, accompanied by anthropological, sociological, and communications studies research, that rethought the involvement of the arts in society, both practically and theoretically" (*Art beyond Itself* 156). The Centro Latinoamericano de Economía Humana (CLAEH) (Latin American Center for Human Economy) in Montevideo, Uruguay, for example, has several degree and certificate programs in cultural management. One of the CLAEH brochures defines cultural management as a profession that "proposes, designs, and executes cultural products and events," and defines cultural managers as those who both promote others' artistic and creative work and create their own: "they are also creators of cultural products; they discover creative circumstances; they organize encounters between creators and the public; they disseminate, administrate, plan, implement, critique, and propose in the field of national and municipal cultural policy; they invent and reinvent spaces; they advertise, promote, and accompany artists; and they create culture themselves."

This chapter introduces high-level cultural management from mayoral ministries and other prominent municipal institutions that took charge of their city's World Book Capital campaigns. Public reading in the context of the two Latin American cities' World Book Capital programming makes literary experiences the stuff of official aesthetic policy, often with political resonance. The concept of managing culture as a profession and of national and municipal policy making in the arts and literature has a long trajectory in Latin America. The education and literacy campaigns discussed in the introduction, from early nation building in the nineteenth century to later revolutionary policies in the twentieth century, connect politics and reading directly. European Marxist analysis developed theoretical positions that were disseminated through groups such as the Frankfurt School and the Centre for Contemporary Cultural Studies at the University of Birmingham. These positions influenced Latin American thinkers with conceptual connections among social class, labor, consumerism, and culture. European literary and cultural analysis, such as that in Raymond Williams's seminal book *The Country and the City*, deeply informs work by Latin American intellectual historians and cultural critics, including Beatriz Sarlo in Argentina and Antonio Candido in Brazil. The work of scholars such as Stuart Hall and Pierre Bourdieu also linked the sociology and economics of culture.

García Canclini, who is based in Mexico, studied with Bourdieu and is one of the most prolific and influential thinkers on culture, politics, and society. Although his first published book analyzes Julio Cortázar's short stories and theories of myth, he is best known for his cultural theory of the hybrid, which considers the interplay between traditional and elite culture in Latin America. Since publication of his book *Hybrid Cultures*, he has extended his analysis to communications, new technologies, consumerism, the visual arts, and even the sociological study of urban commuting in Mexico City. In his book *Art beyond Itself: Anthropology for a Society without a Story Line*, on the global visual arts scene, he asserts that current social science and cultural inquiry have developed a closer dialogue with one another.

According to García Canclini, one cannot understand the socioeconomic without the cultural, and questions of aesthetics must be examined through a social lens. In his *Consumers and Citizens*, he studies how globalized consumer identities began to take over national and local identities through transnational marketing and electronic media innovation, particularly in megacities (16–19), asserting that "culture becomes a process of multinational assemblage" (17). In *Art beyond Itself*, however, García Canclini redirects attention to reception and the public, and urges us to consider "the activities of the targets of artists' actions, who may be not just consumers but participants in art production: 'prosumers'" (157). The World Book Capital programming in Bogotá and Buenos Aires illustrates García Canclini's more recent concept of the participatory public audience: rather than targeting the individual consumer who uses or purchases goods, World Book Capital campaigns reached out to urban citizens to involve them in reading and literature.

Some specialists in the field of cultural management criticize cultural policy that focuses on elite arts and culture, instead advocating for a more inclusive and contemporary approach to promoting cultural life locally, regionally, and nationally. For example, Manuel Esmoris would like to see initiatives that go further than funding specific artists "to demand and justify more public spending on culture" and encourages programs that "should reach out and build audiences that include people who cannot pay or who face other kinds of barriers, such as physical distance, status symbols, and a lack of regular offerings" (38). While theorists of cultural management recognize the field's challenges and vary their approaches according to particular institutions and settings, they underscore the central values of *convivencia*, public access, emotional and personal identification, and generational legacy in cultural content and programming (Esmoris 50–52). The CLAEH program in Montevideo similarly privileges values beyond the economic in promoting events and programming that nurture community belonging and heal social fragmentation: "We recognize the definitive contribution of culture as a factor in social development, and how culture can contribute to minimizing social fragmentation and strengthening policies of sociability" (brochure, my translation). The World Book Capital campaigns in Bogotá and Buenos Aires reveal this multifaceted approach to celebrating local and national literary culture. Both cities sought to strengthen their local publishing industries while embracing the social and political value of books and reading through differing strategies and goals.

"Literary capital is inherently national," points out Pascale Casanova in her landmark study *The World Republic of Letters* (34). Although her conception of *capital* has less to do with geography and more to do with value (economic and otherwise) than the consideration of literary capitals in this chapter, her argument about the "invention of literature," following Benedict Anderson, reiterates a reliance on national consolidation. For all the primacy of Latin American capital cities and the attention of the UNESCO award, the World Book Capital campaigns must be observed and assessed within their national political and cultural contexts.

It is frequently the case in Latin American capital cities that the municipal government and the national government are led by different, often opposing, political parties. The resulting debates and political confrontations can be fierce, and they can directly affect national legislation, international relations, urban planning initiatives, the economy, and the media. Culture is not immune to these confrontations: cultural initiatives, particularly in the realm of print, have important stakes in local and national decision making. In Bogotá and Buenos Aires during their respective World Book Capital years, the tension between the mayor's office and the presidency buoyed some initiatives and obstructed others.

In Colombia, President Álvaro Uribe (2002–2010), who founded the

Democratic Center movement, is a right-wing politician who devoted most of his presidential efforts to the internal conflict with guerrillas and the growing scandals over abuses by paramilitary forces. Uribe's presidency overlapped with two mayoral periods during the proposal and implementation phases of Bogotá's World Book Capital award, those of Luis Eduardo Garzón (2004–2007) and Samuel Moreno Rojas (2008–2011), who both represented leftist parties. In Argentina, President Cristina Fernández de Kirchner (2007–2015) represented the populist Peronist party while Buenos Aires mayor Mauricio Macri (2007–2015) represented the right-wing Republican Proposal (Propuesta Republicana; PRO).[4] In both cases, second-term presidents from political parties at odds with the mayors of their capital cities often contributed to the friction underlying implementation of World Book Capital programming. The following discussion is arranged chronologically according to each city's World Book Capital year. I analyze and compare the campaigns' events, publications, and rhetoric to assess their commitment to expanding literary experiences beyond the lettered elite.

Bogotá as an Open Book: The Broad Reach of Reading

The official logo of the Bogotá World Book Capital campaign features a thick, canvas-bound book with a metal handle emerging from the canvas as if it were a door to be opened (see figure 1.2). This illustration invites the reader of the catalog to enter and participate in the year's activities that promote books and reading throughout Bogotá. The programming is clustered around six themes: today's writers, tomorrow's writers; Bogotá as a grand school: reading and libraries; Bogotá as a city of publishers and booksellers; journalism and criticism; research and history; and inventing Bogotá: the city's inhabitants (Roda Fornaguera, "Libro al Viento" 6). After accepting the honor of the first Latin American World Book Capital designation, the Bogotá coordinators took immense pride in planning a wide array of activities to showcase the city's literary culture locally, regionally, and internationally. From massive projects to local activities, from visits by internationally recognized writers to local writing contests, and from exhibits of children's-book illustrations to student radio programs, Bogotá's World Book Capital planners sustained a citywide campaign promoting reading as a public everyday activity.

Figure 1.2. Bogotá World Book Capital logo; Bogotá Capital Mundial del Libro © Alcaldía Mayor de Bogotá; courtesy of Ana Roda Fornaguera, Secretaría de Cultura, Recreación, y Deporte

The UNESCO award to Bogotá cannot be divorced from the context of the country's continuing struggle against civic unrest and political violence. Although the violence between the leftist insurgents, the military, and the paramilitary forces for decades was concentrated in rural areas, in the 1990s Colombian cities were no longer immune, and politically motivated killings and kidnappings, including attacks on journalists, began to occur more regularly in Bogotá. Colombia has the unfortunate world record for the second highest number of displaced citizens in their own country, following Sudan. Tens of thousands of these displaced people leave their villages when they've been taken over by combatants and come to the cities, particularly Bogotá, to refashion their lives.[5] As municipal secretary of culture Martha Senn remarked in an article announcing the UNESCO World Book Capital award, the uncontrollable pace of growth has been the most significant challenge for the city, whose "configuration changes by the second, where neighborhoods spring up from one day to the next, where entire displaced families arrive by the hour" ("Bogotá es un libro abierto" 2).

In the years leading up to the World Book Capital designation, public tolerance for violence had reached a crisis point in Bogotá. Massive street demonstrations demanded an end to the conflict, and some initiatives to negotiate with rebels began. Under the leadership of several mayors, Bogotá embraced a number of efforts to encourage active civic culture and promote public space in an effort to reclaim an atmosphere of safety and well-being. In the realm of promoting books and reading, the recent expansion and modernization of the country's public libraries had been drawing international attention, particularly when Bogotá's system of public libraries, BiblioRed, received an Access to Learning Award of a million dollars from the Bill and Melinda Gates Foundation in 2002.[6] These funds benefited all the libraries in the Colombian network, including those in Bogotá, by providing computers and internet access. This award arrived on the heels of the 2001 opening of the city's megalibraries: the Tintal, the Parque el Tunal, and the Virgilio Barca.[7]

The UNESCO committee recognized the city's policies and implementation in enhancing public services and promoting cultural opportunities, and viewed favorably the success of some of the city's ongoing programs. Proposed during Garzón's mayoral term and carried out under the Moreno administration, the World Book Capital programming was integrated into each mayoral theme: "Bogotá sin indiferencia" (Bogotá without Indifference) under Garzón, and "Bogotá positiva: Para vivir mejor" (Bogotá: How to Live Better) under Moreno.

In her essay announcing the award, Senn oscillated between pride over some accomplishments and humble recognition of the ongoing challenges of reaching an ever-increasing urban population: "our progress as a city of readers has not improved substantially in recent years" ("Bogotá es un libro abierto" 2). The Bogotá campaign designated some of its programming to recognize and collaborate with established institutions, and funneled other resources to target new or vulnerable readers.

The twelve months of programming during Bogotá's award year not only revolved around the city's major literary institutions, such as universities, museums, famous public libraries, and annual international book fair, but also celebrated local bookstores and publishers, children's literature, and smaller neighborhood activities. Some events linked literature to other favorite pastimes; for example, the city gave away 45,000 books to fans at the soccer stadium.[8] Already existing and successful programs continued with the World Book Capital support and logo to boost them. One such program was Libro al

Viento, established in 2004: a series of free books distributed in public places and on TransMilenio buses.⁹ For one of the year's high-profile events, Bogotá 39, or B 39, thirty-nine international Latin American writers, all under forty years old, were invited to Bogotá for readings, roundtables, and school appearances. A renowned anthology titled *B 39: Antología de cuento latinoamericano* (B 39: Anthology of Latin American Short Stories) includes a short story by each of the guests (Tamayo). This event sought to address the lack of circulation of younger Latin American writers' work outside their own countries. The anthology garnered the writers much attention and helped launch many of them to future success.¹⁰

Along with publishing and circulating books, the World Book Capital campaign in Bogotá sponsored numerous writing workshops to target new talent and encourage people, from children to senior citizens, to engage in creative projects. Intending to capture and record Colombians' urban experiences and their belonging and imagination, these workshops and classes in many different genres invited participation citywide. While the campaign sponsored competitions for novel and short story writing, the workshops and classes drew attention to other genres, such as letters and *crónicas*. Given the fame of the novel in Colombia and the looming figure and oeuvre of Gabriel García Márquez, this focus on shorter nonfiction narrative forms encouraged massive participation by inviting ordinary citizens, even children, to take up a pen or approach the computer keyboard.

One of these initiatives, Cartas de la Persistencia (Letters of Persistence) elicited 5,400 letters from Colombians who answered the call to write about their experiences of perseverance during difficult times. Letter writers were asked to answer the following question: "How do you nurture the perseverance to keep on living in Colombia in spite of adversity?" Sponsored by Bogotá World Book Capital and several other entities (Universidad Javeriana, Biblioteca Luis Ángel Arango, Fundación BAT), the collection included letters that told how their authors "faced obstacles in their daily lives, accounting for not only the tragedies but also the motivation to overcome disintegration and paralysis" (Ospina Pizano 10). These letters give testimony to all kinds of adversity, from family violence to armed conflict, "from the most subtle to the most overwhelming difficulties" (Ospina Pizano 11). While most Colombians do not consider themselves writers, almost everyone has written a letter. These letters give voice to their authors' resilience, honesty, faith, and inventiveness amid both extraordinary tragedies and the challenges of the daily grind. An archive of the letters is available for public consultation at the Biblioteca Luis Ángel Arango, and a selection of the letters is collected in a volume published in the Libro al Viento series.

The published book includes a few historic letters by renowned writers (Miguel de Cervantes, Franz Kafka, José Asunción Silva), together with letters by Colombians of all walks of life, young and old, men and women. There are letters by victims of violence and displacement, by young adults struggling to find their path, by older people seeking understanding and forgiveness. One chapter in the book collects letters written to the dead, another features letters recounting episodes of the country's decades-long armed conflict. Excerpts from a letter by Íngrid Betancourt to her mother, written while she was held hostage by the Revolutionary Armed Forces of Colombia (FARC) guerrillas, is reprinted as the opening to the chapter of letters that address the armed conflict (Ospina Pizano 115–117).[11] Betancourt shares her despair in captivity but expresses how the act of writing a letter to her mother gives her hope: "tu voz es mi cordón umbilical con la vida" (your voice is my umbilical cord to life) (115). Other than the few exceptions of Betancourt and well-known authors, the letters in the volume come from the general public and tell humble stories of economic subsistence, youthful ambitions, grief, regret, and determination and hope for the future. The book's epilogue underscores the massive and public nature of this project: "giving voice to civil words in public space" (Pérez Mejía 147).

In the chapter called "De los trabajos y los días" (About Work and Everyday Life) in *Cartas de la persistencia* (Ospina Pizano), the letter writers express their challenges in finding work, supporting themselves through school, and providing for themselves and their families. Alongside their frustrations and obstacles, they mention reading and literature as a doorway to a better future. Layla Gizeth Cifuentes writes to her friend Ivette that times are tough because she has not found a job. However, she remains hopeful that an opportunity will come through in her chosen field of reading to children, "leerle un cuento a un niño que no sabe leer, que no puede comprar un libro" (reading a story to a child who doesn't know how to read, who has no money to buy books) (17). Reading literature, she says, has given her "fuerzas para no desvanecer, para no rendirme" (the strength to keep from falling apart, to not give up) (18).

Another letter writer, Claudia Rodríguez, constructs her story of persistence around the Paraderos Paralibros Paraparques in Columnas Park, where she is the facilitator.[12] Young adults like Rodríguez manage brightly painted yellow cabinets, extensions of the public library system in Bogotá, opening them regularly for local patrons to borrow and return books. One of their most important tasks is to host story hours for children to introduce them to the collection and encourage them to read. Rodríguez delights in the children's responses to the stories she reads: "se encuentran con tanta intensidad que lloran, ríen, apuestan, pelean, envejecen un poco" (they exhibit such intensity that they cry, laugh, bet, fight, begin to grow up) (35–36). She used to wonder why they kept showing up each day that she opened the cabinet of books for the neighborhood, but "ya no me pregunto por qué vienen las personas, he ido encontrando la respuesta" (I no longer wonder why people come, I've found the answer): in the children's paper airplanes, jokes, and riddles, and songs they sing that are based on the books (36).

In another writing project during Bogotá's World Book Capital year, Crónicas Barriales: Escribir con los Cinco Sentidos (Neighborhood Chronicles: Writing with All Five Senses), a hundred students participated in journalism workshops at public libraries, led by advanced students in media communications. It was cosponsored by the Biblioteca Luis Ángel Arango, the Communications school of the Universidad Javeriana, the city's archival museum (Archivo de Bogotá), and the District Secretariat of Culture, Recreation, and Sports, and the participants included high school and private and public university students. The city's World Book Capital catalog praises the project as a unique experiment in social class mixing: "gathering in one room a group of young people from such dissimilar backgrounds was an interesting experiment in social mobility" (Melguizo and Posada 113). While the students were trained in journalistic methodology and exposed to professionals in the field, the emphasis on producing *crónicas* gave the young writers the opportunity to convert their own local experiences and views of the neighborhoods into original narratives.

The *crónica* as a genre has a particularly Latin American and urban history. More personal than news reporting, it offers an intimate view of a local place or event, a sort of eye witness report in which the subjective nature of the author's observations, environments, and behaviors plays a major role.[13] The focus on the local scene aims to draw a quotidian landscape, "a cartography of Bogotá from all four cardinal directions" (Melguizo and Posada 112). As residents of their neighborhoods since childhood, the young *cronistas* "recount their strong neighborhood attachment and identity" (Melguizo and Posada 113).

Two of these *crónicas* feature reading as an identifying experience for their neighborhoods. Both essays describe a specific place that characterizes the neighborhood: an informal bookstore in one, and the walls and stalls of public restrooms in the other.

Carolina Cuervo G. offers a portrait of Carlos Escobar and a garage that he's turned into a bookstore in La Soledad neighborhood. The chronicle's title, "Refugio en La Soledad" (Refuge in Solitude), with its double entendre around *solitude*, announces this place as "mucho más que otra librería de las tantas que hay en las calles de Bogotá" (much more than any other bookstore you can find on the streets of Bogotá) (Melguizo and Posada 106). Although Carlos calls himself nomadic, he has established a sort of cultural club in this small space packed with over two thousand books, where he lives and where friends and customers stop by for a game of chess and conversation. Carlos sees himself not as a book collector, but as a facilitator for each book along its trajectory; his role is to ensure that each one "queda en las manos de quien debe quedar" (finds its way into the hands of whom it's meant for) (108). His bookstore "no es solo un lugar donde se venden libros. 'Mi relación con los libros es más sensual que comercial.'" (The bookstore is not just a place where books are sold. "My relationship with books is more sensual than commercial.") (109). Carlos runs his store like a lending library or open house, a permeable space for neighborhood sociability.

In "Rayado de lo escondido" (Secretly Scratched), Juan Camilo Herrera Casilimas takes the reader on a tour of graffiti in men's public restrooms on the National University campus in Bogotá. His fascination with the personal messages, philosophical queries, and political pronouncements scratched into the bathroom walls and doors inspires repeat visits with a notebook to copy them down. The smell of dried urine and damp cement permeates the space where

> la publicidad está por todos lados, en cada una de las paredes, incluso en el marco de la puerta, ningún espacio es virgen, sólo el techo. . . .
> Es un buen medio de divulgación el poner lo que se busca o lo que se opina en el baño de una universidad pública, cualquiera que entre está obligado a leerlo y de una forma tan desprevenida.
> [the ads are everywhere, on each and every wall, even on the door frame, there is no virgin space, only the ceiling. . . . It's a good means

of communication to put what you're looking for or what you're thinking about on the walls of a public university bathroom, anyone who comes in is obligated to read it, without warning.] (197–198)

Herrera Casilimas goes beyond chronicling here; he enters into something of an investigative project. Particularly curious about the messages inviting sexual encounters, he tracks some of the frequent names and phone numbers—many of the messages are signed "Eduardo," and the first-floor restroom in the engineering building is often cited as a meeting place—and follows up with a phone call to ask, "quería saber si lo del letrero es verdad" (I wanted to know if what's written in the message is true) (198). From his tentative, nervous phone calls to an unexpected encounter in one of the bathrooms, this chronicle enters into the urban underside of a lettered space: "Encierran sus palabras en esta caja, muro de lamentaciones, . . . rayones escondidos con un fondo gris o blanco turbio, pintura descascarada por el óxido, llena de manchas, tachones e insultos" (They enclose their words in this box, a wall of lamentations, . . . hidden scratches on a grey or dirty white background, paint chipping from rust, full of stains, cross-outs, and insults) (200). Herrera Casilimas reveals clandestine "required" academic reading that physically inscribes an urban lettered institution. His description of these graffiti-covered walls with no blank space—"ningún espacio es virgen"—hints cleverly at the sexually transgressive texts. The chronicler himself emerges from his investigation tainted and vulnerable, but knowing: his question about whether the messages he read were real has been answered.

One of the initiatives launched under the UNESCO World Book Capital award, titled Bogotá, un Libro Abierto (Bogotá, an Open Book, hereafter BULA), most clearly responds to the open book theme evident in the campaign's visual logo. Under the subsection called Inventing Bogotá: The City's Residents, this area of programming invited citizens to "contribute to the cultural enrichment" of the campaign and to propose "new ways of approaching the city" (Melguizo and Posada 103). The most ambitious programmatic effort of the award year, according to writer Javier Monsalve (quoted in Caro Montoya), BULA distributed grants totaling $700,000 for a series of initiatives involving reading and writing in public space. Libraries, publications, organizations, and individuals proposed projects, and the winning proposals were awarded funding to develop their initiatives during the campaign year (see figure 1.3). The projects fell into three

Figure 1.3. Bogotá, an Open Book, call for proposals; published in *Número*; Bogotá Capital Mundial del Libro © Alcaldía Mayor de Bogotá; courtesy of Ana Roda Fornaguera, Secretaría de Cultura, Recreación, y Deporte

main categories: those that worked toward making literature more accessible (nineteen grants), those that highlighted ethnic cultures (five grants), and those with a local focus (six grants). Some of the projects revolved around a particular Colombian work or author, such as García Márquez's *Cien años de soledad* and Andrés Caicedo's work, while others documented important institutions, such as the city's libraries (see Guerrero). Several of the chosen initiatives intervened in neighborhoods through schools and other institutions with creative writing classes, journalism workshops for youth, and collection of local oral histories.

The projects in the first category, Bogotá for Everyone, particularly pertained to public reading. They extended the boundaries of literary experience to new audiences, utilized unconventional spaces, and exploited the city's infrastructure. Moving beyond the expected venues of schools and libraries, these initiatives drew ordinary citizens into the experience of reading by marking public space and offering opportunities for community reading and writing. Throughout the year's programming efforts, which embraced both a local and a global scope, the BULA initiatives underscored the local. Ana Roda Fornaguera, coordinator of the Bogotá World Book Capital campaign, emphasized the attention to international as well as city-based programs. She contrasted the projects that encouraged "*bogotanos* to look outside our borders" (visits by international writers such as B 39 and a literary contest that was open to the entire Spanish-speaking world) with the BULA initiatives, which "looked inward, helped us define who we are as *bogotanos* today" (quoted in Caro Montoya).[14]

Some of the BULA projects consisted of visual interventions in public spaces. One of these, Lugares Comunes (Common Places), projected images on urban information stands installed on busy sidewalks near bus stops. The photographic billboards combined amplified images of elements of the book as an object alongside fragments of literary texts about love, friendship, solidarity, respect, and tolerance. The project aimed to grab the attention of pedestrians and passersby so they "might experience a transformation in their way of thinking and feeling that could generate a social transformation" (Melguizo and Posada 137).

The most colorful and interactive of the urban intervention projects was Leer . . . Severo Viaje (Reading, a Tough Trip), another BULA-granted initiative, which held graffiti workshops for sixty young people who were either at risk for or already involved in gang activity in specific neighborhoods. The organizers proposed art workshops and collective mural painting projects together with readings and visits to libraries and exhibits to motivate the participants to read and write, and "to link these activities—foreign and misunderstood as boring—to their culture, identities, taste, and forms of expression" (Melguizo and Posada 145).

Leer . . . Severo Viaje produced a series of murals in extremely poor sections of Bogotá known for slum housing conditions and gang and guerrilla activity where the young participants had dropped out of school. One of the groups was from Ciudad Bolívar, a slum in the hills above the city leading into rural areas. In a mural painted after the group's visit to the planetarium, panels feature planets, a night sky, clouds, imaginative spaceships, and a few astronomical facts. A dialogue bubble announces, "HEMOS ENCONTRADO UN EXTRAÑO LIBRO ¡AAGGRAAHG!" (WE'VE FOUND A STRANGE BOOK, AAGGRAAHG!).

An editorial introduction to the online magazine that chronicles the program's goals, activities, and results comments: "The experience with each group continually surprised us: we found geniuses hidden up in the hills, who spent years teaching themselves, virtuosos who had never had the opportunity to discover their own artistic talents, poets in search of an audience to hear their insightful take on reality through rap, writers who rewrote classic stories with humor, groups of kids who had scratched out with their bare hands their own path as graffiti artists in the neighborhood" ("Leer . . . Severo Viaje" 2). Similar to the journalism project of neighborhood chronicles, Leer . . . Severo Viaje engaged groups of young people to expose them to reading and other forms of expressive culture in order to produce something new that contributed to the local scene. This kind of urban interventionist pedagogy, which creates new experiences with youth through reading and social interaction, was at the heart of the BULA grants and a major emphasis of the Bogotá campaign overall.

Los que cuentan: An Urban Anthology

The Bogotá cultural magazine *Número*, edited by Guillermo González Uribe, was awarded one of the BULA grants for a short story contest and anthology. The open call announced in the magazine's September 2007 issue stated that "the stories must be related to the city of Bogotá" (Bogotá un Libro Abierto) and asked writers to "look at the city as a generator of stories" (Melguizo and Posada 129). The contest received 443 submissions; 3 winners and 13 finalists were published in the anthology *Los que cuentan* (Those Who Tell Stories), edited by González and Ana Cristina Mejía and distributed to subscribers and to schools. The complex portrait of Bogotá that emerges in the stories communicates an edgy, tense, distrusting, even conspiratorial cityscape. The stories feature urban settings—a school, a brothel, bars and discotheques, buses, movie theaters, residential apartment buildings, shops—where the characters seem trapped by institutional codes or their own fears and traumas. The mountains surrounding the city and the gloom of gray clouds weigh on these stories with their oppressive, unrelenting shadows. One story calls Bogotá "un pozo urbano" (an urban pit): "esa ciudad vigilada por dos montañas y asediada a veces por una neblina que podía hacerla parecer fantasmal" (that city watched over by two mountains and besieged by mist that turned it ghostly) (Tamayo Sánchez 162 and 167). In the midst of this sense of impending dread, violent acts abound: gratuitous, vengeful, politically motivated. They occur in these stories as inevitably and unpredictably as natural disasters like fires or earthquakes.

Not surprisingly, many of the stories in *Los que cuentan* trace Bogotá itineraries, outlined by the major arteries and localized in neighborhoods, that are accessed on foot or by the bus rapid transit system, TransMilenio. The stories move through a variety of neighborhoods and social classes, with destinations that recapture the past or are motivated by vengeance, love, or fantasy. In "Susana y el sol" (Susana and the Sun), by Óscar Godoy Barbosa, a prostitute sits outside a brothel to enjoy the sun. The story opens with her views of the street on a Sunday morning, as cars, bicycles, and skaters zoom by (Godoy Barbosa 23–24); everyone seems to be on the move except Susana. Her boss calls for her to come inside, but she lingers a bit longer, a small act of resistance before she is swallowed up by the grim building with its heavy-curtained windows.

In "Manzanita envenenada" (Little Poisoned Apple), by Alberto Duque López, a stalking protagonist follows his object of desire, whom he calls Audrey Hepburn, through parks and streets, to cafés and concerts, and on buses, then finally stabs her in a movie theater. As he watches her every move, he narrates his urban pursuit as though he is speaking to her, fantasizing about his plans to "devorarte pedacito a pedacito después de desnudarte sobre esa banca del parque de la calle 60, junto al ruido de las busetas y los buses y los taxis que siguen por la séptima o bajan por la calle hacia la 13 o la Caracas o en busca de la 53" (devour you a bit at a time after stripping you on that bench in the park on 60th Street alongside the noise of the vans and buses and taxis that turn onto 7th Avenue or go down the street toward 13th Avenue or Caracas Avenue or toward 53rd Street) (130).

The narrator of Carlos Córdoba Martínez's "Sara" remembers an unusual night out with friends over the weekend while he takes a bus on an ordinary Monday morning. "La ciudad tiene muchas facetas en la noche: si estudias, tiene un orden establecido; si vas de rumba, tiene otros colores, otros olores, otras gentes" (The city has many facets at night: on a day that you have classes, there is an established order; if you're going out partying, it has other colors, other smells, other people) (140). In "Un sombrero para la plaza," by Ana Paula Castro Castro, a middle-aged woman walks through the city and comes to a street full of hat shops. She becomes obsessed with the street and the hats in the shop windows, buys a straw fedora (*gardeliano*) and heads to the Plaza Bolívar to place the hat on the statue of Bolívar. The next morning, on her way to work, she passes through the plaza and is pleased to find the fedora still atop the statue, until a police officer reaches it with his cane to take it down. The selection reflects the contest's stated goal of encouraging the creation of stories that grow out of the city's own spaces and maps.[15]

While the stories discussed above explore city streets and open space, others turn inward and feature fear, paranoia, and disasters. "Con los pies en la tierra" (With Your Feet on the Ground), by Yezid Cepeda Buitrago, centers on an earthquake, and "¿Hay alguien en casa?" (Is Anyone Home?), by Guido Leonardo Tamayo Sánchez, tells of a series of fires. In each case, the anticipation of disaster sends some of the characters into a panic. In Tamayo Sánchez's tale, Bogotá is afflicted by a series of mysterious fires. In spite of the grey mist, "algunos resplandores intermitentes y esparcidos a lo largo y ancho de la ciudad se divisaban en el horizonte como un juego de fogatas sobre una maqueta" (a few intermittent flashes were visible all over the city as far as you could see like a series of campfires on a model) (162). A couple hears the strange noises of approaching fire and closes up their house, barricading the doors and shutting all the hallways. They are consumed by "el miedo avasallador y destructivo" (a consuming and destructive fear) until their home "parecía una caja inexpugnable. Un escondite sin fisuras. Todo estaba herméticamente sellado" (looked like an impenetrable box. A hideout without a crack. Everything was hermetically sealed) (168).

In Cepeda Buitrago's story, "Con los pies en la tierra," the narrator works in disaster prevention, giving lectures to groups about how to survive earthquakes. His wife becomes consumed with fear and takes matters into her own hands. She buys bulkier furniture under which they can hide, insists that they wear special whistles they might blow to alert rescue workers, and schedules rescue drills at home. "Esta ciudad lo era todo" (this city meant everything to them), and as they walk through the streets, they ponder "cuál de estos edificios resistiría, cuál colapsaría primero" (which of these buildings will hold up, which will collapse first) (82). Their worst fears are realized when an earthquake destroys their building, and in the ruins the narrator finds his wife and his boss, huddled together naked among the pieces of their protective furniture.

Through the characters' routines and itineraries, the stories in *Los que cuentan* communicate urban familiarity and an affectionate sense of tradition and belonging. Nevertheless, a menacing uneasiness, sometimes leading to obsession and panic, also grips the stories. A dark atmosphere surrounds these Bogotá scenes. One of the stories calls the city "un feliz campo de concentración. Más que un campo de concentración, era un búnker. . . . Había una preocupación general en el ambiente" (a cheery concentration camp. Rather than a concentration camp, a bunker. . . . There was an overall anxiety in the atmosphere) (Romero Rey 152). The characters' desperation and vulnerability respond to more than natural disasters: violence, corruption, betrayal, and revenge hover around every corner.

Gente y Cuentos: Reading in and with the Community

Another BULA grant was awarded to the group Gente y Cuentos–Colombia, a branch of the US-based nonprofit People and Stories/Gente y Cuentos. Since the 1970s, the program has organized groups of adults in community settings, in both the US and Latin America, to listen to short stories being read aloud. The program aims to reach new publics in unconventional settings that have never had access to these works before, goals very much in line with the BULA grants. Bogotá-based school librarian Patricia Vélez became acquainted with People and Stories/Gente y Cuentos during her Fulbright-funded graduate study in library science at Rutgers University in the early 2000s. Impressed by the methodology and its applicability for Colombia, she wrote a research paper on the program. Upon returning to Bogotá, she started leading Gente y Cuentos reading groups in small neighborhood libraries and established the beginnings of a local program that she hoped to expand. The BULA grant contributed to consolidation of the program by providing funding to train more facilitators,[16] conduct programs, develop a graphic logo (see figures 1.4a and 1.4b), and film a documentary on the group's experiences.[17]

This grant was particularly meaningful for the parent organization in the United States because the program's founder, Sarah Hirschman, first experimented with informal short-story reading groups in Colombia, where she and her husband, development economist Albert O. Hirschman, lived for five years in the 1950s.[18] There she became immersed in Latin American literature at the same time that she was struck by the region's gaping inequalities in education and access to reading. Soon after her Colombia experience, she participated in a workshop with Brazilian educator and philosopher Paulo Freire and

Figures 1.4a and b. Gente y Cuentos folder © Gente y Cuentos–Colombia; courtesy of Gente y Cuentos–Colombia

was inspired by his approach to education, which is based on experiential local knowledge.[19] Out of these experiences Hirschman forged the People and Stories/Gente y Cuentos methodology: weekly sessions with small groups of participants centered on a literary short story read aloud, followed by discussion that interlaces observations about the story with participants' own experiences. Hirschman elaborates how "the conversation will somehow always relate both to our own experience and to the story and yet also take off into all kinds of liberating, playful, and joyful unexpected directions. . . . The literary text becomes the occasion which sparks and sustains an interweaving of private impressions with public debate" (*People and Stories* 57–58).[20] This melding of literary language, personal reflection, group dynamics, and public space at the heart of Hirschman's methodology also defies social class and educational barriers. Gente y Cuentos did help open the book to a broader community of Bogotá readers.

During the BULA granting period, Gente y Cuentos–Colombia conducted thirty-five eight-week programs in prisons, churches, libraries, schools, adult education centers, maternity residences, and drug rehabilitation programs. Some of the trained facilitators were involved in projects that worked with ex-combatants and victims of political violence. Several programs were offered at maternity residences supported by the Catholic Church. These centers care for pregnant women who are still deciding whether to keep their children or release for adoption; they receive room, board, and medical care along with counseling and group activities. During one of the sessions a group of six women of varying ages gathered with a facilitator to read and discuss Isabel Allende's story "Dos palabras" (Two Words), about a woman who had to choose her own name because she was born into a family that was too poor to name their children. The discussion turned to the participants' experiences in naming children; several of them had other children as well as the one on the way. This was particularly poignant in a group of women who were all contemplating giving up their children, women for whom imagining names for their babies must have been very painful.

Another facilitator worked with a group of teenagers who were in a program that provided activities to redirect them away from crime. This was an unusually rough group of participants, and one day as she was leaving the site, she noticed that her wallet was open and wondered if money or credit cards had been taken. When she got home and explored more thoroughly, she saw that not only were all of her belongings intact, but one of the participants had slipped in a poem he had written anonymously. Another group discussed Cortázar's "Casa tomada" (House Taken Over), a tale about a pair of siblings quietly living alone in the family house when they begin to hear strange noises. The brother and sister gradually close off rooms, corridors, and whole wings of the house where the sounds have spread, until they finally abandon the house entirely. This story can elicit a wide range of imaginative interpretations about what kind of force has occupied the house (ghosts, jealous cousins, hidden siblings, imaginary beings), but in Colombia many participants associated the occupiers with leftist guerrillas or paramilitary forces, and some told terrifying stories of being displaced by such invasions. Personal reflection, local knowledge, family anecdotes, and national politics all come into play in these sessions, where short stories unlock individual and collective histories.

Throughout the year, the Bogotá campaign's programming straddled its focus between celebrating the book's institutional and commercial stalwarts—libraries, publishers, educational centers, media organizations—and working toward greater access to books and reading in local, grassroots, community-based settings. Perhaps the project that best bridged these parallel efforts was the installation of Biblioestaciones, which bring the public library system closer to the patrons (see figure 1.5). Modeled on similar small library branches called BiblioMetros in Santiago and Madrid, these are mobile stands located in heavily trafficked pedestrian areas, such as TransMilenio bus hubs. The Biblioestaciones carry a limited selection of circulating library materials, including Libro al Viento books, and are staffed with workers who can help patrons apply for library cards. Yesid Bahuence, who works at one of the Biblioestaciones at a TransMilenio hub, registered some forty library patrons daily; the busiest Biblioestación counted 120 new patrons a day. Because the cost of books and distance from libraries were two main reasons given for lower reading rates among *bogotanos*, the Biblioestaciones helped ensure that "now there's no excuse for not reading." For a commuter, finding a Biblioestación and having a book to read "makes the trip home a return trip to yourself" ("Hágase socio de las Biblioestaciones").

Senn, Bogotá's secretary of culture during the UNESCO award year, encapsulated the pride of and the challenge to the city when the award was announced. She considered it a recognition "honoring the work that, from the public and private sectors, we have been developing in the city to promote reading and the democratization of books"

Figure 1.5. Biblioestación; author photo

Figure 1.6. Banner with Bogotá campaign logo; author photo; Bogotá Capital Mundial del Libro © Alcaldía Mayor de Bogotá; courtesy of Ana Roda Fornaguera, Secretaría de Cultura, Recreación, y Deporte

("Bogotá, Capital Mundial del Libro 2007" 2). Rather than assuming that the goal was already accomplished, the city's Ministry of Culture approached the award as a boost to programming efforts that encompass literacy and accessibility. Reading in the city is "a right of all inhabitants," according to Senn; it is a "factor in human development and social inclusion" (see figure 1.6).[21]

The city embraced reading as a human right, a strategy for cultural development, and a tool for intervening in urban space. Mural painting, journalism workshops, community reading groups, and the writing of personal letters by thousands of ordinary citizens: with these activities the Bogotá campaign relied on community-based pedagogy targeting youth, disadvantaged neighborhoods, and vulnerable citizens to elevate everyday stories into literary reading and writing experiences. The goal of inclusion underscored blending and integrating populations that might not otherwise meet, such as public and private school students in the journalism workshops that produced the urban chronicles anthology, and the confluence of people in public spaces such as libraries and TransMilenio buses. The campaign drew literary reading out of private intimate spaces like the home and pushed it beyond the boundaries of public institutions like schools and libraries to create participatory civic interactions that reached new reading publics. The Buenos Aires World Book Capital campaign a few years later proposed intermedial projects around books and reading that reaffirmed the city's status as a world literary capital.

Buenos Aires, Always the Lettered City: Books and Other Modes of Cultural Expression

Buenos Aires would not be the same without its passion for books.
MAURICIO MACRI, MAYOR OF BUENOS AIRES

In a public address to introduce one of the Buenos Aires World Book Capital events, Hernán Lombardi, the city's minister of culture, insisted on the connection between reading and citizenship underlying the city's programming during the UNESCO nomination. He particularly lauded the experience of reading "for the pure pleasure of it" and as a catalyst for "the possibility of a more productive sociability." Minujín's public art installation the *Tower of Babel of Books* shared these goals. In an interview just before the installation opened, Minujín underscored two main themes in her work: the ephemeral (her sculptures and installations ultimately are disassembled or destroyed) and public participation.[22] The booklet containing a Borges story that was distributed to visitors to the tower also included some basic information about the artist, the installation, and the book donations. A brief section titled "Why a Tower of Babel of Books?" announced the significance of the sculpture in the following bullet points:

- Living together with others in the same space from the most broad to the most specific
- The possibility of building a common foundation out of individual experiences
- The grand metaphor of what happens on a daily basis in our city, where diverse groups live side by side and make up Buenos Aires's identity. (10)

These linked goals of reading for pleasure, engaging actively as a citizen, and improving *convivencia* resonated throughout the Buenos Aires World Book Capital campaign.

The Buenos Aires proposal presented to UNESCO affirms books and reading as "pillars of the city's identity" ("Propuesta" 1). The proposal took as its point of departure the fact that Buenos Aires is already recognized as a literary capital. Its first section, titled "Historical Background," reviews the city's history: its founding by European explorers, the arrival of the first printing press, development of public libraries in the early nineteenth century, the creation of writers' salons that contributed to nation formation, and the establishment of important journals. The city's Ministry of Culture took on the UNESCO designation with pride and with the confidence of possessing all the necessary elements of a literary capital: "the place where literary consecration is ordained . . . where literary resources are concentrated, where they accumulate, where belief is incarnated" (Casanova 23).[23]

Buenos Aires has not only the economic and material infrastructure of a literary capital—publishers, bookstores, universities, print media outlets, critics—but also the imaginary and mythic quality that Casanova ascribes to Paris (30). One of the invited participants in the Buenos Aires World Book Capital event called La Ciudad Contada, the Ecuadorian writer Gabriela Alemán, attests to Buenos Aires's mythical draw on other Latin American intellectuals. She first learned about the city from her mother's stories about her parents' visit to Buenos Aires before she was born: "Tomé lo que me contó y, sobre ese humus, construí una ciudad" (I took what she told me, and on top of that humus, I built a city) (80). The UNESCO award globally confirmed Buenos Aires's standing as a literary capital, which for many Latin American readers, writers, and critics was already an accepted fact. In the same way that Casanova recognizes Paris as a literary capital that "belonged not to France alone, but to all nations" (87), throughout Latin America, whether proudly from within or resentfully from afar, Buenos Aires has long been considered one of the region's literary capitals.[24]

Therefore, the programming generated for the World Book Capital award took the city's literary status as a given and branched out to collaborate with local and international organizations, even embassies, to promote a diverse series of events and programs that revolved around books. The proposal to UNESCO elucidated the program committee's goal of "encouraging networks of participation between public and private institutions that will convert the city into a true map of readers and reading" ("Propuesta" 26). Another goal that underlay Buenos Aires's programming reveals one of the political tensions between the city and the Fernández de Kirchner presidency: "to create citizenship starting with books, an indispensable element for promoting freedom of expression and thought, the foundation of any democracy" ("Propuesta" 26). Josefina Delgado, undersecretary of culture for the city in the months leading up to the UNESCO award, stated that Buenos Aires being named World Book Capital "comes at just the right time" (personal interview, my translation).[25] She emphasized the campaign's attempt to vindicate freedom of expression as an indirect response from Mayor Macri's administration to tensions over President Fernández de Kirchner's 2009 media legislation (Law 26.522 on Audiovisual Communications Service). The press release announcing the UNESCO award also links the designation with freedom of expression, pointing out that in 2011 Argentina would celebrate the centenary of the law guaranteeing freedom of the press. It even quotes that law, emphasizing that it is "introduced with the beautiful phrase: 'the ability to express one's ideas is as natural to man as thinking'" (press release, my translation).

In carrying out these objectives, the programming took an interdisciplinary approach to connect reading with urban space through a broad array of cultural expressions. The proposal refers to the "crossing of registers," activities supported by the Ministry of Culture that combine genres and modes of cultural expression ("Propuesta" 23). Over the course of the year, events highlighted numerous crossings between literature, film, dance, music, photography, and other visual arts. The strategy and business plan outlines a year of planning leading up to the inauguration of Buenos Aires as a World Book Capital. The city government "will be the main financial sponsor" and "will endeavor the financial support from national and international companies, embassies, international organizations, cooperation agencies and associations" ("Propuesta" 18). As the following examples illustrate, the municipal Ministry of Culture expected all cultural events to "be aligned in accordance" with World Book Capital programming ("Propuesta" 18). Cooperation and cosponsoring with municipal and national organizations, such as the city's public libraries, the Argentine Publishing Association, and Argentine writers societies were essential; many events were organized with the support of local cultural organizations, international embassies, and museums.

The Buenos Aires International Book Fair always begins in late April and coincides with International Book and Copyright Day, 23 April, when the UNESCO award officially begins. Thus the book fair was a logical launch event for the campaign. The Buenos Aires book fair has been a major event in the city since the first fair in 1975.

Bogotá and Buenos Aires as Book Capitals   67

Figure 1.7. Feria Internacional del Libro, Buenos Aires; author photo

It is the second largest in Latin America (after the annual fair in Guadalajara, Mexico) and one of the five largest in the world. The theme of the 2011 fair was "Una ciudad abierta al mundo de los libros" (A City Open to the World of Books), echoing the UNESCO award. The sign at the main entrance displayed the theme and was illustrated by a gray silhouette of buildings with familiar Buenos Aires signs for streets named after celebrated writers (see figure 1.7).

The 2011 fair was held from 20 April to 9 May, was spread out over 45,000 square meters of the convention center, hosted more than 1,500 exhibitors representing forty-three countries, and received over 1.5 million visitors. Two parallel booths at the fair celebrated Buenos Aires: one representing the city and another representing the World Book Capital campaign. The campaign's display was prominently located near the entrance to the first pavilion of the convention center and included the program's logo, a streetscape of books (see figure 1.8). The book fair is organized by the Fundación el Libro, a nonprofit devoted to "promoting books and increasing reading habits" ("Propuesta" 10).[26] According to Gabriela Adamo, Fundación el Libro director until 2011, the city government "always made sure to

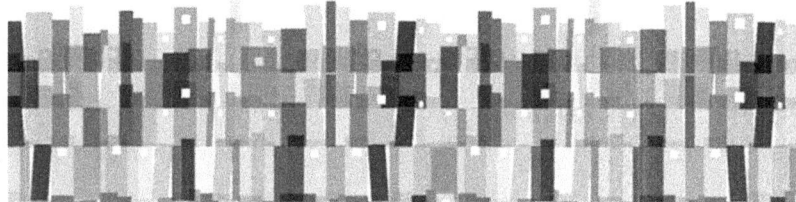

Figure 1.8. Buenos Aires World Book Capital logo; courtesy of Josefina Delgado for the Buenos Aires Ministry of Culture

have a very strong and active presence at the fair" (personal communication, my translation). Although the book fair functions as a commercial showcase for publishers, the entrance fee is reasonable and includes most of the activities, including lectures, readings, book signings, and panel discussions. Several days of special programming are reserved for school groups and teachers.

Buenos Aires Honors Writers and Their Books

As the strategy and business plan indicates, the year's activities fell under three "work axes": promoting reading, promoting the book, and promoting literary heritage. While publishing books under the banner of the World Book Capital was not one of the Buenos Aires campaign's principal activities, some printed books were associated with particular events and were distributed free to those in attendance. The small reprint booklet of Borges's story "The Library of Babel," given to visitors to Minujín's *Tower of Babel of Books*, is one example. These books or pamphlets were not the focus of the events but were a support or extension of the events' experiential aspects. The free books published and distributed during the award year also publicized the city and branded it as a World Book Capital. According to campaign staff member Federico Coulin, the books were a "surprise" or a bonus at the events (personal interview). On the books' covers are printed the logos of the city, the World Book Capital campaign, and all cosponsors. The bright yellow covers visually associate the books with the year of programming, as well as with Macri's political party, the PRO (see figure 1.9).

Most of the books distributed at World Book Capital events in Buenos Aires were not new literary works, but were canonical works reprinted to commemorate events and showcase the city as an arena of cultural production, a hub for multiple art forms. They also presented an opportunity for cosponsorship, from various institutions and organizations, with a concrete material result.

A small book with a short story by Silvana Boschi, "El manto de plata" (The Silver Cover), appeared on Argentina's National Day of

Figure 1.9. Books published under the Buenos Aires World Book Capital campaign; author photo

Dance (10 October). The symbolic date honors a group of Argentine ballet dancers who died in a plane crash in 1971, and Boschi's story incorporates two of the victims, Norma Fontenla and José Neglia. In a brief prologue, Minister of Culture Lombardi insists on the city's role in these dancers' training and performance notoriety and underscores Buenos Aires as the home of the Teatro Colón and as a renowned venue for the arts: "with this publication we honor the world of dance in our City" (Boschi 7).

Some of the published books are associated with a conference or a symposium, such as an anthology of short writings by Julio Cortázar and Georges Perec, *Versiones de la imaginación: Julio Cortázar y Georges Perec* (Versions of the Imagination), which was offered to those who attended a symposium of lectures and readings on the two writers' works. The symposium and anthology were cosponsored by the French embassy and the Alliance Française in Argentina. This homage to Cortázar and Perec also celebrated urban space as a literary construct: in his introduction to the book, Lombardi calls Paris the bridge between the two writers, as both the city they called home and a place evoked and re-created in their work (10). Indeed, Cortázar's short story "El otro cielo" ("The Other Heaven"), included in the book, presents parallel plots that take place in Buenos Aires and Paris during different historical periods that intersect in the covered arcades in both cities.[27]

Buenos Aires events and books recognized other major Argentinian writers as well, including Ernesto Sabato and Oliverio Girondo. Sabato's hundredth birthday on 24 June 2011 provided a natural opportunity to honor him. Unfortunately the author died just a month shy of his milestone birthday, but the festivities went on. They included a film series, a historical tour in the Belgrano neighborhood of significant places in his life and writing, and new editions of some of his works. A photography contest was held to choose the cover image for a special birthday edition of his novel *El túnel* (The Tunnel), with an exhibit of the finalists' photographs and a book launch at a historic museum. On Sabato's birthday, copies of his *Cuatro hombres del pueblo* (Four Men from the Village), re-edited from a 1979 edition, were given away to passengers on public transportation, including the new Metrobus line. The book also commemorates the hundredth anniversary, in 2011, of the Argentine law protecting freedom of the press, which, according to Lombardi "was the first step in transforming Buenos Aires into a city that, since then, cultivates reading and writing as one of its principal symbolic activities" (7–8). Copies of Sabato's books were added to the

Figure 1.10. Oliverio Girondo book offered to tram passengers in Buenos Aires; photo by Buenos Aires World Book Capital; courtesy of Josefina Delgado for the Buenos Aires Ministry of Culture

collections of books in historic bars and cafés, another initiative of the campaign.

Girondo was a vanguard *porteño* ("of the port," colloquial term for Buenos Aires residents) poet whose work celebrated early-twentieth-century urban modernity. On 17 August 2011, his 120th birthday, an array of multimedia events in Buenos Aires recognized his work. First, a guided tour around the city highlighted important places in his work. A one-man performance by Osvaldo Tesser of Girondo's poetry collection *Espantapájaros* was held at the historic Café Tortoni theater. His best-known work, *Veinte poemas para ser leídos en el tranvía* (Twenty Poems to Read on the Tram), was reprinted in a special edition and distributed on his birthday to passengers on public transportation. Passengers who took advantage of the weekly Saturday run of the last remaining tram in the city, in the Caballito neighborhood, also received copies of the book (see figure 1.10). The Isaac Fernández Blanco Museum, which includes Girondo's personal library collection, hosted a book launch of a facsimile edition of *Veinte poemas*. Girondo was also honored among other poets at an event during the World Book Capital campaign of poetry readings, called Flores de Poesía (Flowers of Poetry), in the Flores neighborhood, where he was born.

While the original edition of *Veinte poemas*, published in 1922, was not likely read on trams (its size made it impractical to read on public transportation, and because it was printed only in a limited edition, it could not reach a mass public readership), the poetic gesture of its title introduces the image of reading in public, among the crowd. The collection's content elaborates a modern urban sensibility with wit, sensuality, and surreal images. These poems celebrate urban movement and exalt street scenes and urban encounters. In the prologue Girondo calls them "poemas tirados en medio de la calle, poemas que uno recoge como quien junta puchos en la vereda" (poems thrown into the middle of the street, poems that one picks up like someone gathering cigarette butts on the sidewalk) (13). The pedestrian flâneurie has to compete with automobiles and trams, as in the poem "Apunte callejero" (Street Note), situated in Buenos Aires, where the poetic voice loses its shadow under the wheels of the tram: "Al llegar a una esquina, mi sombra se separa de mí, y de pronto, se arroja entre las ruedas de un tranvía" (Arriving at the corner, my shadow separates from me, and suddenly throws itself under the wheels of the tram) (24).[28] The World Book Capital campaign's homage to Girondo has enormous resonance for the city's self-definition as a literary cosmopolis.

It would have been impossible to bypass Borges in the year's activities, particularly since his birthday, 24 August, was declared Day of the Reader in Buenos Aires in 2008; a law was passed in 2012 recognizing the day nationwide. While the reprint of his short story offered to visitors at the *Tower of Babel of Books* is the only publication of his work by the campaign, seven other events throughout the year honored Borges and his work with readings, exhibits, theater productions, and symposia. The urban focus of some of these events particularly suited the World Book Capital's program, such as in the interactive exhibit titled "Cosmópolis," a display of Borges's relationship to Buenos Aires and the elaboration of cosmopolitan cityscapes in his work. A public reading of his poetry and songs was held in the Plaza San Martín before the *Tower of Babel of Books* was disassembled, paying homage on the anniversary of his death. To commemorate his birthday that year on the national Day of the Reader, the Ministry of Culture unveiled the sculpture "El Libro de la Vida" (The Book of Life), by Raúl Farco. Installed in the main foyer of the Casa de la Cultura, the Ministry of Culture's headquarters, the nearly twenty-foot-tall tree-like form incorporates twenty-five books carved out of stone with inscriptions from Borges's work.[29]

La Ciudad Contada: Buenos Aires from Inside and Out

One of the year's last events in Buenos Aires, and one of the most purely literary, was La Ciudad Contada (The Storied City), a series of public readings by invited international writers at two high-culture bookstores in the Palermo Viejo neighborhood, Libros del Pasaje and Eterna Cadencia. Each of the writers—nine international visitors and three Argentine writers who served as hosts—then wrote a narrative about Buenos Aires that was published as an e-book by the city's Ministry of Culture.[30]

The World Book Capital website included a link to a video of interviews in which the invited writers declare what Buenos Aires means to them. The camera follows them from their readings and dinners to a tour of the city's neighborhoods and well-known sights while a tango soundtrack plays in the background. The guests do not find it easy to define or characterize Buenos Aires; they call it "legendary," "mysterious," "delirious," "a whirlwind," "diverse." Elvira Navarro incorporated being interviewed for the film into her essay, "Buenos Aires: A tomar por el culo" (Buenos Aires: Go to Hell), in which she calls the writers in the group "soldaditos culturales" (little cultural soldiers) of the Buenos Aires World Book Capital campaign. Having been stumped about how to describe the city in a word or two, she admits, "Buenos Aires es luminoso, creo que dije, y por decir algo" (Buenos Aires is luminous, I think I said, just to say something) (Navarro 184). A couple of the writers associate the city with reading and bookstores, mentioning Corrientes Avenue, where many bookstores are concentrated. Nevertheless, other than a few shots of the readings, the film avoids bookstores, libraries, and the teeming Corrientes and instead shows the city's touristy landscapes (La Boca, Recoleta Cemetery, Puente de la Mujer).[31]

In his introduction to the event's published anthology, *La ciudad contada*, Minister of Culture Lombardi calls the collection a new way of looking at the city: "Buenos Aires through words, like balconies from which we can keep gazing on the city" (13). The publication of the anthology as an e-book (see figure 1.11) coincided with one of the campaign's last initiatives in April 2012: the donation of e-readers to the city's public libraries. The last page of the e-book, visually designed as a back cover, introduces the charge to each of the contributors: "How does a *porteño* tell a story about Buenos Aires? Where to begin? And how do those who aren't from here see it?" The essays range from travel chronicles to memoirs to fiction, often toying with several genres in the same text. All of them rely on Buenos Aires as a point of departure—the city's architecture, parks, cafés and restaurants, cemeteries, monuments, bookstores, even the zoo—and they write of lost love, an abandoned building, even an invented visiting writer. An urban nostalgia infuses the essays of both the *porteños* and the international writers.

Several writers express in their essays an uncomfortable anxiety

Figure 1.11. Cover of *La ciudad contada*; digital image from e-book

over what to write. Navarro confesses, "He aquí mi duda fundamental: ¿puedo, como invitada al evento, parir un texto que hable mal de Buenos Aires?" (Here is my fundamental doubt: Can I, as an invited writer, produce a text that speaks badly of Buenos Aires?) (176). Mardero titles her essay "Ya no sé qué camino tomar" (I don't even know what path to take), which communicates doubt about both her urban wanderings in Buenos Aires and her writing of this essay. Frustrated in her attempts to retrace previous itineraries and past loves, she finally comes upon her former lover's street. With resignation, she addresses him and perhaps speaks directly to the city as well: "Buenos Aires tiene tantos vericuetos, puntos y líneas punteadas, tantas alternativas y vías de escape, que no puedo seguirte" (Buenos Aires has so many twists and turns, points, and dotted lines, so many alternatives and escape hatches, that I can't follow you) (49). Juan Terranova, one of the Argentine contributors, titles his essay "La ciudad opaca" (The Opaque City); even for those who live there, Buenos Aires is difficult to see clearly.

What weighs most heavily on these writers are previous readings and versions of the city that seem to obstruct their view. According to Yushimito, "Buenos Aires no ha hecho otra cosa que crear a sus ciudades precursoras" (Buenos Aires has done nothing but create its own precursor cities) ("Los elefantes de Holmberg" 68); this is an intertextual nod to Borges's essay "Kafka and His Precursors." Urrelo Zárate writes that he devoted his visit to searching for the house in Manuel Mujica Láinez's 1954 novel *La casa*, which he had read years before. The title alone indicates his lack of success: "El error del viajero: Buscando una casa" (The Traveler's Mistake: Looking for a House). In "Instrucciones para recordar una ciudad" (Instructions for Remembering a City), Coelho registers the sounds, smells, and sights of Buenos Aires while referencing Cortázar's absurd and humorous "instructions" from *Historias de cronopios y famas*. Paradoxically, these essays seem to confirm Buenos Aires as a World Book Capital by lamenting about how difficult it is to put into words. As Alemán warns, "andar a la caza de paraísos perdidos . . . borró . . . cualquier posibilidad de mirar objetivamente la ciudad" (chasing after lost paradises erased any possibility of looking at the city objectively) (84–85).

The Colombian Antonio García Ángel's contribution "Persona grata/Persona non grata" combines all the anxiety, desire, and bafflement of Buenos Aires with the weight of the city's literary heritage. In a conversational style that blends travelogue, *crónica*, and fantastic fiction, García Ángel's piece also pays homage to Cortázar and Borges with clever intertextual references. The piece begins with all the invited writers gathered for a meal in the Salón Jorge Luis Borges at the restaurant El Histórico in Buenos Aires's San Telmo neighborhood. His chapter incorporates in its urban itineraries the Corrientes Avenue bookstores, the famous street kiosks that sell everything from newspapers to maps and books, the changing face of the city (the new development of Puerto Madero, the proliferation of Starbucks coffee shops), and conversations about boxing and popular music. What at first seems like a teasing version of the visiting writers' event with some local color and architectural commentary transforms into a fantastic fictitious anecdote of literary egos and rivalries. At the writers' first gathering, the group becomes aware that no Paraguayan writer has been included. To fill that gap, they all decide to invent one: a certain Pedro Gómez Bajarrés, whose work is admired but who is personally extremely problematic. The fantastic element enters when the fictional Gómez Bajarrés appears in person among his fellow writers and wreaks havoc on the visit—"fue una verdadera pesadilla" (he was a real nightmare) (161)—to the point of provoking fistfights with other writers and stealing items from their hotel rooms.

García Ángel's tale concludes with urban books and reading. The fictional García Ángel and Alemán devote their free time to hunting for books by the Paraguayan in bookstores all over the city. Of course, their search takes them down Corrientes, "la calle de las librerías. Existen, qué duda cabe, otras mejores lejos de la mundanal profusión correntina, pero de esa abundancia provenía nuestra felicidad. Librería tras librería, en una ristra apenas interrumpida por cafés y teatros" (the bookstore street. There are, without a doubt, other better bookstores further from the Corrientes masses, but it was exactly that abundance that brought us happiness. Bookstore after bookstore, in a row barely interrupted by cafés and theaters) (162–163). When they don't find any of his books downtown, their shopping excursion moves farther afield, "habría que lanzarse a las librerías de viejo, las de barrio, las más polvorientas y caóticas, las más pobres y recónditas" (we had to head to the used bookstores, the ones in the neighborhoods, the dustiest and most chaotic, the poorest and most hidden) (163). Still nothing by Gómez Bajarrés. Finally, at a flea market with some used book stalls they come across two signed copies of his novel *Buenos Aires, humedad* (Buenos Aires, Humidity).

Although the narrator has tried to avoid encounters with Gómez Bajarrés, he discovers that this literary rival has stolen his passport and then his identity when he sees his own name on publications and social media posts that he knew nothing about. García Ángel concludes his essay as he is trapped in a combination of bizarre Cortazarian afflictions, such as an obsession with visiting axolotls in aquariums. He uses his fantastic chronicle on Buenos Aires to joke about Latin American geography and identity.

Sheltered Reading: A Rare Example in the *Porteño* Lettered City

Both campaigns analyzed in this chapter strove to recognize groups of younger "emergente" (emerging) writers, such as those invited to participate in Buenos Aires's La Ciudad Contada and Bogotá's B 39 visits and anthologies. The campaigns in both World Book Capital cities also devoted many events to writers considered *consagrados* (consecrated, canonical), such as Borges, Girondo, Cortázar, and Sabato in Buenos Aires and García Márquez and Caicedo in Bogotá. While activities that honor major literary figures and highlight younger writers are expected in these kinds of broad public literary programming, many fewer events in Buenos Aires featured community initiatives. Bogotá's campaign funneled substantial funding and coordination to community programs, especially through its "Bogotá, un Libro Abierto" (BULA) grants.

One of the only events in the Buenos Aires campaign that integrated grassroots community work into the *porteño* vision of a literary capital was a reading and writing program led by the psychologist and writer Pablo Melicchio at a men's homeless shelter. Although the campaign did not especially recognize his fiction, it did publish his book *Crónica de los hombres que buscan un lugar* (Chronicle of Men Looking for Their Place), recounting his experiences leading weekly reading and discussion sessions at the shelter in the Retiro neighborhood. The book's prologue and introduction refer to crisis in the context of violence and human destruction, underscoring the program's title, Letra contra la Violencia (Writing against Violence). The prologue, by Josefina Delgado, mentions the importance of reading for displaced victims of the Spanish Civil War, and Melicchio's own introduction refers to the Holocaust and the difficulty in giving testimony to unthinkable violence. These two introductory passages set up literature and reading as an antidote to violence, as a humanizing gesture, and as a source of resistance. In the chapters that follow, conversations around reading in community reveal the small deaths of everyday alienation and struggle, "las muertes cotidianas, donde el cuerpo resiste pero muere lo subjetivo, lo social; las mil formas de morir cada día" (the daily deaths, where the body keeps going but the social being, the subjective self, dies; the thousand forms of everyday dying) (39).

Access to literature offers a refuge for the imagination and provides pathways to heal emotional wounds. "El Parador es un puente" (the shelter is a bridge), one of the participants declared. This comment opened the topic of religious beliefs, and a conversation ensued that left Melicchio questioning his own faith: "Yo no estoy seguro de que haya un más allá, pero sí creo en un más acá donde el arte funciona como salvavidas arrojado en medio de un mundo revuelto donde nos toca vivir" (I'm not sure that there's a beyond, but I do believe in something more here where art works like a lifesaver thrown into the middle of this mixed up world that we're living in) (55–56).

As facilitators did in Bogotá's Gente y Cuentos groups, Melicchio read aloud several short literary selections and led a discussion about them, but he went one step further by guiding the participants to write as well:

> Por una noche más tendrán una ducha caliente, un plato de comida y una cama para dormir. Pero también un cuaderno, una lapicera y las palabras que expresamos en el taller. Palabras que, rebotando en sus cabezas o en sus almas, buscarán alojarse, hacer red, construir sentidos, otros modos de ver la vida. Porque las palabras, como los hombres, necesitan cobijo, un lugar donde hospedarse y vivir.
> [For one more night they'll have a hot shower, a plate of food, and a bed to sleep in. But also a notebook, a pen, and the words we exchange in the workshop. Words that while shuffling around in their heads or their souls, will search for a place to rest, to make connections, to construct meaning, other ways of looking at life. Because words, like people, need a blanket, a place to be housed and to live in.] (40)

Along with telling the story of these homeless men's experiences with the texts and their conversations in the group, the book also chronicles Melicchio's experiences. Each chapter begins with him arriving at the shelter, ends with him leaving, and accounts for the gradually developing trust and confidence within the group. The structure of the chapters follows the structure of the workshop sessions, including the itinerary of Melicchio's commute, his anticipation and preparation for each session, and his processing afterward. The prose at times lapses into banal conventionalities; nevertheless, the surprising story of the group dynamic that builds from reading literature aloud with homeless men remains poignant. Melicchio wonders at unexpected responses and moments of disagreement or reminiscence.

The book includes a selection of poems written by the participants themselves. In one, titled "Parador Retiro" (Shelter Retiro), Luis Esteban Contreras writes:

> No olviden que tenemos despierto el intelecto.
> Que la necesidad aguza la fe y la inventiva.
> Que con un trozo de pan, un mate y un abrazo
> Podemos combatir como el mejor de los soldados.
> [Don't forget that we have our intellect awakened.
> That need sharpens faith and creativity.
> That with a piece of bread, some *mate* and a hug
> We can fight like the strongest of soldiers.]

The Buenos Aires Ministry of Culture sponsored a book launch for Melicchio's *Crónica* in 2012, and I was invited to introduce the book.

Three of the men who participated regularly in the reading group attended, shared their experiences, and read some of their own poetry. Two of the three were no longer homeless; all of them discussed how reading with Melicchio helped them grapple with some of their challenges and move forward.

Melicchio's reading and writing program coincided with the annual Buenos Aires book fair, where often he has been invited to speak on panels featuring young writers.[32] He hoped his participants would be able to attend, but the cost of a ticket, although modest at around fifteen pesos per person (about $4.00 at the time), was prohibitive for anyone on the street and without work.

The democratization of the book fair involves vast numbers of visitors who come from broad sectors of society. Journalists marvel at the crowds and the mingling of social classes at the fair each year. One columnist in 2011 called the book fair patrons "the lettered multitude," noting that purchasing a ticket that lets you into the fair "works to ratify a sense of cultural belonging . . . to high culture, lettered culture, culture that occupies a faraway place, that's possible to acquire but difficult to create" (Martínez Daniell 17). He wondered whether the escape into books is a cliché: "in times of crisis, societies take refuge in books; . . . they hope to find there the clues to their misery" (17). But then he reconsidered, pointing out that the legacy of the Argentine 2001–2002 economic crisis ten years later was not only "dramatic material pauperization but also an especially symbolic one" (17). Perhaps as the book fair patrons wander around the exhibits they suffer from class anxiety and are fearful of not gaining entrance and really belonging to the lettered class.

The participants in Melicchio's literary workshop at the shelter embraced their newfound access to books and reading that transcended the boundaries of class and education. If everyone should have access to reading, then everyone should have access to the book fair, so Melicchio asked the Ministry of Culture for tickets for his participants. The week the book fair opened in late April that year, Melicchio posted on Facebook:

> De regreso del Parador Retiro, lectura y ronda de comentarios, acerca del amor, disparado por textos de Abelardo Castillo, Onetti y una letra de Silvio Rodriguez [sic]. Luego, gracias al Ministro de Cultura, repartí entradas gratuitas para la Feria del libro. Los muchachos, felices y con ganas de algo más que el pan nuestro de cada día.

[On my way back from Retiro Shelter, reading and a round of comments, about love, inspired by texts by Abelardo Castillo, Onetti, lyrics by Silvio Rodríguez. Then, thanks to the Ministry of Culture, I gave out free passes for the book fair. The guys are happy, hoping for something more than our daily bread.]

Whether or not the participants would make use of these tickets, what sort of class anxiety they may or may not feel, how they would maneuver through the exhibit halls, and what books they would look at and enjoy, reject, or argue with, would be fodder for discussion at the next session.

Melicchio's program at the shelter stopped not long after his book launch when the Ministry of Social Services discontinued its funding. Although the Ministry of Culture published his book on the experience, it did not provide funds for the program. Emblematic of Buenos Aires's strategy for World Book Capital programming, the Ministry of Culture jumped on board after this program was already running and sponsored by another agency. It funded the published book but backed away from any long-term support. The campaign capitalized on existing programs, established institutions, and collaborations to fill a year with activities, many of which already were scheduled and planned.

Nevertheless, these events did attract crowds, situate literature out in public space, and reassert the city's literary identity. World Book Capital staff member Federico Coulin expressed the goal of hosting events that would "reach publics not so accustomed to literature, putting books in less conventional places," and noted that many of the activities attracted people who "were not big readers" (personal interview, my translation). An emphasis on occupying public space with literary culture underscored much of the programming.

When I spoke with Undersecretary of Culture Delgado in 2011 as the year's campaign was just beginning, she pointed out a particular philosophy that lay behind most of the events: "meeting people, the possibility of sharing, contagious enthusiasm, appropriating new spaces and making more room for cultural activities." Strengthening the link between the city and the book was key: "drawing attention to books, to Buenos Aires's dynamism." Delgado explained that she welcomed new formats such as e-books and digital literature, and proudly told me about the campaign's commitment to provide e-readers to public libraries. When it comes to books and reading, "we need to support everything new." However, her welcoming attitude retained some caution:

"in our current moment of huge competition or at least strong seduction (electronic books, etc.), the territories are still in the process of being defined, everything is being negotiated. . . . We need to be very cautious and not get discouraged, but we all believe in the survival of the book as an object in spite of the challenges." After all, she said, "books don't have to be recharged!" (personal interview, my translation).

Closing the (World Capital) Book

Both campaigns hosted large spectacular events and smaller neighborhood activities. Among the lower-profile, less institutional events planned by both the Bogotá and the Buenos Aires campaigns were massive book giveaways and exchanges held outside in public space. The closing event for the Bogotá World Book Capital campaign took place on World Book Day, 23 April 2008, with a street fair and book giveaways aimed to "bring books closer to all citizens" (Melguizo and Posada 75). The Trueque el Libro (Book Swap) event in Bogotá filled the Parque Nacional on a Sunday as people gathered with their books to trade and exchange. Buenos Aires hosted its Suelta de Libros (Book Giveaway) on 21 September 2011, to honor the International Day of Bibliodiversity. Like the events sponsored by the organization Libro Libre Argentina, this "book liberation" invited citizens to "liberate" a book in a public place, with an inscription on the first page indicating that the recipient was to pass the book on again after reading it, "with the goal of promoting reading and creating a mobile library" ("Propuesta" 25).

These open book exchanges contrast with the annual official, and mostly commercial, book fairs held at each city's convention center: the former are free, occur in open space, and promote interactions among participants, while the latter are institutionalized sales events that primarily promote trade publishers. The Buenos Aires proposal to UNESCO embraces both in their goals for the World Book Capital campaign year; the document concludes with a section of "objectives," of which the first two, in order, are

- To strengthen the publishing and graphics industry, as well as the networks for selling books.
- To sustain the importance of the book as a foundation of social and cultural integration. ("Propuesta" 25)

Rather than representing a tension or contradiction, these objectives are parallel and complementary. The necessity of relying on the commercial book market in these public municipal campaigns—for book fairs, book giveaways, and cosponsorship of events—points to the ubiquitous combination of public and private funding that is inevitable in the postneoliberal Latin American economy.

At the conclusion of the World Book Capital year in 2008, an editorial in *Ciudad Viva*, the Bogotá Ministry of Culture's monthly newsletter, articulated the city's commitment to promoting reading beyond the award period: "Bogotá will continue to support and implement an inclusive reading and writing policy, we will keep launching new books into the wind, the municipal administration will continue to support increasing the availability of reading materials to promote reading as a part of life for all *bogotanos*" (Ramírez Vallejo 2). The yearbook compiled at the end of the Buenos Aires award period in 2012 transmits a steady confidence; rather than recommitting to promoting reading, the city seems to rest on its laurels as a lettered city. World Book Capital campaign director Luciana Blasco states, "Without a doubt, readers are part of the Buenos Aires landscape: anonymous and passionate, every day they enjoy the magic capacity of books to silently transmit sensations and experiences over and over again. People who share the same enthusiasm, like a secret, are capable of reading and transporting themselves anywhere" (*Anuario* 13). As literary self-portraits, the Bogotá campaign upholds an aspirational striving, while the Buenos Aires campaign remains complacently confident.

Casanova states at the beginning of *The World Republic of Letters* that literary space "is not an abstract and theoretical construction, but an actual—albeit unseen—world. . . . As a history and a geography . . . [it] has never been properly traced or described" (3–4). UNESCO's designation of World Book Capitals delineates these borders by consecrating a city each year, and the cities' campaigns aim to take what Casanova considers unseen and to sketch its contours, making it visible. By articulating its literariness, each World Book Capital city reinscribes its lettered identity in multiple acts of reading that occupy public space, reaffirming canonical literary institutions and establishing some new ones. This "literary geopolitics" (36) certainly engages in a relationship with the nation, even if it is a tense and tenuous one in the case of these two capitals; but the geopolitical clout of a World Book Capital designation gives the city's writers, books, and literary institutions a public face by intersecting urban infrastructure with participatory, interactive reading programs. The local, municipal stage for reading gains a wider public.

A story from one of Bogotá's World Book Capital projects, from the collection *Los que cuentan*, expands the dimensions of the city's literary geopolitics. "Con los pies en la tierra" (With your Feet on the Ground), by Cepeda Buitrago, a story about the fear of earthquakes, ends as the protagonist's worst nightmare comes true and his whole world is shaken: his city, his home, his marriage. Not only does this specialist in disaster prevention watch his own home crumble during the earthquake, but he also discovers his wife's betrayal with his boss. A brief episode just before the end of the story foreshadows the earthquake when he sees books falling outside a building. They strike the walls and windows and hit people on the head; their bindings come apart, and pages fly around. "Son sólo libros al viento," a man yells as he's being taken away in handcuffs, "lo único que perdurará, el resto se lo llevarán la miseria y el olvido" (they're just books on the wind. . . . The only thing that will last; everything else will be wiped away by misery and oblivion) (89). The protagonist picks up one of the fallen books to read on the bus on his way home.

The rain of books in Cepeda Buitrago's story ironically alludes to Libro al Viento, one of Bogotá's most successful and enduring public reading initiatives. From the fictional scene of books raining down onto the city and its readers in the first Latin American World Book Capital, we turn to Libro al Viento and other programs on public transportation that put reading on wheels.

CHAPTER 2

Reading on Wheels: Stories of *Convivencia* in Bogotá and Santiago

With an arm fixed to the wall, a dark street light holds the convex vision of the people going by in cars....
Going by: an Englishwoman identical to a street light. A tram that is a school on wheels...
OLIVERIO GIRONDO, *VEINTE POEMAS PARA SER LEÍDOS EN EL TRANVÍA*

At the end of the day, we all use the doors of the subway cars as mirrors.
MARÍA TERESA BERTUCCI, *SANTIAGO EN 100 PALABRAS* (2009)

Heralded as the "tram city" of Latin America in the 1920s, Buenos Aires today conserves one last remaining tram line (Parise 37). A remnant of that decade's rapid modernization, the tram follows a historic loop through the Caballito neighborhood. Writers and artists in the early decades of the twentieth century, such as Argentine poet Oliverio Girondo, celebrated Latin America's urban technological advances, particularly locomotion.[1] Girondo's book *Veinte poemas para ser leídos en el tranvía* (Twenty Poems to Read on the Tram) (1922) registered the transformation in urban landscapes in his poems' contrasts and tensions, where modern horizontal and vertical lines (iron railings, streetlamps, telegraph poles and wires) seem to hold up fluid distorted shapes.[2] *Vanguardistas* like Girondo reproduced cities' changing environment in the sounds, images, and forms of their poetry to establish connections between creative aesthetics and daily urban life (J. Schwartz 143–144).

Girondo's title introduces the image of reading in public while moving through urban space. The Spanish poet Ramón de la Serna, a contemporary of Girondo, confessed to reading the book on the tram in Madrid, where "the tram bell chimed between poems" (de la Serna quoted in Girondo and Schwartz 327). *Twenty Poems* was first printed in France as a large-format book (measuring twenty-four by thirty-two centimeters) in an edition of a thousand numbered and signed copies illustrated with Girondo's own watercolor images. Its impractical size and limited distribution prevented it from reaching a mass public readership, and from actually being read on a tram. But Girondo's collection evolved from that first limited edition until its size was in keeping with its title. In 1925 the journal *Martín Fierro* published a second edition, this one smaller (eleven by eighteen centimeters), printed on less expensive paper, and with the drawings in black and white. This so-called tram edition sold for twenty cents, a price that "gave the book an almost massive distribution" (Greco).[3]

In 2011, to commemorate Girondo's birthday, a special edition of *Twenty Poems* was given out free to the public in Buenos Aires on the historic Caballito tram line and on the city's brand new Metrobus articulated bus system—a nod to the modernity, movement, and public access inscribed in the book's origins. Once again these poems had been put in motion, circulated in a tram edition that reenacted Girondo's initiation of public reading on transportation in Latin America.[4]

Girondo's invitation to read his poems on the tram presages contemporary reading programs in Latin America that intersect with urban infrastructure. Urban reading programs in recent years not only promote reading and literature; their interventions in public space aim to generate positive identification with the city and civic interaction among readers. Since the early 2000s capital cities such as Mexico City, Santiago, and Bogotá have initiated programs that promote reading through their city's public transportation systems. Part of the reinvestment in public programming after decades of neoliberal policies, these projects rely on a combination of public and private funding.

This chapter considers two current reading programs that rely on public transportation: Libro al Viento (Books on the Wind) in Bogotá, Colombia, and Santiago en 100 Palabras (Santiago in 100 Words) in Santiago, Chile. Each of these programs issues huge printings of small-format paperback books and distributes them free on buses and subways. The reading programs in Bogotá and Santiago go beyond Girondo's metaphorical recognition of modernity; public transportation serves not only as a setting for reading but also as a mechanism for circulating books to actively promote reading in public as a collective civic experience.

These reading initiatives contribute to efforts to reclaim public space, strengthen urban identity, and reestablish interpersonal respect and trust in their respective cities. As responses to each city's economic and political context, the programs in Bogotá and Santiago emerged after prolonged periods of violence and political repression. Colombia's history of political violence since the period called La Violencia in the 1950s devolved in the 1980s and 1990s into a vicious fight among various guerrilla groups, drug traffickers, the military, and paramilitary troops. Initially affecting the rural areas, the conflict moved into the cities, where kidnappings and political assassinations aggravated the already widespread climate of internal violence.

More than 6 million displaced citizens who fled rural violence have resettled in Colombia's cities. Often completely unequipped to handle the daily tasks and bureaucratization of urban life, displaced persons have found it challenging to acclimate to their new surroundings. The continuing fear of violence, together with massive displacement, has exacerbated class and neighborhood tensions, put a strain on urban infrastructure, and increased poverty in Colombian cities. By the mid-1990s, Colombia's homicide rate was close to five times that of Latin America generally, and in Bogotá it rose to an annual rate of 80 homicides per 100,000 residents (Cala Buendía 23). President Juan Manuel Santos was reelected in 2014 on a controversial platform of seeking peace negotiations with the armed militants. The Colombian government and the rebels signed a long-negotiated peace agreement in 2016, and it was approved by the national congress; at the time of this writing the parties are still in the process of implementing the terms of the accord.

In Chile under the dictatorship of Augusto Pinochet (1973–1990), imprisonment, torture, and disappearance of suspected members of the opposition resulted in over three thousand deaths and nearly forty thousand people experiencing political imprisonment and in many cases torture.[5] Censorship of publishing and media outlets, revision and control of the curriculum in education, and vigilance in public places established an atmosphere of fear. Creative expression in literature and the arts had to be carefully cloaked to escape the censors, and the monitoring of public spaces by the military regime prohibited any public performances or exhibitions. Of all the neoliberal economic experiments in Latin America, Chile's under Pinochet was perhaps the most comprehensively implemented. The country's emphasis on commercial investment, a free market, privatization of public resources, suppression of labor unions, and a diminished role of the state in managing economic and social welfare led to much greater income disparities and sociocultural inequalities. These economic policies avidly promoted consumerism among the rich and the middle class while the regime's crackdown on artistic and personal expression left a legacy of fear and silence in the arts and literature that is often referred to as an *apagón*, or blackout. Since its return to democracy, Chile has struggled with how to define the period following the fall of the Pinochet regime; many cultural critics and political analysts reject the term *transition* because it assumes a clear temporal destination (an ending to the trauma of the dictatorship years); they prefer the term *postdictatorship* to account for the ongoing process of remembrance and reestablishing justice.

Neither Libro al Viento nor Santiago en 100 Palabras claims to have single-handedly restored peace in Bogotá or revitalized creative expression in Santiago, but the programs' literary intervention into public space via public transportation does aim to contribute to these goals. Such Latin American initiatives connect literature, particularly fiction, with urban transportation by inserting stories into the collective experience of public space to enhance social interaction and a sense of local belonging. Literary reading is harnessed as a socially embedded practice that can facilitate change (Barton 32). Multiple goals coincide, such as fighting crime and promoting new transportation infrastructure that will improve efficiency and air quality. Making written material available to the public via buses and subways provokes interactions among readers that increase public safety and strengthen civic cohesion (Kalman and Street 7). The success of these programs is evident in avid public participation and in their duration. I focus here on Bogotá's Libro al Viento and Santiago's Santiago en 100 Palabras because of their long and uninterrupted duration and their intricate relationship with their respective city's public transportation systems.

The public image of these projects improves the reputation of the transportation system, the municipal government, and the various funding institutions that finance them. They challenge the private and stationary identification with reading by situating the written word in public, and they encourage fluid interaction between the printed page, urban space, and citizenship. This public literature invites, in fact depends on, the municipal citizen and commuter as reader and viewer, and sometimes even as author. By linking reading to *convivencia*, both programs engage the lettered city to redefine urban identity as a collective, participatory, and civic experience.

Transportation Renovation and *Convivencia*

Many definitions of public space incorporate movement, whether they highlight sidewalks and pedestrian walkways or the intersecting roadways of plazas and traffic circles. A recent definition from a renowned interdisciplinary urban studies think tank, the Facultad Latinoamericana de Ciencias Sociales, considers public space "the social sphere where discourses from and about the city travel, are put in circulation, are recontextualized and reproduced" (Buendía Astudillo 258). The innovations in bus rapid transit (hereafter BRT) in Latin American cities over the past decade not only have ameliorated traffic congestion and reduced air pollution but also have manifested the cultural politics of government intervention into public space. The new bus systems in Bogotá and Santiago, the TransMilenio and Transantiago, respectively, were inaugurated with great enthusiasm and promise. Together with Santiago's subway system, the Metro, these bus and train systems circulate books and stories as well as passengers. The transportation companies, in conjunction with other private and public entities, financially support public reading programs by producing and distributing books and devoting publicity space to short stories at bus stops and in subway stations. A brief introduction to these two transportation systems will help clarify the role of public policy and public space in these innovative venues for reading.

The TransMilenio, the Transantiago, and more recently Metrobus in Mexico City and Buenos Aires are all modeled after the BRT implemented in Curitiba, Brazil, in the mid-1970s. These systems were designed to relieve traffic congestion, upgrade mass transit equipment and infrastructure, speed up travel through designated lanes, improve air quality, regulate and coordinate a chaotic arrangement of feeder bus lines, and generally enhance urban mobility. The results are elaborate systems of high-capacity, multicar buses that operate on elevated, special access, high-speed lanes, bypassing traffic lights and smaller intersections.[6] The fares on BRT lines are significantly higher than on conventional buses, and in some cases higher than subway fares. The emergence of these high-speed bus lines has shifted the demographics of commuting in cities that offer these new transportation options.

The planning for TransMilenio in Bogotá began in 1998, and construction was underway in 2000. The system has won awards for its environmental improvements and traffic-related efficiency.[7] It has been so successful that other Colombian cities are planning to adopt it as well, and the system has been copied in other cities in Latin America, including Santiago.[8] However, it has not been without controversy even though it has ameliorated the capital's traffic congestion. The construction impinged on neighborhood businesses and local housing, and it eliminated many smaller, independent bus lines.[9] More recently, deferred maintenance is evident, and the system has deteriorated (Fernández L'Hoeste 162–164).

The transportation landscape in Santiago straddles dictatorial neoliberalism and new urbanist idealism, and encompasses a highly efficient subway as well as a more recent BRT system. Metro de Santiago, a combination private and state-run corporation, has overseen and managed the Chilean capital's transportation system since 1965. Envisioning the new subway system, called Metro, was its initial major project. However, they didn't break ground for the first line until 1969, and it didn't open until 1975. This significant modernizing infrastructure, "which would have been a symbol of liberal democracy under Frei Montalva or revolutionary zeal paired with Space Age idealism under Allende—transporting the workers' city—, was instead baptized as a military-neoliberal marvel" (Gordon-Burroughs, "Red Wine and Gangrene"). The architect and theorist behind Santiago's Metro, Juan Parrochia Beguin, aspired to bring the city up to date with a new system that would provide order and a renewed sense of urban belonging. The language in his numerous lectures and public addresses from the mid-1970s—with calls for efficiency, hope, progress, and optimism—reveals a meshing of technological, social, and political goals. He concludes a long list of "basic principles" of the Metro project by linking its social and psychological benefits to "functional and rational solutions" (Parrochia Beguin 63).[10]

An evaluation of bus transportation in Santiago as the Pinochet dictatorship ended in 1990 was largely concerned with environmental issues, particularly the city's poor air quality and constant smog; it resulted in a proposal for an "economically, socially, and environmentally sustainable service" (Pionér 45). Because outdated vehicles were contributing to dangerous air quality, initial improvements under President Patricio Aylwin (1990–1994) included replacing old buses and regulating the smaller microbuses.[11] A more comprehensive plan was developed during President Ricardo Lagos's administration (2000–2006) to integrate the bus and subway systems for greater efficiency. Lagos promised a new system that would be "efficient, dignified, and integrated" (Rivera, *Transantiago* 23). Transantiago was implemented in 2005 and initially met with broad popular approval. Rather than gradually implementing the new bus system a line or so at a time, Metro opted for a "big bang" and opened the system "with great fanfare" (Mardones Z. 110), but it proved too complex to execute effectively.

A host of financial and implementation fiascos erupted during President Michelle Bachelet's term in 2007, provoking strikes, shutdowns, even riots. Commuters received weeks of free service when fare card readers malfunctioned.[12] The initial rough start, which one analyst called "disastrous" (Mardones Z. 111) was largely due to lack of coordination between municipal planners and the transportation company. Unlike in Bogotá, where the mayor's office has had a major role in planning transportation policy and implementing these kinds of large-scale projects, in Santiago "urban planning . . . was absent" (Weil P et al. 19). Still, despite a troubled start, the integration of Metro with Transantiago has enjoyed success: Metro ridership doubled thanks to integrated bus-subway fares, air quality improved,[13] and the whole system became safer as both crime and the number of traffic accidents declined (crime declined because riders began paying with electronic fare cards, and bus drivers no longer carried cash) (Muñoz, Batarce, and Hidalgo 185–189).

Although the Curitiba BRT system emerged during the military dictatorship, with its goals of industrialization and urban order (goals that were also visible in the planning and opening of Santiago's Metro under Pinochet), both TransMilenio and Transantiago were created under democratically elected national and local governments. The Bogotá BRT was developed under Mayor Peñalosa, as one of his many initiatives to promote citizens' participation in urban life. Known as a New Urbanist, Peñalosa made improving public space a central goal of his administration. As Héctor Fernández L'Hoeste remarks, Peñalosa's mayoral administration (and that of Antanas Mockus as well), "succeeded in convincing many that public space, previously understood as belonging to no one, was in fact the property of all, a veritable redefinition of the urban social paradigm" (154). Peñalosa's administration built and repaired sidewalks, established new parks and refurbished existing ones, planted thousands of trees, and declared an annual no-car day in Bogotá. This period of intense investment in public space under successive mayors in Bogotá shows how public space was a "planning ideal; a symbol and a solution regarded as a comprehensive fix for Bogotá's problems" (Berney 17).

Urban planners who have studied these BRT systems insist that urban revitalization enhances civic integration and *convivencia*. A global study of public transportation delineates three major objectives in new transportation projects: expanding the social role of transportation, relieving urban congestion, and protecting the environment (Faivre D'Arcier 71), and points out how crucial the environmental factor has become in the twenty-first century (70). Latin America's recent transportation initiatives share this cluster of priorities. The TransMilenio not only filled a transportation vacuum, but also was expected to "transform the system of public space" (Hurtado Tarazona 15). Better linkages between neighborhoods promote social integration. The upgraded vehicles and new stations initially improved property values and promoted housing and business development. According to planner Adriana Hurtado Tarazona, "everyone deserves a sophisticated and aesthetic system which promotes togetherness and the interaction among citizens of all socioeconomic levels" (16). Bogotá's mayor Peñalosa's idealistic vision comes through in his speeches:

> First we decide how we want to live and then we create a city for that way of life. . . .
> It's a question of constructing citizenship, a way of life, and the city is only a medium. . . . The most important thing . . . is what it means to have a sense of belonging as a community, a sense of citizenship. (15, 39)

Peñalosa presented TransMilenio as much more than a new mass transit system; he trumpeted it "as a 'structuring element' to (re)organize Bogotá's society and develop a different city model (or model city) for the future" (Vélez, *Third Millennium Modernity* 18). The transformational BRT, along with new sidewalks and parks, were announced as "agents of social change of cataclysmic proportions" (Vélez, *Third Millennium* 18, 46). Juan C. Muñoz, Marco Batarce, and Darío Hidalgo underscore the expectation of major social benefits with Transantiago (184). Similarly, Chilean president Lagos's emphasis on "dignity" in his launching of Transantiago insists on social and ethical goals for their BRT.

The lofty ideals of both systems, TransMilenio and Transantiago, clearly involve social as well as practical dimensions (Valderrama

Pineda 126). According to Andrés Valderrama Pineda, TransMilenio was intended "to reconfigure a whole set of relations, including power relations, spatial and distance relations and identity relations" in Bogotá (133). A revised urban plan for Santiago beginning in the mid-1980s reinterpreted earlier theories and practices and explicitly modified the neoliberal, market-based plans of the Pinochet years. "The deficiencies that arose from considering the market as the only determining factor in developing cities become evident" (Massone Mezzano 58). In seeking more inclusive and environmentally sound planning practices that take into account a broader concept of quality of urban life, the revised plan integrated "the concept of 'community participation'" (Massone Mezzano 60). The objectives of Santiago's 1994 Plan Regulador Metropolitano, which call for "a conception of the city that we hope for and desire for the twenty-first century" and which include the Transantiago, underscore "the most essential element" as "moving toward a more supportive, integrated and efficient city" (Carvacho Duarte 65, 66). The rhetoric around these projects adds the articulation of inclusive and participatory notions of citizenship to the 1970s goals of efficiency and logic.

Creative writing and reading in the city intersect with these modernized systems of transport by committing to the social element of *convivencia*. Such a concept lies at the core of Bogotá mayor Mockus's campaign called Cultura Ciudadana (culture of citizenship), an innovative program of investment in public space and citizen engagement in the city. Mockus's two mayoral terms (1995–1997 and 2001–2003), just before and after Peñalosa's, frame this energetic period. Mockus's policies in the domains of urban congestion and improvements in public space coincide with his sociological work in education and decriminalization. In a book coauthored with Jimmy Corzo, he associates *convivencia* with the following conditions: rational communication, negotiation toward lasting agreements, interpersonal trust, respect for pluralism, and tolerance for diversity (17–22). His campaign for transforming public space and engaging citizens' sense of responsibility relied heavily on "artful interventions" such as mimes at traffic intersections (Cala Buendía). Reading falls in line with Mockus's culture-based strategies for redefining the urban imaginary at a crisis point of violence and pollution in Bogotá.

While Bogotá's mayors promoted TransMilenio for improving public safety and civic interaction, the transportation improvements in Santiago dramatize the process of reclaiming public space in the transition to democracy after the dictatorship. The Metro had been considered a space of surveillance and repression. As Chilean writer and activist Pedro Lemebel states, "With that music of a private clinic and those butchers' tiles that cover the walls of the tunnels, the Santiago Metro is the disciplined evidence of the dictatorship." Similarly, writer Carlos Labbé—whose stories have been included in the Santiago en 100 Palabras anthologies—calls the Metro "extremely controlled . . . a sort of panopticon. . . . Everyone starts looking around, feeling watched" (Schwartz, "La Lituratura" 169).[14] From this repressive past, when hidden cameras captured passengers' every move, the subway stations have emerged as stages for cultural expression, "decorated with the grandiloquence of the dictatorship and the flaws of democracy" (Gumucio 125). Along with Transantiago, the city's transportation renovations enhanced the aesthetics and services of subway stations with public art and branches of the public library (BiblioMetro).[15]

As necessary arteries for moving through urban space, public transportation systems in major Latin American cities become more than tools for increasing mobility; they become metaphors for the cities themselves, story grids for urban imaginaries. Moving through the city entails a reading of urban space, a semiotic deciphering of streets, the built environment, and the rules of urban circulation. For Michel de Certeau, the act of reading, both semiotically and as a literacy practice, is a key example of everyday practices, alongside such activities as cooking, walking, and shopping. His references to movement and the stories of urban life resonate with these programs that move literature on public transportation:

> In modern Athens, the vehicles of mass transportation are called *metaphorai*. To go to work or come home, one takes a "metaphor"— a bus or train. Stories could also take this noble name: every day, they traverse and organize places; they select and link them together; they make sentences and itineraries out of them. They are spatial trajectories. . . . Stories, whether everyday or literary, serve us as a means of mass transportation, as *metaphorai*. Every story is a travel story—a spatial practice. (115)

Certeau's theories of individual and social movement through urban space propose a discursive occupation of space, a writing into and onto the urban topography. Libro al Viento and Santiago en 100 Palabras install literature on public transportation and make it visible on billboards and available in circulating books. Stories, poems, and essays become part of the cities' built structures and passengers' spatial itineraries.

Promoting reading on public transportation supports municipal governments' official interest in *convivencia* and interpersonal dignity through the aesthetic and human dimensions of literature. A similar initiative in Mexico City, Para Leer de Boleto en el Metro (Reading on the Run in the Metro), a model for Libro al Viento, also strove for enhanced civic interaction through literature: "The long term goal is to make travelers into better citizens"; the experience of reading on the metro "helps rebuild civic confidence and solidarity" ("Para leer"). Echoing the municipal rhetoric of *convivencia*, the Centro Regional para el Fomento del Libro en América Latina y el Caribe (Regional Center for Promoting the Book in Latin America and the Caribbean; CERLALC) encourages generating "more agile and open distribution channels . . . and sponsoring communal reading spaces," including buses and subways (25). A follow-up survey of TransMilenio commuters gauging the public response to Libro al Viento found that after encouraging reading habits, promoting solidarity and civic culture was the next most recognized objective of the program (Seguimiento 38–39). Libro al Viento and Santiago en 100 Palabras capitalize on the social experience of public transportation for collective reading and writing.[16]

Libro al Viento: From Urban Reading to Book Collecting in Bogotá

When award-winning fiction writer Laura Restrepo and former Biblioteca Nacional director Ana Roda Fornaguera invented Libro al Viento, they had in mind "not only promoting reading but also demonstrating that reading, literature, could be part of people's everyday lives" (Roda Fornaguera interview, my translation).[17] Libro al Viento was conceived and implemented in conjunction with Bogotá's TransMilenio and was part of the municipal government's widespread campaign to promote TransMilenio and stimulate pride in the city (see figure 2.1). The campaign for a positive urban image shows up in the city's mid-2000s slogan under Mayor Luis Eduardo Garzón, "Bogotá sin Indiferencia" (Bogotá without Indifference), which was printed on posters, banners, and advertisements. Financed by the city, Trans-

Figure 2.1. Libro al Viento logo; photo courtesy of Libro al Viento © Alcaldía Mayor de Bogotá; courtesy of Ana Roda Fornaguera

Figure 2.2. Books at TransMilenio stations; Libro al Viento © Alcaldía Mayor de Bogotá; courtesy of Ana Roda Fornaguera

Milenio, and several corporate sponsors since it began in 2004, Libro al Viento publishes a series of literary anthologies of all genres and distributes them for free in public spaces. During Libro al Viento's first two years, its books were available at TransMilenio hub stations, where passengers were invited to take a book to read during their trip and then to return at another station (see figure 2.2).[18] Libro al Viento turned out to be a key factor in Bogotá's successful application for the UNESCO World Book Capital designation, which was awarded to the city in 2007. In fact, the brochure for Bogotá as World Book Capital describes Libro al Viento as one of the programs "that facilitates the road to the book and makes reading more attractive" (Roda Fornaguera, *Bogotá Capital Mundial del Libro* 15).

Roda Fornaguera, who directed Libro al Viento during its first few years, identifies two main goals: first, to publish high-quality literature, selections that are "seductive, enjoyable, fun, sharp, intelligent"; and second, "to have the books circulate, be shared, recommended, passed from hand to hand, by word of mouth, to reach houses, to be read aloud and to oneself, be loaned out, talked about, and to eventually become part of all *bogotanos*' lives" (Roda Fornaguera, "Libro al Viento, un verdadero milagro" section M, p. viii). Libro al Viento's objectives stress enjoyment of literature over reading skills or functional literacy. The organizers hope that readers will "find pleasure in reading, diversion, illumination, sources of reflection, knowledge, a broad vision of the world" (Libro al Viento). The program invites citizens to engage in reading literature as a right rather than a privilege: "Reading is everyone's right, and it should be in everyone's reach" (Roda Fornaguera interview, my translation). By expanding access to and availability of literature in everyday contexts, Libro al Viento offers what New Literacy Studies considers a "literacy practice" that "has social implications concerned with relationships of power" (Barton 127). All those involved in Libro al Viento, from the founders to the various editors and promoters, underscore the goal of expanding the pleasure of reading to an increasingly large and diverse public.

The books published and distributed in the Libro al Viento program include a combination of works by Colombian authors in several genres, books by other Latin American writers (Julio Cortázar, Julio Ramón Ribeyro, Roberto Fonseca), works by authors beyond Latin American (Tolstoy, Chekhov, Maupassant), and Greek classics. The first two books published in the series illustrate this broad range of authors and titles: *Antígona*, by Sophocles, inaugurated the program, followed by selections from Gabriel García Márquez's autobiography. By launching the series with a classic, the program directors wanted to highlight "links of correspondence" through language and stories as universal experiences (Paredes Castro interview, my translation). That wide range, alternating among Colombian, Latin American, and world writers, continues. Recent titles include a volume by French poet Guillaume Apollinaire, a collection of essays by Colombian Álvaro Mutis, the classic fables of Jean de La Fontaine, and an

Figure 2.3. Libro al Viento books; author photo

anthology of essays on war and reconciliation called *Breviario de la paz* (Breviary of Peace).

The selection process relies on an editor who proposes a series of titles for the coming year and an advisory committee that meets annually to review, revise, and approve the editorial plan. The advisory committee includes representatives from various municipal ministries; Ana Roda Fornaguera, who founded and first administered the program; and other city officials. The editorial program strives to avoid paternalism by insisting on drawing from multiple genres and literary periods. Former Libro al Viento editor Julio Paredes Castro stated that the program aims to redefine and open up the hermetic "sacred space" of literature to create a more natural relationship with readers: "all readers ought to be able to approach and find something that interests them there" (personal interview, my translation).

In the first few years, the program published one title each month; more recently the program has put out four to six books each year. The titles are printed in editions of various size, from fifteen thousand to one hundred thousand copies,[19] and more than one hundred titles have been published as of this writing. The volumes are small-format paperbacks, easy to fit in a purse or a large pocket (see figure 2.3). The books were initially distributed on bookshelves at six TransMilenio hubs, as well as in open-air food markets, hospitals, municipal offices, parks, schools, libraries, and over two hundred soup kitchens. The practice of circulation is the foundation of Libro al Viento; the program's association with and reliance on TransMilenio buses only underscored its goal of moving books among readers in public spaces. Paredes Castro mentioned that each book is assumed to reach at least six readers because books are shared with family members, distributed to school groups, and passed on to friends. A book that is returned to a bookshelf in a public area finds its way into other hands (personal interview, my translation).

The relationship between the city and books is at the center of Libro al Viento's mission. Paredes Castro identified "a connection among space and culture and books. . . . The books are just there, and people can take them—there's no barrier; rather, it's completely available" (personal interview, my translation). Carlos Ramírez, who was handling distribution for the program at the time of this writing, considers each title "not a free book but a book that belongs to the city," that rests upon "a vote of confidence in people" (personal interview, my translation). A message printed on the back cover of each book offers basic instructions, suggesting that rather than being a giveaway of free books, the program puts books into circulation "like a public good" (Ramírez interview, my translation). During the period that TransMilenio sponsored the program, the message on the back cover highlighted the transportation company:

This is a Book on the Wind
It's for you to read, and for
Many others like you to read it too.
So, when you finish it, leave it
at a TransMilenio stop and,
If you enjoyed it, take another.

The books published after the TransMilenio support ended had a different message on the back cover: "The city belongs to everyone and so do its books. Contribute to the success of this campaign; it's a vote of confidence in Bogotá." The most recent books' back cover message underscores Ramírez's view: "This copy of Books on the Wind is a public good. After reading it, keep it circulating among other readers." The front covers also include a circular, stamp-like emblem with the program's name surrounded by "FREE CIRCULATION," reminding readers that the books are free and to be circulated. An elaborate distribution plan allocates a specific number of copies to parks, municipal offices, public and community libraries, universities, prisons, bookstores, and public transportation hubs, and reserves some copies to be given away at book promotion events. Free downloads of some forty Libro al Viento titles are available on the website for IDARTES, the branch of the municipal government that oversees Libro al Viento, and on the Banco de la República's website.[20]

Among the Colombian Libro al Viento titles are selections that highlight indigenous folklore, such as the two-volume multilingual collection *Pütchi Biyá Uai*, edited by Miguel Rocha Vivas. These titles, alongside other Latin American and world literature, confirm the program's goal of "the effective and increasing inclusion of new readers and new voices" (Paredes Castro, "Introducción" 8). One or two books each year address a topic related to Bogotá, with such volumes ranging from a short story anthology of *bogotano* writers (Suescún et al.) to historical essays and chronicles about the city. Since 2012, the program has employed color coding that identifies four broad categories related to readership and genre, "in the hope of reaching readers in a more specific way" (Gerencia de Literatura 19): young readers (green), world literature (orange), hybrid or less conventional genres (blue), and the Colección Capital (violet). This branding of the Colección Capital, with a commitment of at least two titles per year that highlight Bogotá's history and culture, anchors the program in urban themes.

The Bogotá collection merits particular attention for the purposes of this study because it most concretely underscores the theme of urban identity and the program's *bogotano* sponsorship from the mayor's office. The collection offers historical, documentary, and imaginative sources that encourage local belonging, with selections from nineteenth-century *crónicas* (*Crónicas de Bogotá*, by Pedro María Ibáñez) and *costumbrista* tales (*Semblanzas poco ejemplares*, by José María Cordovez Moure). The first title in the new Capital series offers *bogotano* recipes culled from various sources; the book stands out "for its gastronomic value and for its historical representation of identity" (García Ángel, *Recetario santafereño*). These titles feature *bogotano* writers and recognize regional history and local customs to promote pride in the city through the rediscovery and re-creation of local folklore.

Along with showcasing historical writing from earlier periods, Libro al Viento's Colección Capital highlights contemporary writers who reflect on current urban issues. One of the volumes, titled *Cuentos en Bogotá*, includes the top ten stories (one winner and nine honorable mentions) from a creative writing contest sponsored by TransMilenio. The judges' comments serve as an introduction, praising the ordinary citizens who submitted stories that offer readers a version of the city not from above but from ground level (Arias, Giraldo, and Durán 9). Several of the stories incorporate characters traveling by TransMilenio and are punctuated with the names of stations and cross streets. Violence marks these fictional urban itineraries, suggesting how Libro al Viento mines the literary imagination to process recent history. The winning story, "La paga" (Pay), by Héctor Manuel Hoyos, concerns a violent attack involving a paramilitary vehicle. The story indirectly critiques the proliferation of armed bodyguards hired by upper-class *bogotanos* to ferry around their children, referencing the 1990s, when moving through the city was terribly dangerous. In the final story in the collection, "El hombre de la silla azul" (The Man in the Blue Chair), by Álvaro Guillermo Reyes, written in fragments subtitled with the names of TransMilenio stops, a construction worker's disillusioned love leads to a crime of passion.

Bogotá contada, another title in the Capital series, is a more recent collection of original texts written about Bogotá, this time by a group of invited writers.[21] Three Colombian authors who served as hosts and twelve writers from other parts of Latin America and Spain were invited to visit Bogotá, tour the city, participate in readings, and write a selection for this anthology. Their visits coincided with important historical and literary events (the celebration of the 475th anniversary of the founding of Bogotá, and festivals such as Bogotá Literaria and the Festival of Children's and Youth Literature). The narrative texts they produced span a wide range of genres from *crónicas* to memoir, short story, travel writing, and children's fantasy. Two of the pieces are called "postcards," and a third, a "drawing," designations that characterize them as fragmentary verbal sketches. Of the twelve pieces by non-Colombian writers, seven feature public transportation by mentioning bus or TransMilenio routes. They offer personal reflections on the urban scene and incorporate the city's topography from the geographical to the institutional: the altitude, the hill of Monserrate, the mountain ranges surrounding the city, major avenues, neighborhoods, libraries, and bookstores. From observations of the clouds and the weather to glossaries of linguistic *colombianismos*, comments on hotel accommodations, and even an account of being mugged, the visiting writers trace their *bogotano* itineraries.

Two of the Colombian writers chose to commemorate in their essays significant cultural institutions in the city: Miguel Ángel Manrique writes a brief history of the Lerner bookstore, and Ricardo Silva Romero remembers Bogotá's classic movie theaters. Violence is an inevitable topic, as editor Antonio García Ángel notes in his introduction (11). The third Colombian writer in the collection, Pilar Quintana, writes a *crónica* titled "Las guerras" (Wars), which recognizes violence as another sort of urban institution. Quintana recounts a series of violent events in the city: the 1948 Bogotazo, the 1985 guerrilla occupation of the Palacio de Justicia (when *bogotanos* were shocked into recognizing that "en Colombia la guerra solo occuría en el campo" [in Colombia the war was going on only in the countryside] was no longer true [75]), and frequent bombings during Pablo Escobar's reign of terror from the late 1980s to the mid-1990s. She recalls a bombing at the university during her teenage years, and her family's fear until she returned home safely by bus.

Several of the visiting writers indicate how their own local experiences with violence unite them, giving them points of reference with respect to Colombia: "en la negociación social con lo latinoamericano, el miedo nos une" (in Latin American social negotiations, it's fear that unites us) (Yushimito 23). Several essays begin with transcribed bits of conversation among the invitees, in which they joke about whose country wins the prize for the most people displaced or disappeared (Yushimito 23). Rodrigo Blanco Calderón recalls his first evening in Bogotá with the group of visiting writers, who chatted about natural disasters until they moved on to "una radiografía más profunda: qué tipo de violencia nos caracterizaba. A pesar del famoso comienzo de Anna Karenina, era la infelicidad lo que nos permitía reconocernos" (a deeper analysis: what kind of violence characterized us. Despite the famous beginning of Anna Karenina, it was unhappiness that brought us together) (43). He structures his essay around the story of Jaime Garzón because the date of his visit coincided with the anniversary of Garzón's tragic death.[22] Blanco Calderón finds himself in "el país de los muertos" (the country of the dead), where portraits sold on the street and graffiti on walls emit shadows of violent episodes that hang over his urban exploration (54).

Neither a panorama nor a catalogue of the city as a place or an experience, the combination of essays and stories in *Bogotá contada* offers a prism of multiple perspectives and angles that resists any comprehensive or conclusive vision. Catalan writer Sebastià Jovani calls his *Bogotá contada* essay "(Vana) tentativa de agotamiento de un lugar colombiano" ([Vain] Attempt to Wear Out a Colombian Place); from Monserrate to the Museo del Oro, he is unable to characterize the city, and he transmits a combination of fascination and frustration. Jovani mentions failure, paradox, fragments; "orden y caos también se funden" (order and chaos also blend) (117). He sums up Bogotá's "incomposibilidad" (uncomposability) (112) in a passage that might describe this whole collection: "una narración se vierte ineluctable sobre la ciudad. Un relato que se complica progresivamente hasta transformarse en un palimpsesto de relatos que se superponen, se suceden y se contaminan mutuamente" (an inescapable narration pours out over the city. A story that becomes progressively more complicated until it transforms itself into a palimpsest of stories that overlap, follow and contaminate one another) (109). However, this difficulty in capturing the city verbally is a challenge rather than an impossibility. It is a tantalizing collective writing exercise just as the book will become a collective reading experience. In all of these selections, the city emerges as inscrutable yet inviting, mesmerizing but indescribable.

The cover of *Bogotá contada* features a drawing of an iconic Bogotá monument, La Rebeca, originally installed in 1926 in Parque Centenario and now displayed in a plaza on Calle 26. The statue positions Rebeca kneeling in a pool of water, one hand outstretched with a conch shell; but the cover design replaces the conch shell with a book, and Rebeca's arm is bent and her gaze is on the open pages (see figure 2.4).[23]

Libro al Viento published a second volume in 2015 titled *Bogotá contada 2.0*. To promote the forthcoming volume a few months before its release, the program published on its Facebook page a short video interview with Diego Zúñiga, one of the invited authors. It opens with images of Bogotá's downtown traffic: TransMilenio lanes splay across the screen as one of the buses zooms by.[24]

After Libro al Viento's first two years, the city government administered questionnaires to commuters and readers on the TransMilenio to assess the program's impact. The results revealed TransMilenio's crucial role in disseminating the program: the greatest percentage of respondents reported learning about the program by using the BRT (52.6% in 2005; 60.6% in 2006), as compared with media publicity, printed flyers, or hearing about it from a friend or family member (Castro Osorio 38). Beyond the stated objectives of the program—"facilitating access to books and promoting the practice of reading"—the evaluation discovered that one of Libro al Viento's greatest achievements, according to respondents, was "promoting

Figure 2.4. *Bogotá contada* cover; author photo

solidarity and civic culture" (38–39).[25] A majority of respondents reported that they had begun to read more since being exposed to Libro al Viento (54% in 2005; 72.8% in 2006, 49). These newfound or rediscovered reading habits reflected enjoyment of literature, just as one participant defined literary works as "works that one reads for pleasure" (n.p.). The transcribed comments from the questionnaires mention reading as an antidote to stress, recognize that reading is not elitist, value reading books that are not required for a class, and point out the pleasure of reading with others (48).

Libro al Viento redefines literature and reading, for citizens and readers have come to assign "more value to reading" (Castro Osorio 48) after being exposed to these free circulating books. Participants in the evaluation expressed their admiration for people who read; they have an impression that readers are cultured, as these two responses indicate:

> When I see someone reading, they interest me. One says, "Hey, that really interesting person is reading." I feel sympathetic toward that person, reading in unconventional spaces moves me. I admire people reading on buses or in parks. . . .
>
> A person reading seems nice, I think he's educating himself, he's

opening up new horizons, seeing other worlds, other cultures, knowledge. (Castro Osorio n.p.)

Reading on public transportation creates new impressions among commuters; Libro al Viento expands reading experiences and affects how citizens view one another. Paredes Castro asserts that a program like Libro al Viento could never exist in Europe or the United States: "The publishers and bookstores would never allow it—100,000 copies given out free every month! But in Colombia, the people who buy books don't ride public buses or shop at marginal urban markets, so Libro al Viento reaches new readers without competing for consumers" (personal interview, my translation).

The follow-up report revealed that about 30 percent of the books were returned and continued to circulate; the directors and editors of the program began to worry about the remaining two-thirds that were not returned. Roda Fornaguera, Paredes Castro, and Ramírez all assert that the program was never intended as an "editorial collection" for personal libraries; as Roda Fornaguera states, "the idea was not to create an editorial collection, . . . but rather to bring people closer to books, to expand the number of readers" (personal interview, my translation). Nevertheless, its very success through public accessibility and attractive design prompted readers to keep the books. To combat this collectionism and promote circulation, Libro al Viento has become more associated with the public library system. Biblioestaciones, mobile library modules with a limited selection of books, have been installed in many of the major TransMilenio stations, and they all carry Libro al Viento books. No longer free to keep, the books circulate and help promote library membership. Similarly, where the books appear in open-air food markets and municipal offices, they are available for people to read while shopping or waiting for an appointment, but they must be returned to the shelves.[26]

Thus the books become fixtures of urban spaces, and reading an experience integrated into urban life: "the objective, along with promoting reading, is to revive the plaza as a space for meeting, as a tradition, and to promote collective memory" (Ávila 8). This emphasis on reclaiming public space corresponds to recent theories of the commons and efforts to reinvigorate the role of the public, particularly in cities. In urban geographer and former Barcelona mayor Jordi Borja's overview of contemporary urban planning, public spaces take precedence. In the revalorization of collective spaces, "the marginalized are included, the passive bystander acquires rights, the resident establishes

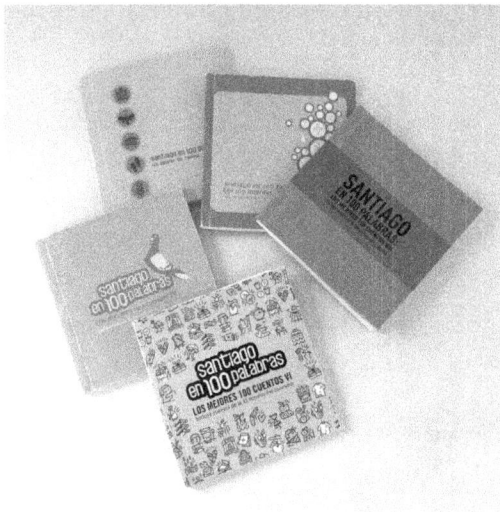

Figure 2.5. Santiago en 100 Palabras books; author photo

his surroundings, everyone acquires self-esteem and dignity, accepting and responding to the challenges of urban dynamics and policies" (Borja 72). Bogotá's Libro al Viento, with its focus on the citizen-as-reader, reaches beyond an elite and privileged precinct and inserts literature into public space. Books in circulation create an inclusive cohort, in which ordinary citizens become "participants in a project for the public good" (Paredes Castro interview, my translation).

Santiago en 100 Palabras: The Urban Citizen as Reader and Writer

Since 2001, Santiago en 100 Palabras has been promoting not only reading but also creative writing in the city in conjunction with public transportation. The minifiction contest of narratives of no more than a hundred words is cosponsored by the magazine *Plagio*, the copper mining company Minera Escondida, and the public transportation company Metro de Santiago. The objective is to prompt literary expression out of the common experiences of urban life in order to promote urban interaction and a sense of belonging. The winning stories are published in small paperbacks and printed on billboards featuring the authors' names and illustrated with colorful graphics (see figures 2.5 and 2.6). The contest is judged by a panel of writers, including well-known authors such as Diamela Eltit, Alberto Fuguet, Alejandro

Figure 2.6. Winning story displayed on bus billboard; © Santiago en 100 Palabras; photo courtesy of Fundación Plagio

Zambra, and Alejandra Costamagna. In a special edition commemorating ten years of Santiago en 100 Palabras, Costamagna calls the program "democratic" and "egalitarian," "a live exercise, a dialogue in public space. . . . that tells a collective story" (189).

The hundred-word limit for the stories is not random, but rather coincides with the transportation medium: it is the maximum number of words that can be read in the two-minute stops at the stations or in the time between trains on the platform (Mujica). During the first few years of the contest, the stories were submitted on paper in mailboxes in the metro stations; when participation ballooned, the program developed a digital submission system, along with public voting on selected stories. Cash prizes of between $500 and $2,000 are awarded to the winning stories,[27] and the hundred best stories are collected every two years in the tiny paperback books that are given away free on the buses and subways, to "give back to the citizens what belongs to them" (Arnold, García, and Dümmer 13).[28]

Sponsored by a combination of public and private institutions, and a mix of the municipal, the cultural, and the corporate, the project's seemingly disparate elements and institutions all coincide in new and dynamic interventions into public space. The magazine *Plagio*, a free biannual publication since 2000, launched the project and administers the contest. The private multinational mining company Minera Escondida uses the project to boost its public image by showing support for local culture. Metro de Santiago contributes to this collaborative public/private venture by lending its public image and helping to distribute information on the prize, display winning stories, and circulate the books.

Temporarily replacing advertising with short stories and their illustrations in a space normally devoted to promoting consumer spending is one of the program's critical strategies for occupying public space and reaching a mass audience. On the one hand, the use of the billboards subverts consumerism and indirectly critiques the neoliberal economic policies of postdictatorial Chile. Instead of marketing global consumer goods in what Jane Griffin calls "unidirectional communication," stories on the billboards are free, reach an enormous population of readers, and reconfigure publicity space "into a locus of social dialogue between Chilean citizens" (*Labor of Literature* 136). Urban planner Pablo Allard calls use of the billboards "a new art form that mixes opportunism and the ephemeral character of publicity infrastructure with the beauty of art and literature" (131). On the other hand, visible signs of Minera Escondida's corporate sponsorship are evident in the company's logo, which appears on all the billboards and books, perpetuating patterns of neoliberal consumerism. This contradiction is emblematic of the tensions and compromises of these combined public/private reading programs. Griffin points out that "the increased power of corporations in the cultural sphere is an inherent product of neoliberalism . . . [that] dissolves the demarcation between commercial and public interests" (*Labor of Literature* 145–146).[29]

Brief essays in the biennial books by the editors and sponsors underscore the civic and social goals of the contest. While applauding the growth of the story competition, Metro de Santiago simultaneously congratulates itself on the expansion of the Metro: "In 2004 we added six new stations to the system, which will continue to grow with more new stations proposed for 2005 and 2006 totaling 87 km; definitely more space for promoting culture" (vol. 2, n.p.).[30] In another volume, Metro's introduction identifies "social profitability" as part of its development plan (vol. 3, n.p.). The company alludes to Transantiago's problems in the next volume, calling the period the "era of Transantiago" (8) and committing to "take literature further and bring it to more people" (9). Whether on billboards or in the anthologies, the stories "will flood the streets of Santiago with good literature" (vol. 5, p. 9). Metro's introduction to volume 8 articulates the contest's objectives from its point of view: to facilitate high-quality culture for a broad public, to promote new literary talent, and to support initiatives "that resuscitate and disseminate local patrimony and identity" (4).

The growing civic dimension of Santiago en 100 Palabras is evident in the numbers. The quantity of stories submitted for the contest has soared, from around 2,600 the first year to more than 50,000 annually. Santiago provides the theme as well as the venue for the stories, and the contest stresses ownership and invites readers (referred to as a collective "we" in the books' introductions) to "transcend reality and transform it into a story, and in this way, to discover the essence of a city that speaks about us and about who we are . . . and to diminish the distance between us" (vol. 2, n.p.). Each printed story on the huge posters and in the books identifies the author's name, age, and neighborhood, further mapping the city through the authors' residential identification.[31]

From children to senior citizens, the authors of these stories broach urban life in chance encounters, dog walking, childhood memories, dialogues, street intersections, romance, and mystery, often highlighting public spaces such as parks and street scenes as arenas for intimate dramas. A common theme in the stories reveals how the dreary routine of everyday itineraries can explode into startling surprises. Some of the writers who have been judges in the contest appreciatively refer to these stories as vignettes, greetings, scenes, notes, lists, love letters, confessions (Gumucio 125), or urban postcards and still lifes (Jeftanovic 131). Giving the city this human dimension in tiny anecdotes contributes to another aim of the contest: to improve Santiago's image among its residents, from its "collective low self-esteem" (Labbé 172) as "a city with nothing to write about it" (Gumucio 125), through creative writing and collective participation.

In these minifictions about Santiago, public transportation often serves as a setting integral to the stories, which feature mutual attraction between strangers in crowded spaces or elaborate efforts to escape the drudgery of the office or domestic life. An overview of the prizewinning, honorable mention, and thirty or so jurors' choice stories published in the anthologies suggests some notable tendencies. Twenty of the one hundred stories in the first volume and eighteen in the second volume make bus or subway transportation a major part of the action, and several others in each volume include passing mention of public vehicles. The Metro and buses appear more prominently in the earlier volumes, tapering off for a few years but maintaining a consistent presence.[32] Even taking into consideration the lack of statistical comprehensiveness in this sample (the published stories may or may not be representative of all stories submitted, and the printed stories may reflect judges' biases), the trend points to some tentative conclusions. These stories confirm how travel through public space with fellow inhabitants functions as an emblem of urban life. The contest's association with the Metro begins with the company's financial sponsorship and extends to the Metro's visible role in the contest each year from start to finish: from providing the sites for the mailboxes where stories were initially submitted to displaying the winning stories on billboards along the platforms. I hypothesize that as the competition shifted toward electronic submission, the Metro became less imaginatively central to the contest.

A study of one year's corpus of submitted stories confirms these conclusions. In his urban planning master's thesis, Ricardo Greene F. analyzed all the 18,434 stories submitted to the contest in 2005. After organizing the full corpus according to age, gender, and neighborhood of the author, and overall theme, Greene found that nineteen percent of the stories focused on some form of transportation (79), and nine percent concerned the Metro itself (153).

I share Greene's hesitance to draw firm conclusions regarding the Metro as a theme in these stories, given how intricately connected it is to the contest's publicity, prizes, and results (141). He mentions in his introduction that the contest's name was originally proposed as "Microcuentos en el Metro" (Microstories in the Metro), but the Metro refused to accept anything that included "micro," the slang term for buses, so as not to be associated with the city's ailing bus system. Similarly, the logo was changed from yellow, associated with the buses, to red and blue, which were more associated with the Metro. Carlos Labbé also notes how "the aesthetic of the illustrations and graphic design has a strong relationship to the corporate quality of the Metro, in its colors and dimensions" (169–170). No stories criticizing the Metro are allowed to win; this adds a layer of restriction and control to the judging process.[33] Although Greene considered the stories anonymously (authors' names were removed before Greene was given access to them), his geographical analysis revealed that the neighborhoods most represented among the stories' authors were along Metro lines.[34]

The transportation-related stories fictionalize personal interactions on buses and subway cars and reveal how much transportation occupies the public spatial imagination in Santiago. Bus and subway travel provide a platform for the poetics of urban movement in these often elliptical tales, whose brevity is a result of the hundred-word limit, but is also a stylistic element adding suspense and mystery. The story "Calipso," by Pablo Morales, for example, scarcely traces the outlines of a plot: "Cuando bajé en la siguiente estación, vi que ella había cumplido su promesa" (When I got off at the next station, I saw that she had kept her promise) (vol. 2, 59). The transport station mentioned in the middle of the story becomes the temporal and spatial hinge on which the story turns. The relationship between these two travelers, or perhaps a traveler and a woman waiting on the platform, relies on the bus or subway ride to confirm her "promise."

Transportation's movement through and structuring of urban space engineers literary anecdotes by providing dramatic spatial scenarios as well as discursive familiarity. Many of the public transportation stories are love stories or tales of attempts at interpersonal connection. They recount intimate encounters—unexpected meetings, breakups, seductions, and tensions between couples—facilitated or hampered by public transportation's movement, darkness, window reflections, speed, and anonymity. The exchange of gazes in crowded public vehicles is practically inevitable, and many of the stories are built around allowing, avoiding, or insisting on making eye contact, as are the two stories here:

"METRO DE LOS HEROES," BY MICHEL MONTECINOS
Aquí llega el Metro, atestado de gente como todas las mañanas. Escojo con la mirada desde el andén a mi víctima, mientras repaso mentalmente el plan. Se abren las puertas. El último en bajar es un hombre todavía somnoliento. "Mi víctima", digo para mis adentros. El me mira de reojo y entonces ataco: "Hola, ¿Cómo está?" le digo, mientras subo y avanzo por el carro. El gira. Las puertas se cierran y veo con satisfacción su cara de incertidumbre. Pobre hombre, pensará todo el día quién lo saludó, y yo, no puedo esperar hasta mañana a mi siguiente víctima.

["LOS HEROES METRO"
Here I arrive at the Metro, teeming with people like every morning. I choose my victim from the platform, with my gaze, while I mentally review my plan. The doors open. The last one to get off is a man who

is still half asleep. "My victim," I say to myself. He gives me an odd look and then I jump in, "Hello, how are you?" I say to him, while I get on and move into the car. He turns. The doors close and I see with satisfaction an uncertain look on his face. Poor guy, he'll be wondering all day who said hello to him, and I can't wait until tomorrow for my next victim.] (vol. 1, 43)

"NO ME MIRES," BY RODRIGO LEÓN
¿Qué me mira tanto señora? ¿Por qué no hace como todos, ver cómo se curva el tren boa, leer avisos? Bien, allá voy. Grandes ojos azul pálido. Diez segundos. Los abre más, sus pupilas se contraen. Veinte segundos. Bajan algunos, interceptando el haz de nuestras miradas. Treinta segundos. Me lloran los ojos, pestañeo. Perdí. Segundo intento. Miro fijo sus zapatos, eso nadie puede soportarlo. Son elegantes, caros, impecables. Levanto la vista y ¡está mirando los míos! Touché. Definitivamente es una profesional. Los limpio disimuladamente en el pantalón y casi tropiezo al bajar en Tobalaba. Ella sigue su viaje. Sonríe.

["DON'T LOOK AT ME"
Why is that woman looking at me so much? Why doesn't she act like everyone else, watch how the train curves along like a boa, read advertisements? Well all right, I'll go ahead. Big pale blue eyes. Ten seconds and she opens them more, her pupils contract. Twenty seconds. A few people get off, intercepting our gaze. Thirty seconds. My eyes start to water, I blink. I lost. Second attempt. I look straight at her shoes, no one can stand that. They are elegant, expensive, impeccable. I look up and she's looking at mine! Touché! She's definitely a professional. I clean them off discretely on my pant leg and I almost trip getting out at the Tobalaba stop. She stays on. She smiles.] (vol. 1, 12)

These two stories dramatize the anonymity of public transportation and the flirtatious games commuters play with glances, generated by men or women. From a playful, cynical approach in the first story to a curious guessing game in the second, the narrators exploit the close quarters of strangers packed into subway cars. The passage of time on the trains is evident in each of the stories: the seconds between stops, doors opening and closing, the comings and goings of other passengers. Both are anecdotes about being caught off guard by someone's gaze. The narrator of the first story seems to relish the daily challenge of finding another "victim," while the narrator of the second story seems bothered, almost taunted, by the woman staring at him. But he accepts the task in the end and turns it into a contest.

The stories not only feature riding on the Metro and Transantiago, but also begin to inscribe the contest itself into their plots, showing how it has become part of the city's urban imaginary. Beyond its graphic presence on billboards along the subway platforms and the Transantiago stops, the contest appears as the subject of one of the competing stories:

"RECURRENCIA," BY PABLO VÁSQUEZ
Más influenciado por la perseverancia de su padre que por una verdadera disposición artística Maldonado escribe sobre Luis Pezoa, un poeta olvidado que en la estación Baquedano lee las bases del concurso "Santiago en 100 palabras". Rejuvenecido ante la posibilidad de pagar algunas deudas y de reposicionar su nombre en los impasibles círculos literarios, Pezoa sale a la Plaza Italia, busca un asiento y crea la historia de Maldonado y su desesperada necesidad de buscar un deseo, una vocación lejos de las pretensiones de un padre obstinado por tener un hijo escritor.

["RECURRENCE"
More influenced by his father's perseverance than by a true artistic disposition, Maldonado writes about Luis Pezoa, a forgotten poet who in the Baquedano station reads the rules for the contest "Santiago in 100 Words." Rejuvenated by the possibility of paying some debts and gaining acceptance in exclusive literary circles, Pezoa gets out at Plaza Italia, looks for a seat, and creates a story about Maldonado and his desperate need to search for a desire, a vocation far from the pretensions of a father insistent on having a son who is a writer.] (vol. 2, 85)

This story's mise en abyme fictionalizes the contest within the contest, in a story about writers who write about writers, creating a Möbius strip that tricks the reader with an ending that does not end. The displacement of the writer, who starts out as Maldonado but ends up as Maldonado's subject, shifts the creative impulse onto the poet. This deferral reviews Pezoa's motivation of receiving prize money and enhancing his reputation as he considers entering the contest announced publicly in a metro station. The story incorporates movement through the city on the Metro only to subordinate the transportation function of the Metro to its role as the locus of information on the contest, of which it is also the sponsor. Here the narrative source of the story elusively slips to trap the reader in a continuous loop, ever searching for Maldonado's vocation or Pezoa's acceptance into that impenetrable literary world.

Another story fictionalizes the printed posters of the winning stories:

"LO PERDÍ," BY MARÍA INÉS PERANCHIGUAY
Tuve el mismo celular por tres años. Mismo número, 100% ubicable por todos y a toda hora. Si me llamas hoy, no te contestaré yo, sino otro. No tengo cómo avisarte, pues todos los datos estaban allí y sólo allí. Si lees ésto, te enterarás y quizás nos encontremos al afiche, yo deseando que lo leas y tú riéndote de la despistada que perdió el celular.

["I LOST IT"
I had the same cell phone for three years. The same number, 100% reachable by everyone and at any hour. If you call me today, I won't be answering, someone else will. I don't know how to let you know, since all the information was kept there and there alone. If you see this, you'll find out, and perhaps we'll meet at the poster, me hoping that you'll read it and you laughing at the scatterbrain who lost her cell phone.] (vol. 3, 33)

Here the narrator and her friend have lost track of one another when the narrator loses her cell phone, their only means of communication. She hopes that if her story is chosen by the contest, its graphic display in public with her name will help them reunite. The latest technology has failed them, so she resorts to the publicly printed version of a written message that inscribes the city to restore contact.

Another example from Santiago en 100 Palabras brings together reading, writing, and movement through the city with particular resonance for this exploration of urban public reading by inscribing the vehicle that delivers the story:

"ESCRITO HALLADO EN UN RESPALDO
DE ASIENTO DE MICRO," BY JULIO GUTIÉRREZ
No se me ocurrió otra forma de ubicarlos para que lo supieran. Mamá, papá: estoy bien y los perdono.

["NOTE FOUND ON THE BACK OF A BUS SEAT"
I couldn't think of any other way to find you to let you know. Mom, Dad: I'm fine and I forgive you.] (vol. 3, 14)

The title of this short piece announces the public transportation setting for the text itself, immediately enveloping the reader in the plot. The title also contains literary allusions through the image of a found document, a frequent metafictional move in Latin American fiction. The text to be discovered is inscribed directly on the vinyl of the back of a bus seat, exposed to any commuters who sit there, circulating along with the vehicle. The title indicates an intertextual genealogy that includes Edgar Allan Poe's famous tale "Manuscript Found in a Bottle" and Julio Cortázar's "Manuscrito hallado en un bolsillo," all texts moving through space in search of readers. The intertextual relationship between Cortázar's and Gutiérrez's stories pertains not only to the title, but also to the settings, as Cortázar's story takes place almost entirely in the Paris Metro.[35] The intricacies of public transportation in both stories motivate interpersonal encounters. Uncertainty and chance govern all of these tales of found written messages. The tension of Gutiérrez's story hinges on the uncertainty of the implied readers, the narrator's parents. Will they find the story, or will the story find them? As readers, we are interlopers who have found this text destined for someone else. The public bus not only is the setting for the action, but also becomes the vehicle for delivering the message. In an extreme economy of language, this microfiction develops movement in varying directions and with multiple destinations: the narrator's movement away from the family, the note's travel to deliver its message, and the readers' trajectory to the text.

The act of reading also becomes incorporated into some of the plots, as in Gutiérrez's story. His "Escrito hallado en un respaldo de asiento de micro" depends on the note being read by those to whom it is addressed, the narrator's parents. Literary reading also appears in the stories as a "practice of everyday life" just as Certeau highlights: reading among friends, in libraries, in bookstores, and in parks. Some stories unite out-of-touch friends or estranged family members, while in others the characters read for imagination and entertainment while riding on public transportation. Reading in these stories can be a solitary aesthetic experience, but it's carried out in the midst of the crowd.

"SOBRE AZUL," BY RENÉ ALLARD

Hoy es viernes y tengo que despedir a Sanhueza. Mi jefe piensa que ya se lo dije. Pero no es tan fácil. Sanhueza es como veinte años mayor que yo y, cuando llegué a la empresa, fue el único que no pensó que mi puesto lo merecía él. Desde mi oficina observo el Paseo Ahumada y podré ver cuando llegue. Él siempre anda acompañado de un libro. Ahora mismo debe venir en el Metro releyendo alguna historia de Cortázar o Borges, sus favoritos. "¿Para matar el tiempo, Sanhueza?", le pregunté cuando recién nos conocíamos. "No", me dijo, "para hacerlo vivir".

["PINK SLIP"36
Today is Friday, and I have to fire Sanhueza. My boss thinks I've already told him. But it's not so easy. Sanhueza is about twenty years older than me, and when I joined the firm, he was the only one who didn't think that my job should have gone to him. From my office I can see Ahumada Boulevard, and I watch him coming to work. He is always carrying a book. Right now he is probably approaching in the Metro reading some story by Cortázar or Borges, his favorites. "To kill time, Sanhueza?," I asked him when we had just met. "No," he said, "to keep it alive."] (vol. 1, 76)

The tension in this story rests on the conversation that lies ahead of the narrator, one that we as readers will only imagine. By order of a supervisor, the narrator must fire his coworker despite their mutual respect. In anticipation of this sad and difficult encounter, the narrator recalls an earlier conversation with him, when he discovered that he reads literature on his commute. For Sanhueza, fiction doesn't kill time, it enlivens it. Remembered in the context of the pressure to fire him, his habit of reading humanizes him.

Despite their brevity, some of the stories manage to incorporate neighborhoods, parks, historic architecture, and secret spots in the city, superimposing interpersonal anecdotes over a map of urban planning and transportation design. In the following example, the characters discover an abandoned tunnel, where they cover the walls with poetry, writing and reading on the city itself:

"TAJAMARES," BY POLETT BODY
Cuando me llamó el Nico, su bus venía llegando de Valpo. Le dije que me esperara en las banquitas que dan a la Alameda. Cuando lo encontré, nos pusimos a caminar hasta Meiggs, y al Nico se le ocurrió robarse una cajita con tizas. Tomamos una micro y nos bajamos en Salvador. Le dije que conocía una galería abandonada en el parque. Entramos. Estaba tan oscuro que iluminó con su encendedor. Sacamos las tizas y llenamos las paredes con poemas de Pizarnik. Estuvimos

como una hora conversando. Al otro día volví y estaba con candado. Mañana mismo compro un napoleón.[37]

["DIKES"
When Nico called me, his bus was just arriving from Valpo. I told him to wait for me on those benches that face the Alameda. When I found him, we started walking toward Meiggs, and Nico decided to steal a box of chalk. We took a bus and got off at Salvador. I told him I knew about an abandoned alleyway in the park. We went in. It was so dark that he used his lighter so we could see. We took out the chalk and filled up the walls with poems by Pizarnik. We stayed there, talking, for an hour. We went back the next day, and it was locked. Tomorrow I'm going to go buy a wrench.] (vol. 6, 79)

This story of transgression revolves around interurban bus travel, reading, and writing. The narration not only traces the characters' bus riding itinerary, but also intensifies movement in the story through transportation associations with particular Santiago neighborhoods. Meiggs, a neighborhood named after the entrepreneur and railroad engineer Henry Meiggs, who built the railway line between Santiago and Valparaíso in the middle of the nineteenth century, is adjacent to railway station Estación Central, where the engineer's mansion is located. The *tajamares* of the title refer to brick ramparts built along the Mapocho River in the colonial period to prevent flooding. The ramparts were mostly destroyed in the 1970s with the construction of the Metro, but some of their ruins were discovered recently, particularly in the park near Salvador that the story mentions.[38] The underground tunnel in the story, remains of the dikes whose walls they chalk over with Pizarnik's poems, allows readers clandestine entry into a public but hidden space. The end of the story continues the adventure, as the narrator is not deterred by the lock on the tunnel, but is determined to return and break in. Here reading and writing are forms of resistance that accompany friends who reunite to explore their urban surroundings.

Reading, writing, and public transportation come together in Santiago en 100 Palabras in stories that not only fictionalize commuting but even metafictionalize writing about commuting. The itineraries, intersections, bus stops, and platforms in this last example trace a cartography of the city while searching for the grammar that will tell the story:

"GRAMÁTICA DE TRANSPORTES," BY MAXIMILIANO GARCÍA
¿En qué persona gramatical se debe relatar un viaje en micro a las 7:30 de la mañana entre Pudahuel y Vitacura? ¿En la primera-persona-singular y solitaria que viaja las cuatro horas diarias? ¿En la primera-persona-plural que el hacinamiento sudoroso reinventa en cada parada? ¿Quizás en la tercera persona de ese narrador omnisciente y omnipotente, a quien le pedimos—por favor—que abra la puerta? En cualquier caso, el diseñador del plan no puede haber sido un gran narrador.

["TRANSPORTATION GRAMMAR"
From what point of view should one tell about a bus trip at 7:30 in the morning between Pudahuel and Vitacura? In the first person, singular and solitary, who commutes four hours a day? In the first person plural that the sweaty overcrowding reinvents at every stop? Maybe in that third person omniscient and omnipotent narrator whom we ask—please—to open the door? In any case, whoever designed the plan could not have been a great narrator.] (vol. 7, 38)

The trip's geographic borders tell only part of the story, as the two bus stops frame the spatial dimensions but are not able to account for the personal ones. From solitude (first person singular) to solidarity (first person plural) to the impotence of the impersonal (third person omniscient), the story tells of the frustrated attempt to capture a daily urban trek, only to conclude with the self-reflexive irony of an incompetent cartographer-narrator. Through this contest, Santiago's citizens become narrators, mappers, and designers of urban life; masters of their travels as well as of their travelogues. As Griffin notes, the contest "allows Chileans to occupy the position of literature's object and subject at the same time and thereby creates the possibility of replacing a structure of cultural elitism with one of cultural democracy" (*Labor of Literature* 131).

Santiago en 100 Palabras gathers citizens' private stories and makes them public as a strategy for reestablishing ties and communal identification among *santiaguinos*. Along with the anecdotes that they narrate, "the stories from Santiago in 100 Words also tell about the ways inhabitants produce social cohesion and the feelings of integration in current Chilean society, such that the concepts of sociability, individuation and subjectivation always seem to be present" (Campos Medina 110). The value of *convivencia* is not a surprising result, but rather a programmatic intention built into this collective public reading and writing initiative.

The sponsors of the contest reiterate these goals in their introductions to the anthologies. María Olivia Recart, vice president of BHP Billiton, the multinational that owns Minera Escondida, said in a brief statement introducing the anthology commemorating the program's tenth anniversary that she considers the contest "a social catalyst that promotes values like governability, civic cohesion, and quality of life, ... space for civic participation" (Recart 9). Plagio's preface to the volume celebrates the contest by acknowledging that "it's no longer ours; rather it belongs to the thousands of people who participate in it. We and our partners only act as mediators of an initiative that has come to life" (Arnold, García, and Dümmer 13).

Along with a selection of colorfully illustrated stories spanning all ten years of the contest, the anniversary anthology prints short essays by writers, urban planners, cultural directors, social scientists, and architects who offer their views on Santiago en 100 Palabras. According to sociologist Manuel Tironi, the contest has redefined citizenship: "If instead of that random 'citizen' we hear about in public policy we were to talk about the thousands of these little stories[,] . . . it would be a much more accurate snapshot of the *santiaguino*. . . . We could use S100P to redesign civic participation" (32). Alejandra Wood, director of the Centro Gabriela Mistral, goes so far as to assert that "sociability is built on the foundation of all of these stories. . . . 'Santiago en 100 Palabras' has been transformed over time into a space for expressing citizenship" (104). Similarly, for writer Rafael Gumucio, all the stories together compose "the succinct biography of this city that is nothing more than an accumulation of these never-ending little miniatures" (125). The collective nature of the contest has multiple dimensions, from the thousands who write stories to the many more who read them as they travel through the city or enjoy them in the anthologies.

The cumulative effect of years of undiscovered citizen-authors and anonymous citizen readers contributes to this grand biography of Santiago. According to the contest's director, Carmen García, Santiago en 100 Palabras has changed the character of the city, creating a sense of belonging and of ownership in Santiago:[39]

> The citizens take ownership of the city because their stories intervene in public space. Although there are only twelve winners, the fact that people's stories are published generates a connection, and that con-

nection generates integration because it's not some random citizen or stranger, or someone threatening. One sees in the stories that the same kinds of things happen to everyone, that there is a common perspective. Conceptually, this is one of the major gains of the contest, integration through literature. The theme of urban interaction has been a fundamental element in reestablishing social and cultural identity that was rather hidden. (personal interview, my translation)

The brief stories from Santiago and the traveling books in Bogotá take the printed page and set it in motion, circulating fictions in new itineraries outside the trajectories of their vehicles. Although the two programs differ in a number of respects—Libro al Viento stresses reading, while Santiago en 100 Palabras promotes creative writing; the Bogotá program has official municipal backing, while the Santiago program relies more on private funding—both programs draw ordinary citizens into literary reading through public transportation and stage urban reading in public space. They capitalize on imaginative written culture as a strategy for promoting *convivencia* and civic interaction in their respective cities. This emphasis on *convivencia* does not emerge from an abstract concept but lies at the core of concerted programmatic efforts to reclaim public space and reinscribe urban belonging in both cities. These programs have become part of broad strategic policies for diminishing urban violence in Colombia and reestablishing democracy after the dictatorship in Chile, policies that incorporate community-wide reading and writing as an integral part of redefining citizenship.

Reading in the Market for Public Culture

The attempts to foster inclusivity across social class in Santiago and Bogotá through reading programs that benefit from both public and private funding indicate a shift in priorities in the wake of neoliberal economic policies. Chile, in particular, became the prime territory for testing Milton Friedman's economic approaches, which favor the free market and private global investment, with significant impact on cultural industries (Cárcamo-Huechante). After decades of boosting of free-market privatization and diminishment of the state's role in cultural, economic, and social welfare in much of Latin America, an emphasis on the public has begun to reemerge. The eclectic blending of public and private sponsorship on which these reading programs depend parallels a wider trend of cautious reinvestment in the public sphere.

In these programs' urban expression, innovative dimensions of writing the city also mesh what is considered elite or high literature with popular street expression, challenging the boundaries that supposedly distinguish them. The goals and objectives of Santiago en 100 Palabras and Libro al Viento, as defined by their corporate and municipal sponsors, share those of public art. More than decoration and embellishment, art and reading in public space should motivate "the activation in their users of a *reflective civilized consciousness*; of their being in a place shaped both to specific uses—learning, healing, debate, diplomacy, etc.—and to those general purposes beyond immediate utility, of the human project, which include the contemplation of matters of value, the pursuit of happiness, and a sense of well-being" (Gooding and Public Arts Commission Agency 19–20, emphasis added).

Literary or visual expression in public places, particularly in cities, is built on a paradox, wrestling between the freedom of aesthetic expression and the institutional and financial constraints of urban planning. The extent to which critical messages and political opposition can be conveyed in public art depends not only on the artist but also on the mechanisms of funding, patronage, and civic planning at a given site. CERLALC stresses the social, interactive benefits of reading in public policy and programming when it recommends "strategies and plans based on common interest that seek to guide, articulate, and promote, through coordination, the activities developed by diverse sources: the state, private business and civic organizations, in specific areas of social life" (182–183). Encouraging *convivencia* and promoting engaged citizenship is often the motor behind public culture projects, particularly literature as considered here, and serves as a justification for their funding.

Libro al Viento and Santiago en 100 Palabras reflect the hybrid stories of their production—literary reading that relies on official financial backing from public, municipal institutions as well as private investment. These projects underscore the contradictions of urban institutionalization and have important implications for public space in the urban realm. The transformation of elevated bus lanes or underground passageways into avenues of fantastic adventures through public, free fiction stretches the confines of industrial structures and urban lettered institutions. Stories on billboards in Santiago and books given away and circulated in Bogotá confound the false dichotomy between elite and popular culture by inaugurating new uses for urban space. By empowering citizens as mobile readers and writers, public reading reassigns agency regarding who controls urban spatial functions.

The urban reading programs reviewed here reveal not only the role of cities in promoting the reading of literature but also the role of literature in rewriting urban identity and providing a route for reimagining the city during periods of political transition. The networks that connect public space and public policy with literature involve heterogeneous sources, with some expected institutions—such as public libraries, ministries of education, and literacy campaigns—and diverse sources of corporate sponsorship. The innovation of programs like Libro al Viento and Santiago en 100 Palabras lies in their participatory structure, which moves outside of the conventional institutions of the lettered city, passing over their physical walls and renegotiating their bureaucracy to incorporate a much wider citizenship of public readers. Travelers' private readings lead to collective conversations that promote public consciousness and a shared experience of location and urban belonging.

Throughout Latin America, municipal programs now strive to capture the urban imaginary and circulate it through everyday infrastructure. The subway in Buenos Aires announced in 2013 that it would discontinue Line A's historic wooden train cars, and it temporarily closed Latin America's oldest running subway line until new cars could be installed.[40] The city government's Ministry of Culture plans to relocate ten of the iconic cars to city parks, where they will serve as public libraries. Instead of books and stories in Santiago and Bogotá descending underground or gliding along designated lanes to provoke conversation among commuters, the subway cars in Buenos Aires will emerge from below to house and circulate books rather than commuters. Several parks slated to receive a subway car are located along this very subway line, including Parque Rivadavia, which already has a vibrant book culture, with permanent stands selling used books daily. The public interaction of these new library branches will begin with the collection itself: the books will be gathered from users' donations, in the spirit of book "liberations" that many cities sponsor throughout Latin America (Rivas).[41] Access to reading on a moving vehicle, or even in a stationary one like the historic retired subway cars in Buenos Aires, drives urban citizens to reclaim the lettered city as they traffic in the wide circulation of letters.

CHAPTER 3

Cacerolazos y bibliotecas: Solidarity, Reading, and Public Space after the Argentine Economic Crisis (2001–2002)

Assemblies: a place for everyone.
NEWSLETTER TITLE, ASAMBLEA POPULAR DE LINIERS

Florencia Abbate wrote her novel *El grito* (The Scream; 2004) during Argentina's economic crisis of 2001–2002, while she was unemployed and living off of her dwindling savings. Comprising four interrelated stories with shared characters, each one narrated in a different voice, the novel offers an intergenerational view of this period's economic and political events. Each of the four chapters recounts a personal crisis: depression over turning thirty, separation from a partner, a failed suicide attempt, and a cancer diagnosis. These experiences of disillusionment, vulnerability, and instability in the crucial days of late December 2001 and early January 2002 coincide with the climax of the nation's economic and political crisis.

The scream referenced in the title recurs in each chapter: the cry of an impoverished family picking through the garbage or the shout of an angry man before he breaks a window. The shadow of the dictatorship years looms over the overlapping stories. Several of the characters were militants in the 1970s and spent years in exile, and although they have been back in Argentina for years, they continue to face unresolved challenges. Connections between the personal and the political parallel tensions between the individual and the collective; the characters enact their private anguish within, and exacerbated by, the national scenario of chaos, collapse, and collective despair. Scenes from Abbate's novel frame this chapter's focus on literary reading and community libraries as priorities in the solidarity movement's response to economic crisis in Argentina.

El grito's first chapter, entitled "Warhol," is narrated by Federico, who just turned thirty and is resentful and disillusioned.¹ He grew up in exile, living in various countries with his activist mother; he now lives in Buenos Aires but is lost professionally and personally. When his parents separated, his gay father remained in Buenos Aires, living with his partner and running a series of music shops. Disdainful of his mother's outdated leftist activism, Federico is loath to participate in any political activity. Nevertheless, he finds himself inadvertently thrown into the street drama the morning after the *cacerolazo* protests, when angry citizens demonstrated by banging on pots and pans in their neighborhoods.

Totally unaware of the political tumult the night before, Federico wakes up on December 20 and decides to launch a fresh start on his new decade by joining a health club. As he walks to the gym, he wonders why so many shops are closed, why so few cars are in the street, why armed police officers stand on many corners. A young punk outside the gym, who turns out to be the owner, says that he fears the country is on the verge of a civil war. He shows Federico a book he's carrying called *How to Write a Poem*, and says he wants to write a poem about the current national situation. Slowly Federico begins to realize that the protests and demonstrations of the night before, "eran acontecimientos de dominio público" (were events in the public domain) (37), and that he is totally in the dark about what happened. After wandering on empty streets he hails a taxi for a labyrinthine ride of constant detours around closed roads, a cartography of a city under siege. Suddenly,

> ocurrieron una serie de fenómenos que nunca olvidaré. Una auténtica batalla campal se desplegó de pronto alrededor de nosotros. Enjambres de personas huían de la policía, retrocedían para reagruparse y volver a avanzar hacia la casa de gobierno. Yo corrí como un condenado. . . . Sentía un pavor irracional, aunque en definitiva muy real. Vi que la montada venía siguiendo a una oleada de tipos con palos, y me oculté en el hall de un negocio de electrodomésticos.
> [a series of phenomena occurred that I will never forget. An authentic battle erupted suddenly around us. Groups were fleeing from the police, slowed down to regroup, and kept moving toward the governmental palace. I ran like someone condemned. . . . I felt an irrational terror, although it was definitely very real. I saw the crowd was following a wave of guys with sticks, and I hid in the foyer of an appliance store.] (47)

An old man complaining that he had to spend all his money on medicine yells, "ya no aguanto" (I can't take it anymore) and breaks the window of the appliance store. Suddenly Federico sees his father on the illuminated television screens, interviewed on the news because one of his music stores has been looted. "Aquello fue lo último que vi, puesto que en ese instante una bala se incrustó en mi pantorrilla y caí desmayado" (That was the last thing I saw, since at that very instant a bullet penetrated my calf and I fainted) (48).

This last scene of the first chapter reveals some key structural and contextual elements of the crisis: the failure of the neoliberal economy (in the vulnerability of the local appliance store and health club), the public taking to the streets, the dire consequences for the middle class that will prompt their participation in an alternative solidarity economy, and, of particular relevance for this study, the presence of literature and reading as a resource in the midst of economic and political collapse.

In Abbate's re-creation of the despair of the crisis, she introduces creative expression as an avenue for resistance, perseverance, and change. Most of the main characters' vocations or professions—theatrical sound engineering, sculpting, art education, and music retail—are in the arts and culture industry. Through their creative endeavors, despite the current circumstances and after years in exile, these characters persist and strive to situate themselves and stabilize their relationships in Buenos Aires. Even Peter, after his failed suicide attempt, affirms that "existe algo indestructible en cada uno. . . . Es aquello donde mora nuestra fuerza para seguir viviendo, aun cuando se hayan conmovido todos los cimientos en que nos apoyábamos. Hoy sé que la mayor misión consiste en descubrir estos principios que velan sobre los escombros, que nos permiten soportar el horror consustancial a la vida, superar las peores catástrofes y reencontrar en nuestro interior la fuente de los nacimientos" (there is something indestructible in everyone. . . . That's where our strength to keep on living resides, even when the foundation that we stand on is shaken. Today I know that the greatest mission consists of discovering the principles that watch over the embers, that allow us to survive life's intrinsic horror, to survive the worst catastrophes and rediscover within ourselves the source of all beginnings) (162–163). The crisis period in Argentina seems to be framed in this duality of hopefulness and disillusionment, where cultural expression plays a crucial role in bolstering solidarity efforts. The rest of this chapter explores the urban survival strategies

Figure 3.2. "Out with them all!" flyer; author photo; courtesy of Princeton University Library

vertibilidad (law of convertability), paving the way, over the rest of the decade, for a sharp increase in foreign imports and a decline in manufacturing, forcing many factories to close. Unemployment rose to 18.3 percent by late 2001 and soared to 55 percent in some sectors in 2002. When the International Monetary Fund refused to go through with a loan to Argentina, the entire economy collapsed. A run on the banks pushed President Fernando de la Rúa's administration (1999–2001) to pass a law in early December 2001 limiting withdrawals and thereby ending the one-to-one relationship of the peso to the dollar. The move unleashed the fury of the middle class, whose savings were lost. De la Rúa and his cabinet resigned, and a revolving political door saw five presidents come and go in the span of two weeks. The slogan "¡Que se vayan todos!" (Out with them all!), printed on banners, painted as graffiti, and shouted in the streets, expressed the citizens' complete lack of confidence in all elected officials, and in the legitimacy of representational politics overall (see figure 3.2).[2]

In the midst of this economic and political collapse, a solidarity movement emerged that provided economic, logistical, and social support to neighborhood residents on the local level and strove to replace

Figures 3.1a and b. Pots and pans, symbols of the street protests; author photo; courtesy of Princeton University Library

employed just after the crisis, to reveal how reading is integrated into the urban solidarity economy through community libraries and cultural programming.

Anatomy of the Crisis and the Emergence of Neighborhood Solidarity Associations

The street protests, looting, and *cacerolazos* that took place on the evening of December 19, 2001, have become emblems of this difficult period in Argentina (see figures 3.1a and 3.1b). Although the events of this day were dramatic, they did not emerge suddenly or without warning. Rather, they were the culmination of economic and political failures after a decade of neoliberal policies that exacerbated income disparity and unemployment, particularly since the presidency of Carlos Menem (1989–1999). In order to stabilize the economy after the previous economic collapse, which brought the highest inflation in the country's history, Menem implemented conservative neoliberal policies, counter to his Peronista party's platform, including privatization of natural resources and key infrastructure.

The peso was pegged to the US dollar in 1991 in the *ley de con-*

party politics with direct democracy. Along with political organizing and economic solidarity through bartering of goods and services, the solidarity movement often highlighted culture, where reading and literature had a persistent presence. According to María Sáenz Quesada, former Secretary of Culture for Buenos Aires's city government, "in the rigorous test we've had to go through in 2002, culture came out with a high grade" (145). Argentines turned to culture as a form a resistance and demonstrated "its capacity and willingness to create, to entertain, to imagine new paths" (Sáenz Quesada 145).

Although book publishing came to an abrupt halt and a spike in the price of imported books made them inaccessible, alternative forms of literary culture emerged, particularly at the neighborhood level.[3] A notable example is the publishing cooperative Eloísa Cartonera, founded in 2003 in Buenos Aires by the writer Washington Cucurto and the artist Javier Barilaro as a response to this dearth of literary publishing. They bound books in reused cardboard purchased from the city's garbage pickers (*cartoneros*), whose ranks had burgeoned because of the crisis. Eloísa Cartonera inadvertently launched a phenomenon of dozens of cardboard book publishers throughout Latin America and elsewhere internationally.

Like these grassroots publishing initiatives, the strategies employed by people trying to survive the crisis and rebuild emerge from the intimacy of close associates and the local neighborhood. One cannot overstate the historical importance of the *barrio* in Argentina. As architect and cultural historian Adrián Gorelik comments regarding the rapid growth of Buenos Aires in the 1920s, "The barrio was a social and cultural creation that transformed urban expansion into a new public space incorporating popular sectors" (153). Neighborhood associations often coalesced around a local soccer team or a tango bar and served as a buttress against the waves of European immigration and the unprecedented expansion of the city. These clubs and *asambleas* functioned as the "active cores of civil society" (Gorelik 153).

James Scorer's book *City in Common* explores Buenos Aires's role as an agent in maintaining a "commons" through culture, from the dictatorship through the neoliberal period and the economic crisis. His chapter on the suburban response to the crisis underscores local barrios "as privileged sites of urban identity in Buenos Aires . . . as site[s] of belonging" (131–132).[4] Most of the neighborhood groups established in the early decades of the twentieth century had disintegrated by the 2001–2002 crisis, but the practice of small, local organizations of neighbors persisted in historical memory and became the principal mode of organizing and activism after the crisis, particularly in Buenos Aires, as well as in other cities, such as Córdoba, La Plata, and Rosario.

The rage and dismay of the public fueled the famous *cacerolazos*. There were more than 2,000 protests between December and March, and in December 2001 alone there were an average of sixty-six *cacerolazos* per day. However, the numbers of protests tapered off in the new year,[5] and angry, disillusioned citizens sought more effective ways to organize. As Stella Calloni writes, "the 'rebellion of the pots and pans,' at first a spontaneous step, later searched for ways to stay, remain, grow, mature in the neighborhood Assemblies" (19). Weary of chanting "Out with them all!" and convinced that the democratic system of representational government was not going to meet their expectations or demands, they set themselves "to search for new ways of organizing and community building within the method of horizontal participation, with consensus, respect for differences, and exercising solidarity" (*Boletín Asamblea de la Plaza Estación Coghlan* 1.4 [2002]: 11).[6] By March 2002, more than 270 neighborhood associations, called "asambleas barriales" or "asambleas populares," had been established and were active in urban areas across the country.[7] An experiment in direct democracy, the *asambleas* attempted to fill the breach left by the collapsed national political structure. By functioning on the local neighborhood level, a personalized and subjective form of political organizing encouraged individual participation and action.

One of the outstanding characteristics of the neighborhood associations was their mix of social classes, a result of the severity of the crisis, particularly for the middle class, which served to unite groups who otherwise shared few common political interests. While the groups' adherents depended in part on the social-class composition of the neighborhoods, the barrios became heterogeneous "connecting spaces" (Svampa 267) that brought together the chronically unemployed, members of labor unions, small business owners who had lost everything, and young people interested in political activism for the first time.[8] The *asambleas*' activities and initiatives included bartering fairs (*ferias de trueque*), food pantries and soup kitchens, communal buying, community gardens, job fairs, and cultural events. In the realm of political organizing, the *asambleas* planned protests, painted murals, and challenged the city's bureaucracy by occupying abandoned buildings and empty lots. Some of the groups promoted neighborhood pride by renovating historic buildings, painting murals, and leading walking tours. Although there were some attempts to connect the neighborhood associations into citywide *interbarriales* (interneighborhood groups), coalescing among the groups was short-lived, and the autonomy of each group prevailed.⁹

While the *asambleas* emerged as a direct response to the crisis of 2001–2002, they often incorporated a commitment to remembering and denouncing the 1976–1983 dictatorship. The groups' neighborhood initiatives, committee work, and public art projects recalled the dictatorship's censorship of communication and repressive restrictions on group associations. They commemorated the neighborhood's victims, who had been detained, tortured, or disappeared. It is not an exaggeration to claim that the *asambleas* were part of the ongoing transition to democracy, a concrete way to reclaim the right to meet in groups and organize, which was outlawed during the dictatorship: "The associations confront the desolate panorama of social unraveling, which had reached such a state that one could almost consider it dissolving. The process that started in 1976 had decimated the carefully constructed structure of organizations up to that point. In 2002 the neighborhood groups, community building associations, local libraries, neighborhood clubs, parish activities, cooperative and mutual societies had practically disappeared" (Feijóo and y Salas Oroño 24). The neighborhood associations' protests and efforts to organize an alternative solidarity economy not only responded to economic and political collapse but also took on the continuing effort to rebuild the democratic society that the authoritarian military junta had destroyed. The connection between these efforts—on the one hand addressing immediate circumstances, on the other turning to the memory work of the recent past—lay in their participatory and local nature, and in the community reclaiming its rights and basic values.

Cecilia Marteau points out a sequential progression of violence against the public and a loss of power in Argentina that began with the dictatorship and culminated in the 2001–2002 collapse: "There had been a sort of sequence of disappearances in the country. Thirty years ago people began to disappear, then money disappeared and now the political structure has disappeared. . . . Violence is the disappearance of language" (quoted in Caram 33). Several groups painted murals in the neighborhood to commemorate the barrio's victims of the dictatorship. Many organized marches and demonstrations on March 24, the anniversary of the 1976 coup. The Barrio Hipódromo association in La Plata named their Centro Cultural Favero to memorialize Daniel Favero, a disappeared poet and musician. The Villa Pueyrredón asociación renamed (they called it a rebaptism) Plaza Lonardi as the Plaza del Nunca Más (Never Again) and erected a sign with the names of

Figure 3.3. Centro Azucena Villaflor flyer; author photo; courtesy of Princeton University Library

twenty-seven people who had been detained or disappeared from the neighborhood (*Prensa Asamblea Popular Villa Pueyrredón* [September 2002]: 4). The Asamblea Popular Boedo y San Cristóbal's newsletter announced a mural commemorating the victims of the "noche de los lápices" (night of the pencils), when ten teenagers were arrested and tortured and six of them disappeared in La Plata (no. 20: 1).

In San Telmo, Buenos Aires, the *asamblea* mobilized around the Club Atlético, a former clandestine center for torture and disappearance early in the dictatorship. When the club was destroyed for highway construction, the *asamblea* held memorial events and demanded an archeological dig and forensic investigation. The Avellaneda neighborhood in Buenos Aires established the Centro Azucena Villaflor in the former Mayo Bank building. This cultural center for the community was named after one of the founding members of the Madres de Plaza de Mayo, who was arrested, tortured, and disappeared when the group was infiltrated by an informer. The center, whose logo incorporates the emblematic white handkerchiefs of the Madres, sponsors food programs and political organizing workshops (see figure 3.3).[10]

The spontaneous emergency organizing in the neighborhoods in late 2001 that coalesced into the *asambleas* "emerged out of the embers, but the impulse had started long before and was accompanied by the ghosts of those who fought before and are no longer here" (Calloni 19).

Press and Politics: The Role of Newsletters in Solidarity Organizing

The work of the *asambleas* was accomplished through committees, called *comisiones*, that were devoted to health care, women's issues, housing, political organizing, communications, and culture. The committees met regularly (in some cases weekly) and recruited members through announcements in the groups' monthly newsletters. These newsletters, called *boletines*, documented the *asambleas*' activities and organizing efforts. Neighborhood efforts to provide food, distribute clothing, and exchange resources and skills through bartering attempted to relieve some of the concrete hardship neighbors were facing, but the commitment to cultural activities, emphasized in each and every *asamblea*, offers a surprising dimension to the local response to the crisis. Books and reading were a persistent priority in the groups' festivals, workshops, public readings, and use of public space (see figure 3.4).

The *comisiones de cultura* actively promoted reading and literature through weekly meetings and frequent events. All the *asambleas* supported a committee for culture and defined its scope according to the neighborhood's needs and interests. Cultural *ferias* were very common, sometimes held every weekend, and included puppet shows, theater workshops, and poetry readings. The cultural fairs, which were announced in the newsletters and on flyers distributed in the neighborhood, promoted a party-like atmosphere, aiming to draw people together and encourage them to look beyond the current misery and hardship. Flyers advertised music, games and other activities for children, and inexpensive snacks, and they called for donations to the neighborhood food pantry. The flyer for the Jornada de Resistencia, a fair held in the Parque Avellaneda neighborhood in 2002, asked attendees to "bring one book and/or non-perishable food item to benefit soup kitchens and food pantries," showing that books were as urgently needed as food during the crisis. Some groups led historic tours of the neighborhood to promote pride and belonging, and they often high-

Figure 3.4. Newsletter cover; author photo; courtesy of Princeton University Library

lighted writers who had resided there with readings, homage events, and lectures. Alongside workshops on political organizing, women's health, and housing advocacy, the cultural committees sponsored literary classes and workshops on creative writing, theater, puppetry, and *murgas*.[11]

Along with announcing events, meetings, and initiatives that promoted reading, the newsletters themselves were a source for reading; they published poetry, printed quotes by writers and philosophers, and used poetic language in their essays and articles. Poetry by leftist writers such as Mario Benedetti and Eduardo Galeano and quotations from playwright Bertolt Brecht appeared regularly. Reflecting on the role of the newsletters themselves, sometimes an opinion piece or editorial praises the *boletines* as the mouthpieces of the *asambleas*, "a place to make language our own. . . . And the word turned into ink, and any little bar became an editing studio. . . . Word by word, we are scratching out oblivion, we are writing history" (*La Cacerola de Zapiola*, Boletín de la Asamblea de Colegiales 1.16 [20 June 2002]: 20). Another example, with an allusion to Tolstoy, claims that language holds the potential for change, revealing the newsletters as a key tool of the solidarity movement. The *asambleas* relied on the newsletters as:

> a channel of expression for the potentiality that, it seems, is ready and waiting for us to give it free rein. And giving it free rein means cleaning out resentment, suspicion, inhibitions and whatever ties us down so that we can speak, propose, invent, debate, expose, create. A Newsletter that speaks up, with gloves off, an open mind, a probing gaze, finger on the pulse. . . . a Newsletter that, like Tolstoy, in telling about the neighborhood tells about the world. . . . For the Newsletter to be the true symbol of this collective construction that we all hope for, we have to take hold of language and open it up like a ripe piece of fruit or a window; let's turn it inside out like a glove and, if necessary, reinvent it until we find a way to say something new. (*La Cacerola de Zapiola* 1.12 [18 April 2002]: 1)

The metaphors, literary allusions, humor, and idiomatic expressions transmit a playful, poetic, ebullient attitude about the power of language for social change. The Buenos Aires Balvanera neighborhood newsletter's cover illustration offers a graphic confirmation of the importance of reading to the solidarity movement (see figure 3.5). Dialogue bubbles hovering over an urban streetscape highlight the group's five main objectives: where a book to represent reading joins symbols for housing (a house), food (bread), jobs (a factory), and health (a cross).

One of the most significant projects of the neighborhood associations, and one that supported the promotion of reading, was occupying abandoned buildings and empty lots in order to convert them into useful, productive spaces for the neighborhood.[12] A list of complaints and demands printed in one of the newsletters states, "public spaces do not belong to 'them,' they are ours, we are reclaiming what is rightfully ours" (*Boletín de la Asamblea Vecinos de Constitución* 2 [July 2002]: 1). The Parque Saavedra association in La Plata declares that one of its principle objectives is to "recuperate public spaces for the good of the community and at the same time provide opportunities" (*La Cacerola de Cornelio* 1.1 [12 October 2002]: 12).

The various groups' efforts to occupy and "recuperate" abandoned spaces served to "reactivate a dead place and make it belong to everyone" (*Carta abierta* [Asamblea Vecinal de Boedo] 1.3 [September

Figure 3.5. Balvanera newsletter cover; author photo; courtesy of Princeton University Library

Figure 3.6. Brukman Factory newsletter ("Desde Brukman estamos enhebrando sueños" [At Brukman we are stringing together dreams]); author photo; courtesy of Princeton University Library

2002]: 5). Empty lots were cleaned up and repurposed as community gardens, often with playground equipment and bread ovens. The associations worked to regain use of structures—from former pizzerias and car washes to empty bank buildings—for tutoring, childcare, food pantries, soup kitchens, and community libraries. A literary newsletter edited by a group of workers at the famous Brukman textile factory places the word *poetry* above and in larger lettering than the names of the other genres (editorials, essays, memoir) that the publication includes. This workers' group is an extension of the community building among the labor force that led to a successful takeover of the factory when the owners and managers were losing money during the crisis and planned to shut it down (see figure 3.6).[13]

Bibliotecas para el barrio: Reading through the Crisis

Neighborhood or "popular" libraries in Argentina were first established in 1879 by Domingo Faustino Sarmiento under the umbrella organization of the National Commission of Popular Libraries (CONABIP).[14] More informal and less imposing and institutional than major urban, academic, or government-sponsored public libraries, these small libraries were meant to serve their neighborhoods. Because they were independent of the networks of municipal public libraries and frequently were set up in rural towns, it was difficult to oversee and maintain them, and many were neglected, fell into disrepair, or disappeared altogether. A number of the community libraries that the *asambleas* publicized and supported were CONABIP libraries that the groups reopened and revitalized, while others were completely new initiatives. Whether resurrected or new, in the wake of the crisis neighborhood libraries overtly countered the pattern of neoliberal privatization by supporting reading as a publicly accessible right. The Biblioteca Popular de Bella Vista in Córdoba makes this explicit on its webpage: "Popular Libraries have survived all the avatars of so-called capitalist 'development' in Argentina, conservative fraud, dictatorships, populism, the clientelistic mechanisms of bourgeois democracy. They survived book burnings, the flood of best-sellers, and marketing" (Fiorito). Susana Fiorito calls the neighborhood libraries communitarian institutions, "refuges for culture" that are working to protect against the "danger that they might privatize public reading."

The *asambleas* stepped in to reactivate community libraries, which offered a range of services for the neighborhood. The Biblioteca Popular Cornelio Saavedra was established in the 1920s and originally provided the neighborhood with public health services and adult education, as well as books. During the solidarity response to the crisis, the library's newsletter boasted about a collection of 20,000 volumes, 16,000 of them "literature" (*Claraboya* 1 [December 2004]: 1). The Club Imperio Juniors, a social and sports club that also had a community library in the Santa Rita neighborhood, was founded in 1935. When it was in danger of being shuttered in 2002, a group of neighbors intervened to preserve it. The Biblioteca Popular housed in the Club Everton in Parque Saavedra in La Plata, another CONABIP library, which was established in 1943 by the writer Mario Sureda, had been closed for seven years when the neighborhood association stepped in to reopen it in response to the economic crisis (*La Cacerola de Cornelio* 2.6 [May 2003]: 4). The library of 10,000 volumes became a public resource that was no longer restricted to club members.

Neighborhood libraries were frequently mentioned in newsletter announcements and articles, as well as highlighted on event flyers (see figure 3.7). The layout of a page from Villa del Parque's neighborhood newsletter indicates the significance of reading literature: an announcement asking for book donations for a mobile library is printed at the top of the page, above a call for donations of food, medicine, blankets, and clothing. The note enumerates literary genres as well, mentioning "novels, stories, magazines, poetry books" ahead of textbooks, cookbooks, and books on philosophy (*En la Plaza* [6 July 2002]: 6). A citywide charter, "Proyecto de Ley de Comunas de Participación Directa" (Project for the Neighborhood Law of Direct Participation), written collectively by Buenos Aires *asambleas*, confirms this dedication to reading: Article 22 of the document points out libraries as a priority for the movement: "to oversee the maintenance, development and promotion of buildings such as schools, libraries, museums, sports centers, cultural centers, theaters, and other buildings that pertain to the city of Buenos Aires or to nongovernmental community organizations" (5).

In the Caballito neighborhood in Buenos Aires, the association sought to connect its solidarity efforts with an existing community library, Biblioteca Popular "Los Libros de la Buena Memoria" (*Boletín Asamblea Popular de Caballito Parque Rivadavia* 1.10 [29 June 2002]: 1). A year later, the Asamblea Caballito Gastón Riva, a nearby group named in memory of one of the victims of the repression in De-

Figure 3.7. Newsletter cover ("La Asamblea decidió armar su modesta biblioteca" [The Association has decided to set up a little library]); author photo; courtesy of Princeton University Library

cember 2001, published an advertisement for this library in its newsletter, indicating the collaboration between the solidarity group and the library (*Boletín Asamblea Caballito Gastón Riva* 2.8:2).

One of the most striking examples of prioritizing reading in the recuperation of abandoned spaces revolves around community efforts to occupy the mansion that belonged to the soldier and writer Lucio V. Mansilla in the Belgrano neighborhood of Buenos Aires.[15] The Asamblea Popular Belgrano-Nuñez's newsletter extensively documents the process of gaining access to the "Casona de Mansilla." The building had been used as a teacher training center by the Ministry of Education from 1914 to 1982, but was closed due to the high cost of maintenance. Declared a historic monument in 1999, the building was soon after abandoned by the city government and fell into disrepair. The *asamblea* made recuperating the house and converting it into a neighborhood cultural center one of its top priorities. The project is mentioned in the first issue of the group's newsletter in July of 2002, and a photo of the building occupies the cover of the second issue (*Boletín Asamblea Popular Belgrano-Nuñez*, September 2002). Subsequent flyers, articles, and questionnaires continue to document the initiative.

One questionnaire that was distributed through the newsletter and

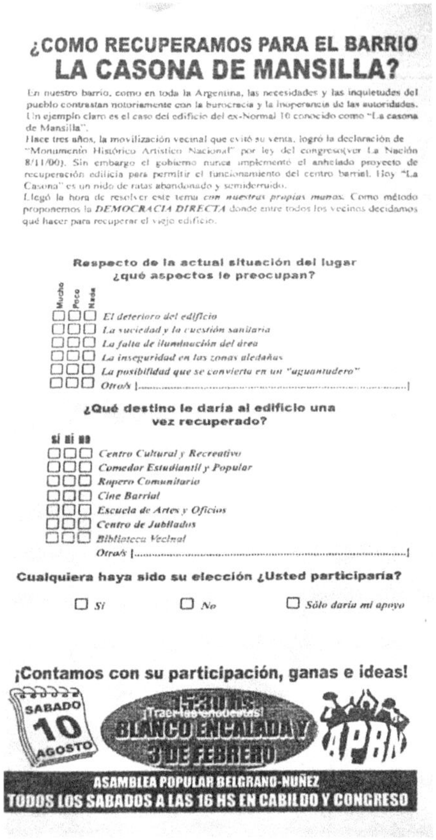

¿COMO RECUPERAMOS PARA EL BARRIO LA CASONA DE MANSILLA?

En nuestro barrio, como en toda la Argentina, las necesidades y las inquietudes del pueblo contrastan notoriamente con la burocracia y la inoperancia de las autoridades. Un ejemplo claro es el caso del edificio del ex-Normal 10 conocido como "La casona de Mansilla".

Hace tres años, la movilización vecinal que evitó su venta, logró la declaración de "Monumento Histórico Artístico Nacional" por ley del congreso(ver La Nación 8/11/00). Sin embargo el gobierno nunca implementó el anhelado proyecto de recuperación edilicia para permitir el funcionamiento del centro barrial. Hoy "La Casona" es un nido de ratas abandonado y semiderruido.

Llegó la hora de resolver este tema *con nuestras propias manos*. Como método proponemos la ***DEMOCRACIA DIRECTA*** donde entre todos los vecinos decidamos qué hacer para recuperar el viejo edificio.

Respecto de la actual situación del lugar ¿qué aspectos le preocupan?

Mucho Poco Nada

- ☐☐☐ *El deterioro del edificio*
- ☐☐☐ *La suciedad y la cuestión sanitaria*
- ☐☐☐ *La falta de iluminación del área*
- ☐☐☐ *La inseguridad en las zonas aledañas*
- ☐☐☐ *La posibilidad que se convierta en un "aguantadero"*
- ☐☐☐ *Otro/s* [......................................]

¿Qué destino le daría al edificio una vez recuperado?

sí ni no

- ☐☐☐ *Centro Cultural y Recreativo*
- ☐☐☐ *Comedor Estudiantil y Popular*
- ☐☐☐ *Ropero Comunitario*
- ☐☐☐ *Cine Barrial*
- ☐☐☐ *Escuela de Artes y Oficios*
- ☐☐☐ *Centro de Jubilados*
- ☐☐☐ *Biblioteca Vecinal*
- *Otro/s* [......................................]

Cualquiera haya sido su elección ¿Usted participaría?

☐ *Sí* ☐ *No* ☐ *Sólo daría mi apoyo*

¡Contamos con su participación, ganas e ideas!

SABADO 10 AGOSTO

15:30 hs

BLANCO ENCALADA Y 3 DE FEBRERO

APBN

ASAMBLEA POPULAR BELGRANO-NUÑEZ

TODOS LOS SABADOS A LAS 16 HS EN CABILDO Y CONGRESO

Figure 3.8. Questionnaire, Belgrano-Nuñez newsletter; author photo; courtesy of Princeton University Library

in flyers asked residents to register their concerns and preferences for the building. The first part of the form posed questions regarding the building's safety and appearance, while the second part requested input on how the building should be used after renovation. The last option on the list in that part, following culture and recreation, community meals, clothing, a film series, arts and technical classes, and services for senior citizens, is "neighborhood library." The results of the questionnaire appear in the following issue of the newsletter (*Boletín Asamblea Popular Belgrano-Nuñez* 1.2:8), and show strong support for dedicating space for a library (46%, almost equal with training in arts and technical skills); it was among the top four activities preferred by the members (see figures 3.8 and 3.9). This example of the Belgrano-Nuñez group polling and being accountable to the neighbors regarding the use of the recuperated building demonstrates the practice of horizontal community organizing during the crisis and the value of reading as a public resource.

The neighborhood commitment to libraries and to reading literature is not an end in itself but a strategic tool for solidarity organizing and the exercise of direct democracy. The horizontal structure, which values every voice and every vote, requires—according to the *asambleas*' solidarity principles—a critically thinking, informed, and empowered citizenry. Not only are books and reading essential tools for academic tutoring and technical skill building, the articles and flyers produced by the neighborhood associations consistently announce creative writing workshops and justify public space for literary reading in their centers and events.

The vast majority of the volumes collected in these community libraries, according to the accounts in the newsletters, represent literary genres. An article in Parque Lezama Sur's newsletter *El Puente: Encontrando Palabras*, titled "The Reasons for a Neighborhood Library," elaborates on the link between reading, solidarity, and local participatory action: "Where readers are much more than just consumers of knowledge and they begin to find the language for thinking about their life, . . . to generate a productive space for socializing knowledge, . . . a space where readers have direct contact with books,

Figure 3.9. Questionnaire results, Belgrano-Nuñez newsletter; author photo; courtesy of Princeton University Library

contact that helps them shed fear and awe" (1.2 [October 2002]: 3).[16] Rather than serve a didactic function, the libraries and reading activities occupy public space to promote socializing, support local pride in the neighborhood, and contribute to the solidarity movement. Another short article in a newsletter warns that "books do bite": "Yes. Books do bite the brain, and wake it up. That's why our Assembly has a library open to all who want to read or donate books" (*Boletín de la Asamblea Popular Florida Puente Saavedra* (2.6 [January 2004]). As Luisa Valenzuela comments about her book titled *Libro que no muerde* (The Book that Doesn't Bite), "this is a very Argentine phrase: 'Grab some books, they don't bite!'; for example, when you tell a kid to go study.... In the end, books do bite, ... if only they would" (19).[17]

Both of the quotes above from neighborhood newsletters underscore the value of literary reading for the solidarity movement. Community libraries, literary workshops, and other events encourage reading as a strategy for neighborhood cohesiveness and demonstrate the appreciation of books as a public resource. Instead of viewing books and reading as a frivolous pastime, an academic necessity, or an elite luxury, the *asambleas*, like the cartonera publishers, harness literature as an essential tool for community building.

The Collective Scream: Between Utopia and Despair

The scream in Abbate's novel *El grito* is a metaphor for both an individual and a collective expression of anguish. In an interview, the author calls this a pessimistic novel but also underscores a sense of liberation in the midst of crisis. The scream "has more to do with liberation, with a collective scream that allows something contained to loosen up and break free.... There was a very tense social climate, people were living with tremendous personal anguish, without any possibility of finding channels for expressing that anguish, leading to isolation. Beyond what happens after that liberating cry, that scream has value. Even if it ends there, I celebrate liberating screams" ("Dulce fuerte grave" 80). Although she draws characters who are weak, disillusioned, and lost, she still sees them as a source of hope.

This exploration of reading under crisis in Argentina rests in the paradox of utopia and anguish, of hope and despair. As political commentator José Pablo Feinmann states, "We are the picture of failure:

that of our political classes subjected to the economic power through the International Monetary Fund's decisions. And we are also the face of a horizon of possibilities: an airy, new, noisy gesture in the struggle against the globalization of capital" (33). Two more examples from the newsletters, in the form of published poems, frame this tension that is evident throughout the *asambleas*' activities. In the parallel contexts of loss and defeat on the one hand, and resistance through collective solidarity on the other, the newsletters' consistent inclusion of poetry contributes to their rhetoric and visual layout.

La Cacerola de Zapiola, newsletter of the Colegiales neighborhood in Buenos Aires, devotes considerable space to the role of the newsletters themselves and to self-conscious musings on language. The cover design of their issue commemorating one year since the economic collapse features a cooking pot with the word *cacerola* and its definition: "cylinder made of steel, aluminum, or brass, used for cooking. Banged on continuously, with a spoon or stick, it becomes a weapon for getting rid of thieving ministers of the economy, ending states of siege and making corrupt presidents resign" (1.25 [19 December 2002]: 1; see figure 3.10). An earlier issue from 2002 further exploits the imagery of the *cacerola* by printing a passage by Galeano, "Utopía," between a photograph of an old pot and a metal spoon, the lines arranged as the percussive sounds emanating from banging it (see figure 3.11):

"LA UTOPÍA"
Ella está en el horizonte.	[She's on the horizon.
Yo me acerco dos pasos,	I advance two steps,
Ella se aleja dos pasos.	She moves away two steps.
Camino diez pasos	I walk ten steps
Y el horizonte se corre	And the horizon moves
Diez pasos más allá.	Ten steps further away.
Por mucho que yo camine	No matter how much I walk
Nunca la alcanzaré.	I'll never reach her.
Y entonces . . .	And so . . .
¿Para qué sirve la utopía?	What good is utopia?
Para eso sirve:	It's good for this:
Para caminar.	For walking.] (1.18 [20 June 2002]: 1)

The Galeano passage combines the hopeful idealism of utopia with discouragement, urging readers to continue even when goals seem unattainable.[18] This bold visual-verbal message on the anniversary of the

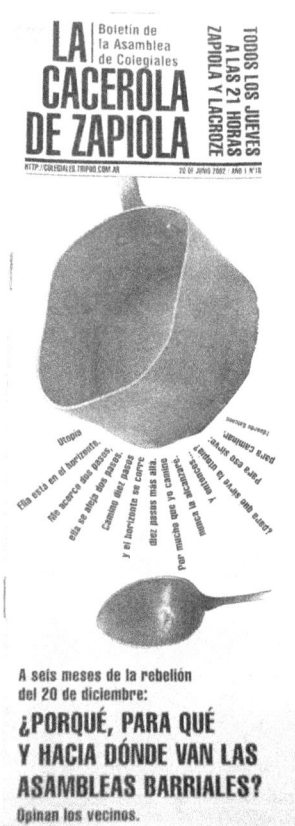

Figure 3.10. Newsletter cover; author photo; courtesy of Princeton University Library

Figure 3.11. Newsletter cover; author photo; courtesy of Princeton University Library

cacerolazos, with the battered pot occupying the center of the page, is less triumphant than cautionary as it encapsulates the contradictory emotions of a long struggle.

Another poem published in a newsletter in La Plata reproduces the sounds of the *cacerolazos* through onomatopoeia while adding the sinister presence of mad dogs. "Soltando los perros" (Letting the dogs out), printed in 2002 and signed with the pseudonym "cacaai-cacaí," has a menacing message of raw street violence in the midst of solidarity protests:

USA (y tira)
USP (United States of Police)

Cache!
cache cache
Cache!
cache cache

Guau guau guau!!

(perrosterriblementeágiles,
deojocerteroentrenado,
atodacarreravienen
luciendo
impecabledentadurablanca)

Cache!
cache cache
Cache!
cache cache

Ay!, ay!, ay!

(sehunden
afiladasdentadurassehunden
saltan
borbotonasdesangrefrescayroja)

Cache!
Cache, cache, Guau!
Cache!
Cache, cache, Ay!
Cache!
Guau, guau, guau!!

(perrosterriblementeágiles,
se alejan
moviendosutraseroinmundo
contentos).

[Cache!
cache cache
Cache!
Sic sic

Bow wow wow!!

(terrificallyagiledogs
sharptargettrained
theycomerunningatfullspeed
showingoff
theirimpeccablywhitefangs)

Cache!
cache cache
Cache!
Sic sic

Ay!, ay!, ay!

(theychompdown
sharpteethsinkin
dropsoffreshredbloodfly)

Cache!
Cache, cache, Guau!
Cache!
Cache, cache, Ay!
Sic!
Bow wow wow!!

(terrificallyagiledogs
moveaway
waggingtheirfilthybutts
content.)] (*Boletín de la Asamblea Barrio Hipódromo* (0.6 [October 2002]: 12)

The repeated percussive "cache cache" (equivalent to the English imperative verb *sic*) encourages the dogs to attack while imitating the rhythms of banging on pots and pans. This poem relies on onomatopoeia to re-create the noise and rhythm of the *cacerolazos* and the barking and growling sounds of the dogs. The use of the space on the page also transmits the movement in the streets of the protests contrasting with the concentration of crowds and the threat of the violent dogs. Perhaps the dogs are metaphors for the revolving door of presidential failures and corrupt politicians preying on citizens. Alternatively, they might be dogs trained to attack the agents of neoliberal economic policies who have bled the country of its resources. The title of the poem introduces this critique of global capital with its play on words: "USA" doubles as a form of the verb *usar* and the abbreviation for the United States of America; the parenthetical "y tira" (use and throw away) indicates the parasitical relationship between Argentina and the first world. Once the country's resources are used up, the country is thrown out. The sharp-toothed, blood-thirsty mongrels are "agile," alert, and readied, and they leave the scene "content." The street has quieted as the "cache cache" dies down and the barking, growling dogs wander off. Where the street has been the scene of protests, demands, occupations, and voices, a frightening emptiness remains.

Similarly, a dog plays an important role in structuring Abbate's *El grito* in relation to the economic crisis. The presence of a dog in the first and last chapters guides the characters toward a tentative sense of hope and a connection to the larger collective crisis. Unlike the noisy, rabid, aggressive, dangerous dogs in the poem just reproduced, the dog in Abbate's novel is a passive, dependent, and vulnerable creature who is associated with the street and reunites characters in a newfound solidarity. Federico, the narrator and the main character of the first chapter, faces his thirtieth birthday with despair, and the gifts he receives—a dog from his father, a life-size sculpted roly-poly figure of Munch's *The Scream* made by his girlfriend—leave him overwhelmed. He ignores the dog and moves the Munch figure to the laundry room, out of sight. This figure, called a *tentempié* in Spanish, is another emblem of the hope–despair continuum along which the novel is structured; when pushed, it rocks from side to side, only temporarily losing its balance and always bouncing back.

After returning to his apartment several days after getting caught up in the protests, Federico finds the dog listless and barely alive. In a desperate attempt to save the dog, knowing he is incapable of caring for it, he gathers the animal in his arms and searches for a solution. He gives the dog to his brother Agustín in the novel's last scene, at the end of a chapter narrated by Agustín's girlfriend, Clara, who concludes: "Salimos al balcón y nos sentamos a mirar la calle. El perro estaba parado entre nosotros y movía la cola. Agustín se rió y dijo que la presencia del perro nos hacía parecer una extraña familia" (We went out on the balcony and we sat down to watch the street. The dog was standing between us and wagged his tail. Agustín laughed and said that with the dog there we seemed like an odd family) (221).

The novel ends in the interstitial space of the balcony, where the characters are situated in a precarious position between inside and outside, a perch from which to watch the street. They form a new, tentative, "odd family," vulnerable but united. In relief from their own anguish, or perhaps in a feeble attempt at solidarity, they turn toward the street to watch and listen to others.

Although most of the *asambleas* became less active or even dissolved by the time Argentina elected Néstor Kirchner as president in 2003, the extraordinary local organizing that emerged after the crisis marks 2002 as the year of "recuperating protagonism, the capacity for action, through the return to street politics" (Svampa 274). "THE STREET IS OURS" is emblazoned in bold letters on the cover of a newsletter, below the cooking pot definition. Occupying the street, taking public space within the local neighborhood, is the impulse behind the *cacerolazos* and the primary tactic of the *asambleas*. Reading literature—at cultural fairs, in creative writing workshops, in newsletters, in neighborhood libraries—also occupies the neighborhoods' reclaimed public sphere. In the face of economic and political collapse, it is in the streets that citizens' outrage and frustration channels into festive and creative solidarity:

> In the middle of the national drama, repression and anguish of all kinds, it's impressive to note the festive atmosphere in demonstrations, the tendency to work together, to build solidarity in the exact Latin meaning of the term and that furthermore goes beyond the corporate spirit that has been destroying us historically in favor of leaving behind the security of gated communities (of the rich) and locked doors (of the poor) and to embrace the street as our own. These changes in collective subjectivity are the most relevant information of the moment. (Mattini 46)

In a cover illustration of a neighborhood newsletter from Liniers, a suburb bordering on Buenos Aires, the street features prominently in a graphic interpretation of citizen participation in reconstructing public engagement (see figure 3.12). A simple line drawing of a corner building depicts the Cultural-Political-Social Center, whose hyphenated name indicates the multifaceted and intersecting goals for the space. A handwritten sign next to the front door announces, "do not delegate, let's take things into our own hands" (*Asambleas: Periódico Mensual de la Asamblea Popular de Liniers* 2.5 [September 2003]: 1). Bricks already installed announce specific activities offered by the cen-

Figure 3.12. Newsletter cover; author photo; courtesy of Princeton University Library

ter: English classes, debates, and workshops in music and philosophy. Neighbors work together to construct the center, and a smiling pair in the forefront hold in their arms bricks labeled "CULTURE" and "POLITICS." These two principal building blocks not only form the foundation of this center but were the basis of the wider solidarity movement during the crisis in Argentina; as Svampa notes, "Culture constitutes a mode of reconstructing individual experience, and at the same time an expression of collective resistance" (265).

On the list of announcements to the right of the Liniers newsletter illustration, "Literary Meetings" appears just after a workshop on the external debt and is followed by workshops on philosophy and music. Reading fuels both the cultural and the political, and it plays a consistently prominent role in activism and survival during the crisis. From the *cacerolazo* protests to neighborhood organizing, "feeling that the street is ours" relies on both political rage and cultural resistance. Literature occupies new public spaces—out in the street, recited at festivals, and inside recuperated buildings, collected in libraries. It is an essential building block of solidarity organizing.

The jubilation and creativity that fueled horizontal political structures and economic solidarity in Argentina after the crisis spurred other cooperative ventures in literature and art. The next chapter turns to the cartonera publishing collectives, the first of which emerged in Buenos Aires following the economic and political collapse. These independent publishers have expanded and multiplied. They demonstrate flexible and sustainable models for reading that endure crisis and continue beyond it.

CHAPTER 4

Recycled Reading and the Cartonera Collectives: Publishing from the Ground Up

The book cannot be reduced to the text that it holds, nor is the text independent of the concrete object in which it is incarnated. Neither can the concrete object be disassociated from the concrete uses of that object.
GABRIEL WOLFSON, "DOS O TRES CAMINOS—ENTRE OTROS POSIBLES—PARA ENTRAR Y SALIR DE ALIAS."

Literature is recycled material, a pretext for making more art.
DORIS SOMMER, THE WORK OF ART IN THE WORLD

Opening the Box

When Fernando Acosta, Princeton University's librarian for Latin American acquisitions, first purchased some new books bound in cardboard by independent Latin American publishers, he sent them to be cataloged, as he does with all additions to the collection. He was shocked when, a few weeks later, the books were returned to him, now processed and cataloged but unrecognizable. Instead of the hand-painted cardboard covers, Acosta saw a stack of books covered in buckram, a durable acrylic material often used for library books, that hid all outward signs of alternative publishing. He asked his colleagues why they had covered the books, and they told him they found the cardboard books fragile and thought they should be protected. He insisted that the rest of these new acquisitions, despite their apparent fragility and peeling paint, should be left as they were. The University of Wisconsin–Madison's archive of more than 1,200 cardboard-bound books is stored in special collections along with rare books and doc-

Figure 4.1. Cartonera archival materials, University of Wisconsin–Madison; author photo

uments. Each book is wrapped in an acid-free sleeve inserted into an acid-free envelope and stored in an acid-free box (see figure 4.1). In Madison these books do not circulate; they can be read only in the special collections reading room.

The Biblioteca de Santiago, Chile's premier modern public library, has hosted annual Encuentros of cardboard book publishers since 2012. The library has a circulating collection of about one hundred of these books and displays them together in their literature collection. At the Rutgers University library, the collection of some fifty cardboard-bound books from Latin America is shelved according to call number, intermingled in the stacks with conventionally published books in order to allow readers to discover them as they search for other books.

I came across my first cardboard-bound book at a museum gift shop in Buenos Aires; next I saw them being made and exhibited at the São Paulo art biennial; now they also are sold in a downtown newspaper kiosk.[1] Why are there such divergent practices in cataloging and distributing these books? Are they literature or art or artists' books? How should they be used, stored, and circulated? Are their archival homes or modes of circulation in sync with or at odds with their origins? This chapter proposes answers to these questions by exploring Latin American cartonera publishing as an urban public reading initiative.

These independent publishing groups generate so much discussion because their products are not conventional literary objects, nor do the groups' goals coincide with those of most mainstream publishers, which are primarily oriented toward literary recognition and capital profit (see figure 4.2). These books—on the inside and on the outside, in terms of what they publish on their pages, as well as how they are produced—question the relationships among the reader, the text, the market, and circuits of distribution. They engage in a new ecology of reading. Eloísa Cartonera in Buenos Aires, the first cartonera publisher in the current generation of cardboard book collectives, transmits its mission in the phrase "Mucho más que libros" (much more than books). The slogan is painted in vibrant colors on the windows of its bookstore and studio (see figure 4.3). Eloísa Cartonera not only

Figure 4.2. Selection of Eloísa Cartonera books; author photo

Figure 4.3. Painted storefront window of Eloísa Cartonera, Buenos Aires; author photo; courtesy of Washington Cucurto and María Gómez

publishes books but also creates a collective community through environmentally sustainable cultural production. This alternative publisher that spearheaded the binding of books in reused cardboard collected in the street has inspired dozens of cardboard bookmaking collectives all over Latin America, as well as in Mozambique, Spain, France, Germany, Sweden, and Finland.[2]

This chapter features cartonera publishers from Argentina (Eloísa Cartonera), Brazil (Dulcinéia Catadora), Peru (Sarita Cartonera), and Colombia (Amapola Cartonera) whose books and programming promote collective public reading in the city. The groups share three interconnected characteristics: their urban location frames and guides their work, their initiatives reach out to the public, and their books and other projects overtly problematize material and physical resources. A brief section introduces the process of cartonera bookmaking and some commonly shared goals, objectives, and philosophies among cartonera groups. The chapter then elaborates on particular groups' bookmaking projects that intervene in public space (urban interventions such as selling handmade books at a kiosk), involve the community (in local schools and with housing advocacy groups), and reflect on the books' materials and processes. The section devoted to Dulcinéia Catadora is more extensive; this group not only is one of the earliest and longest-lasting but also has produced a wide array of books and projects that demonstrate the commitment to urban intervention that this book highlights.

I hope to underscore the intricate and highly developed connection between what these groups publish, how they publish, and their activism and outreach with their publications. All of these groups maintain a focus on the street and connect their initiatives with local circumstances. The books they publish raise consciousness about vulnerable urban populations and champion marginal writers, and the way they produce the books dignifies those who participate. These groups' simultaneous commitment to product and process, to books and to collective bookmaking and reading, inscribes the process into their product. The chapter concludes with examples of the cartonera metadiscourse that is incorporated into both the texts and their packaging.

Cartonera publishing dramatizes the move toward collective rather than individual initiatives to confront the consequences of neoliberal economic policies, particularly in the publishing industry. In the 1990s, the consolidation of established national publishers into huge multinational conglomerates—what Malena Botto calls denationalization—sought to emphasize commercial profits via big-selling authors over taking aesthetic risks with less established writers. For example, Argentina's Sudamericana was acquired by Random House Mondadori in 1998. According to Botto, by the late 1990s multinational conglomerates controlled 75 percent of the industry.[3] Jania Kudaibergen notes the "tremendous reconfigurations" in the last few decades in the Mexican publishing industry as well (130). Mexico has the largest number of multinational publishers in Latin America, but fewer and fewer bookstores, according to Kudaibergen. In this publishing economy, many smaller presses either disappeared or were subsumed by the few large corporations, and opportunities for younger and experimental writers shrank. The number of copies per title plummeted and books that did not sell fast or were not considered commercially viable were given little visibility in bookstores and were eventually relegated to discount stores.

As the publishing industry consolidated into fewer large conglomerates, a number of new independent presses emerged to counter the publishing policies of the conglomerates by developing less commercial and more alternative catalogs.⁴ They embraced the "quixotic position that the book is a long-lasting product, and that publishing production is a high-risk activity in terms of economic profit" (Botto 225). They do not conceive of themselves as competition for the multinationals or even for one another; rather, "they consider the emergence of new presses as assurance for the continuity of a cultural project in which common intentions count more than distinguishing nuances" (Botto 225). This cooperative attitude of solidarity is evident among the cartonera collectives as well.

It was in this contracted economic and publishing climate that the first cartonera publisher emerged. Eloísa Cartonera was established in Buenos Aires following the Argentine crisis of 2001–2002, when "economic crisis catalyzed the process of shifting the aesthetic order in a more collective direction" (Epplin, *Late Book Culture* 61). As Paloma Celis Carbajal states in her prologue to *Akademia cartonera*, the first book to consider Latin American cardboard book publishing in a comparative context, these independent presses questioned "the publishing process within the neoliberal economic system . . . by establishing a new method of book production that attempts to democratize literature" (Bilbija and Celis Carbajal 16).⁵

Poet and fiction writer Washington Cucurto⁶ founded Eloísa Cartonera with artist and writer Fernanda Laguna and artist Javier Barilaro in 2003 following the economic and political crisis in Argentina, when the ranks of *cartoneros* (cardboard pickers) in Buenos Aires swelled.⁷ Each cartonera collective has its own reason for being and mode of operation and was not necessarily founded, as was Eloísa, in the wake of economic collapse. Nevertheless, the continually expanding wave of cartonera publishing responds to decades of contraction in the public sector, to ever widening socioeconomic inequality, and to urban environmental degradation that disproportionately affects the poor. As Gisela Heffes notes in *Políticas de la destrucción, poéticas de la preservación*, cartonera publishers are collective initiatives that bring together the aesthetic, the political, and the environmental, for with them, "recycling has been transformed into something not only environmental but also social, in that it has prompted and continues to encourage the emergence of a network of multiple shared efforts in which poverty and the creative imagination intersect" (229–230). In these alternative publishing initiatives, environmental and economic principles converge; the groups are autonomous and diverse but share "ecological concerns and the constant and radical redefinition of the relationship among the book, the market, and the reader" (Álvarez Oquendo and Madureira 6).[8]

The Medium Is the Message: Cartonera Process and Product

The process of making a cartonera book involves a few simple steps that each group adapts to its own circumstances: the group buys cardboard from the *cartoneros* (cardboard pickers); they hand-cut the cardboard with utility knives or box cutters; they photocopy or print the short texts; they fold, paste, and staple or sew the paper to the cardboard; they decorate the covers with stencils and tempera paints or collage. Bookbinding techniques differ slightly from group to group. For example, some groups cover the binding with cloth or tape, although they are all artisanal and extremely low-tech.[9] The authors offer their texts free of copyright as a way of supporting the collective independent press, as well as participating in what has become a trendy aesthetic. Most of the groups pay above-market value for cardboard, which helps sustain the *cartoneros*. The aesthetic of the covers varies more widely than production methods across cartonera collectives. The classic tempera-painted cartonera cover is first whitewashed with a stencil indicating the author and title, and then colorfully hand-decorated (see figures 4.4 and 4.5). Some of the groups use a variety of collage techniques with cardboard layering and alternative shapes, sizes, and formats for the books (see figures 4.6 and 4.7). Many of the collectives employ the *cartoneros* who sell them cardboard to make and decorate the books. Each group determines how those who produce and sell books retain the profits.[10]

Producing books is not the only goal of these alternative and environmentally sustainable publishing initiatives. They emphasize the process along with the product, and the product retains the signs and signature of its process. In the current media environment of increasing reliance on the internet and digital platforms, the cartonera project represents a determinedly retrogressive move. Cutting paper and cardboard, adhering with glue and staples, decorating with paint, and hand-sewing pages to bindings constitutes a return to bookmaking as an artisanal activity. Even the printed pages, either photocopied or, when funds permit, printed on small presses, seem to rediscover an outdated technology. As a member of Bogotá's Amapola Cartonera

Figure 4.4. Lúcia Rosa of Dulcinéia Catadora working with a stencil; author photo; courtesy of Lúcia Rosa

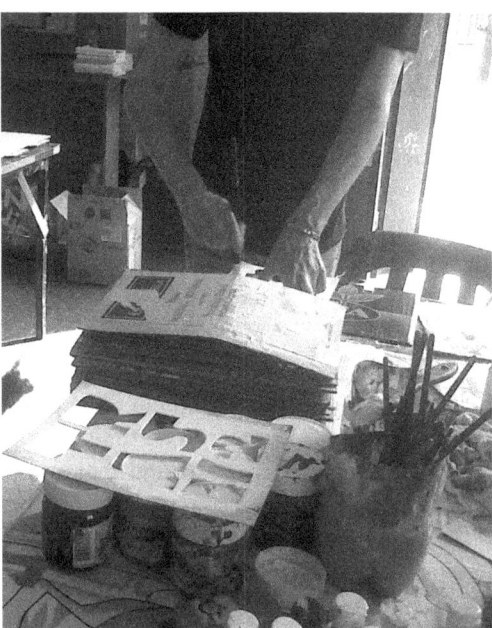

Figure 4.5. Bookmaking at the Eloísa Cartonera studio; photo courtesy of Washington Cucurto and María Gómez

Figure 4.6. Cartonera publishers' binding and decoration; author photo

Figure 4.7. Dulcinéia Catadora books; author photo

declares, cartonera publishing "brings back to life not only used and thrown out cardboard boxes but also those old printing presses that still have plenty of life left in them, and that in the context of digital publishing and so-called new media, have been displaced by a capricious and arbitrary technological mandate" (Espinosa Caro 65).

The local and mostly urban situatedness of the cartonera collectives also goes against the grain of digital media experience. As Craig Epplin notes, "the imaginarily disembodied, geographically dispersed social interactions often associated with digital culture would seem to have their polar opposite in the sort of small-scale, site-specific collectivity" of these groups ("New Media" 393–394). Cardboard books embody the paradox of evanescence and permanence: they are fragile in comparison with industrially produced books (the paint smudges or chips, the pages unfasten from the binding, they are easily damaged by water), yet permanent in comparison with the transience and instability of digital culture. Reusing already spent and discarded boxes, cartonera books reassess the value of what is viewed as garbage and elevate it as an archival material, making cartonera books archives of their own fleeting performance (Epplin, "New Media" 395).

Cartonera publishers, despite all their variety and independence, share the goal of bibliodiversity. As Jaime Vargas Luna elaborates, for these collectives *bibliodiversity* refers not only to the books' alternative artisanal format but also to the wide range of authors published and to the cooperative culture among the different groups (personal interview). Diego Recoba, founder of La Propia Cartonera in Montevideo, Uruguay, underscored the cartonera orientation toward antihierarchical, egalitarian relationships: "what matters is to take the author off the pedestal and have booksellers, authors, readers, and publishers all on the same level" (personal interview, my translation). Most of the collectives publish a broad selection of works, including some by *consagrados* (canonical writers) such as Mario Bellatin, Ricardo Piglia, Diamela Eltit, and others by new and young writers and by a mix of local, national, and international authors (Vargas Luna, "La rumba" 124–125). Intergroup initiatives also contribute to bibliodiversity through the cartonera culture of interaction and cooperation. For example, thanks to authors waiving copyright, multiple editions of some texts are produced by several publishers. The experience of exchange and interaction at regional independent publishers' fairs and exhibits occurs in the spirit of sharing techniques and appreciating one another's products (see figure 4.8).[11] This alternative culture of collab-

Figure 4.8. Encuentro Cartoneras, Santiago, Chile, 2015; © Olga María Sotomayor Sánchez; photo courtesy of Olga María Sotomayor Sánchez

oration instead of competition among cartonera presses is another key contribution to bibliodiversity.

Cartonera groups consider books a tool for solidarity, a way to bring people together, and instruments that foster reading and new writing. Cucurto commented in an interview, "beyond reading, books are useful for other things, like bringing people together. Books help people meet, relate to one another, show affection, become closer, establishing bonds" (my translation). María Gómez, another member of the Buenos Aires cooperative, added, "the book must be more than this, it's a social necessity, it has a humble but powerful path" (personal interview, my translation). The books they produce are not the cooperative's only aim; the group also has expanded the canon to include younger writers, has produced music CDs, hosts literary festivals and theater events, and operates a street kiosk. Cucurto and other collective members travel to train and mentor new collectives throughout Latin America through workshops and residencies. The communal effort in making the books, along with the events they organize and participate in, encourages collective over individual reading. Cucurto admitted that perhaps one day they will no longer make books, but will devote their energies to new projects. In fact, soon after Eloísa Cartonera became a nationally registered cooperative in 2008,[12] the group bought land outside of Buenos Aires and has ventured into organic agriculture (see figure 4.9).

Cartonera publishing emerged out of economic crisis and support

Figure 4.9. House on Eloísa Cartonera's rural property in Buenos Aires province; photo courtesy of Washington Cucurto and María Gómez

for marginalized groups, and its well-developed but flexible aesthetic, which varies from group to group, often includes a commitment to social practice. Some of the collectives produce carefully wrought objects. La Cartonera in Cuernavaca, Mexico, and Pelo Malo Cartonera in Panama, for example, lean toward artists' books. Others "mass produce" artisanally with a more haphazard aesthetic, what Epplin calls "imperfect publishing" (*Late Book Culture* 68–70). A certain tension exists between the old-school groups, borne of crisis and conceived as a literary necessity, and the new-school collectives whose aesthetic goals override those of accessibility and sustainability. Ximena Ramos Wettling and Tanya Núñez Grandón, founders of Animita Cartonera in Santiago, Chile, in 2005, call Animita "a publishing house with a social, cultural and artistic purpose" (Bilbija and Celis Carbajal 92). Sarita Cartonera, also founded in 2005, in Lima, Peru, considers its publishing endeavor a "social, cultural, and communitarian project, not for profit" (statement printed on most of their books). Its goals go beyond the literary; its "integrated project" has to do with publishing in connection with other goals (Saldarriaga and Silva, my translation). While several cartonera groups share this social dimension, they emphasize economic sustainability for all participants and reject any association with charity (Dulcinéia manifesto in Bilbija and Celis Carbajal 153).

Eschewing the trappings of established publishing houses, most cartonera groups lack basic studio space and work in precarious settings. This nomadic existence adds to the street dimension of their projects. La Propia Cartonera in Montevideo, Uruguay, meets at a bar. Ramos Wettling and Núñez Grandón of Animita Cartonera in Santiago leave their supplies in borrowed office space above a car dealership and carry around their cardboard, paints, glue, and brushes to make books in a marginal neighborhood.[13] They say they consider Animita's existence "very gypsy" (personal interview, my translation), referring to the group's movement and uncertainty. Dulcinéia stores supplies and makes books in a recycling cooperative under a highway. Like Animita, the first Brazilian cartonera group is fairly mobile and often travels around Brazil with some of the women garbage pickers from the cooperative to lead bookmaking workshops. A combination of characteristics, such as the design of their books, the writers they publish, and the material conditions of their workspaces, identify most cartonera publishers with a grassroots, low-art dimension. From their physical spaces and materials to the programmatic stance of their catalogs, cartonera publishers push back against the literary establishment and neoliberal consumerism.

Sarita Cartonera: Lumpen Street Pedagogy

Founded in Lima in 2005, Sarita Cartonera followed the Eloísa model closely but adapted it to the situation in Peru at the time. Unlike Eloísa, the group did not emerge as a response to a particular economic crisis. Rather, it arose from the founders' diagnosis of the city's "state of severe cultural inertia" (Sarita manifesto in Bilbija and Celis Carbajal 74). Grassroots production, distribution, and access on the street is reflected in the group's name, taken from an unofficial Peruvian saint "who goes by foot . . . to find hope in the streets among the drunks and the whores" (74). Sarita Cartonera also identifies as *chusca* (slang for "streetwise" or "funky") and deliberately feminine "to accentuate the exclusion. . . . We are all *chusca* here" (78). Its inside covers refer to the books' material origins in the street from findings of local cardboard pickers (called *caladores* in Peru), who both sold their cardboard and painted the book covers:[14] "copy made by *cartoneros* from the city of Lima. Bound and covers painted by them at the Municipal Neighbor House #5."

Milagros Saldarriaga, a founding member of Sarita, describes the group's mission as a desire to "intervene in the space of the book and the circuits of reading" (Saldarriaga and Silva, my translation). Vargas Luna, another of the group's founders, mentions the paradox of creating inexpensive books for nonexistent readers (personal interview). One of their big challenges was to create readers, particularly in the context of Lima, where although cartonera books were inexpensive, they cost more than many used and pirated books available all over the city.[15] Whereas Eloísa offered cheap books in Buenos Aires, a city with high literary demand, at a time of almost no book production, Sarita had the complicated task of creating demand and a niche in its own local literary landscape.[16] A statement printed on the inside back cover of their books invites potential new readers to commit to reading: "for putting up with the bother of the van or bus, for not despairing in line, to cast a spell on any kind of ghosts, or just for when you simply feel like reading. A cartonera book, your best friend" (my translation).[17] They propose reading as an antidote to the tedium of riding on public transportation or waiting in line, common experiences for people moving about in public space, and they re-situate reading and literature from the classroom or private space to the street.

Sarita bookmakers went into classrooms as well, as sites of intervention in the group's efforts to produce readers. Sarita Cartonera developed Libros, un Modelo para Armar (LUMPA; Books, a Model Kit), a concrete strategy for extending their project to youth and creating new readers. Saldarriaga describes LUMPA as a "pedagogical proposal, an axis of action, of intervention in society" (Saldarriaga and Silva, my translation). They made cartonera books with schoolchildren in a project that brought together environmental sustainability, literature, and visual art. LUMPA promoted not only bookmaking but also interpretation: the intervention involved collective reading and discussion that "makes creation an avenue of very powerful and very serious reflection" (Saldarriaga and Silva, my translation).

This interactive project inspired the program Pre-Texts at Harvard University's Cultural Agents center, which Doris Sommer describes as a productive combination of "literacy, art-making, [and] citizenship" (111).[18] Sarita staged playful and artistic extensions of the texts. Students began by making books out of reused materials and then read them together; next, they interpreted, reenacted, and played with what they had read. The broad range of LUMPA activities included drawing portraits of characters, choreographing scenes, role-playing alternative endings, and empowering young readers to engage with the books physically, linguistically, spatially, and visually. "Books are not sacred objects; they are invitations to play" (113), Sommer declares, something that is expressed in her outreach program in the Boston area as well as in initiatives her center sponsors internationally. Reading literature as a catalyst for imaginative play and artistic re-creation made the cartonera project in Lima an activist public reading and art initiative.

The proliferation of new cartonera publishers dots the Latin American map with bookmaking put to the service of many different needs and missions. Although Sarita Cartonera is no longer active, in Peru alone there are more than twenty active cartonera collectives as of this writing, including several new groups that have responded to particular circumstances and needs. A new cartonera group in Lima founded in 2015, Sullawayta Cartonera, follows the philosophy of Sarita in its dedication to a social mission. The group's Facebook site states: "we are a cartonera publisher that was created to use and offer our tool—bookmaking—for social and popular causes and needs" (my translation). In another example, a group of rural bilingual teachers in Lamas, Peru, met with members of Sarita. Inspired by Sarita's projects and motivated by a lack of materials in the Quechua language, they established Qinti Qartunira in 2010. As Bárbara Rodrigues explains, "our main goal is to make books exclusively in Quechua for bilingual schools in the area, since this is one of the major difficulties facing students and teachers: . . . training readers in language acquisition with the potential to reach high levels of both reading and writing" (Rodrigues 15). She distinguishes Qinti Qartunira from what she calls the "radical urban context" of most of the cartonera collectives in Latin America: instead of working with street *cartoneros*, they rely on regional storytellers and artisans, "the Quechua speakers' language arts that integrate into their stories the knowledge of weavers, ceramicists, musicians, farmers, carriers, healers, and hunters" (15). This variety of objectives and missions reveals each group's local situation; as Cala Buendía emphasizes, each group "responds to its own cultural, economic, political and social context. . . . [They] are highly localized and in no way function as a network" (134).

Dulcinéia Catadora: Urban, Literary, and Artistic Interventions

Artist and activist Lúcia Rosa founded Dulcinéia Catadora in São Paulo in 2006. The collective emerged out of a collaboration with Eloísa Cartonera during the São Paulo art biennial, where the Buenos Aires collective had an exhibit with daily workshops (see figure 4.10). Dulcinéia Catadora's name honors not only Don Quixote's love interest in Cervantes's seventeenth-century novel but also one of the first cardboard pickers to join Rosa's bookmaking project.

The São Paulo collective echoes Eloísa's slogan, as translated into Portuguese: "muito mais que livros" (much more than books). The group offers art workshops for children, erects cardboard sculptures, and stages urban interventions in the street. Dulcinéia makes "hybrid books" that bring together writing, visual art, and artisanal skills. Rosa underscores the significance of cardboard, a devalued material picked out of the garbage, in all of their projects:

> Cardboard pickers start to see another way to use cardboard, an artistic way, when they see cardboard as a material they can use to express themselves. Perhaps it has the power to start a revolution deep inside them. When you make something that others consider beautiful, this gives you a chance to see something beautiful inside yourself. Working with cardboard transforms the way they see such a common material and helps to build self-esteem. (personal interview)

Rosa's revalorization of garbage is the foundation for all these publishers, as Ksenija Bilbija asserts regarding cartonera pioneer Eloísa Cartonera: "the 'garbage' that *cartoneros* collect—technically the product from which all value has been used up—actually does have worth, just like the *cartoneros* themselves, people who have value despite the fact that they had been relegated to the status of social detritus" (17).[19]

Dulcinéia commits to incorporating the *catadores* (street recyclers) into nearly every aspect of the production process. Arivaldo, one of the *catadores*, proposes an attitudinal change that leads to looking at garbage in a new way: "[T]hey're going to have to pay special attention to garbage that for us is not garbage." He goes on to compare recyclables to gold that is melted down and refashioned into a new piece of jewelry: "from gold you make a ring and it lasts for many years, and later you melt it down again, and you make a new ring" (D'Angelo 20). There is no difference, he says, between garbage and gold.

Figure 4.10. Eloísa Cartonera stand at the Twenty-Seventh São Paulo art biennial; author photo; courtesy of Washington Cucurto and María Gómez

The writers published by Dulcinéia are not only well-known, established writers or emerging young experimental writers; the group has published anthologies of peripheral poets and people living on the street to underscore urban challenges such as the housing crisis and migration from other parts of Brazil to São Paulo.[20] One of their books, *Catador* (edited by Ana D'Angelo), is devoted to the stories of the garbage scavengers themselves. The selection process, as Rosa explains, "is far from that of commercial publishing, since we envision a work that deserves to be seen, disseminated, that has a language and a proposed vision of the world that coincides with ours" (in Bucchioni). She elaborates, "it's important for us to publish writers from the periphery, the surroundings of this gigantic city, poets who don't have a chance to be included in the [conventional] editorial market" (personal e-mail communication). The press's diverse list of writers and genres is not limited to those representing these concerns, but Rosa admits that "the great majority of our work has to do with social and political questions" (personal e-mail communication).

Dulcinéia's hybrid visual-verbal books incorporate graphics, color, drawings, and photography, and nearly always include an urban focus. Some of the titles feature concrete poetry, a form that exploits the space on the page and for which Brazilian poets such as Augusto de Campos are renowned. Titles such as Paulo de Toledo's *Concreróticos & outros versos* exemplifies Dulcinéia's literature-art interface. One of Toledo's poems, "Cidade" (City), is composed of the repeated word *gente* (people) arranged in rows and columns to form a rectangular block (n.p.). The large red lettering of the title contrasts with the smaller black lettering of the rectangle. The poem opens in the middle, with extra space for one *gente* in red, the letters spread out, the *n* of *gente* inverted above it as a *u*. The center's single red *gente* moves like an urban dweller who after walking in the city has met up with others. Through space and color the poem's design communicates density but also draws its own public plaza.

In the collection *SigniCidade* (SignCity), by Frederico Barbosa, the poems take place on the streets of the city, registering the rain on the pavement and the sensation of returning to familiar places. Susanna Busato's introduction associates Barbosa's urban poetry with Charles Baudelaire's apprehension of modernity via the senses. She particularly underscores the sense of sight in Barbosa's poems, where the flaneur's gaze works to "reveal in the retina's memory of the word an image in that moment. . . . The city, that sign that emerges in front of our eyes, is born in order to be destroyed or rediscovered in fragments of sounds-words-movement" (3). The book includes two photographs by Maurício de Paiva, urban scenes that at first glance are iconic of São Paulo visual design but alongside the poems become metadiscursive meditations on reading, guiding the reader to decipher the city as well as to decode the verbal text. The photograph of a silhouetted man walking on the sidewalk (4) accompanies the epigraph, a fragment of a longer Barbosa poem (see figure 4.11). The photograph and the poetic excerpt serve together as epigraphs:

Seguir tantas tramas	[To follow so many paths
Impressas	imprinted
na rua, nas bancas,	on the street, on the benches,
nas paginas.	on the pages.
En cada nova leitura	In each new reading
uma antiga descoberta	an old discovery
reverbera.	reverberates.] (5)

The verbal fragment evokes roads, public benches, and book pages all as potential spaces for reading. The overlapping patterns in the photo-

Figure 4.11. Photograph by Paiva and poem by Barbosa in *SigniCidade*; author photo; courtesy of Lúcia Rosa

graph—sidewalk tiles creating iconic Brazilian waves, chain-link fencing, painted curbs, painted traffic lanes, horizontal railings—envelop the man walking so his legs, torso, and head occupy distinct zones. Because the photograph and poem are on facing pages, the man appears to walk toward the poem. The reader then is invited to read the photograph and walk into the book to discover ("descoberta") the rest of the poems. Through its integration of texts and images and its overall design, the book meshes the discourses of walking, reading, and viewing to map a composite urban discourse.

Dulcinéia's commitment to the street is also evident in anthologies that emerge from specific places or urban experiences, such as encounters among writers in particular neighborhoods or bars. The poetry collection *Cátia, Simone e outras marvadas* (Katia, Simone, and Other Wonders), edited by Sebastião Nicomedes, focuses on the vulnerability of the homeless. The book is dedicated to both the National Movement for the Struggle and Defense of the Rights of the Homeless and the National Movement of Garbage Pickers and Recyclers. According to the introduction by Eliane Brum, Nicomedes was working in construction, installing a sign on a building, when he fell from a height of twelve feet and became disabled (6–7). As he writes in the poem "Dignidade ou nada!" (Dignity or nothing!), "Se chega à rua por vários motivos, / se levanta em proporção desigual" (people wind up in the street for various reasons, / and they rise up in uneven numbers) (13). The cardboard that covers the speaker at night also combats stress and fear: "O papelão que cobre o corpo é também o lençol, o cobertor, o colchão, / o estresse, a depressão e o medo vencidos" (the cardboard that covers the body is also a sheet, a blanket, a mattress, / stress, depression and fear are vanquished) (13). That same cardboard might become the cardboard that covers this book.

Other poems in the collection that mention homelessness overtly—"Ocupação" (Occupation) and "Ao relento" (In the Damp Night)—enumerate the urban structures of buildings, houses, and windows viewed "Da torre do prédio mais alto" (from the tower of the highest hill), from afar, as the speaker finds himself "sem teto / sem um lugar para morar" (without a roof / without a place to stay) (30). Negation, positioned in contrast to what is viewed but not accessible, becomes part of the grammar of the poem, imposing a binary logic on the structure that punctuates the rhythm of the verses. "Ao relento" concludes with a negative: "á rua é onde moro / o endereço / lugar nenhum" (the street is where I stay / the address / is no place) (31).

Along with publishing works that focus on urban street life, Dulcinéia makes interventions in public space that have a performative dimension. The group creates a form of participatory and sustainable visual art, always using cardboard bookbinding put to the service of raising awareness about the rights and dignity of recyclers and about socioeconomic inequality more broadly. Heffes underscores the disproportionate burden of environmental devastation that falls on the poor and the disenfranchised in Latin America, and offers numerous examples of *cartoneros* and *catadores* serving as the new face of this intersection of the ecological, the aesthetic, and the political. According to James Scorer, *cartoneros* are urban political actors who "enact political change . . . on the level of their everyday habits and rhythms, they constantly transform the city" (157).[21] Heffes writes that street recyclers "have become a pragmatic model for how a political act related to the environment comes about as a result of dire economic necessity, which lacks a priori political ideology" (241). The Dulcinéia collective organizes events, publishes books, creates art, and stages street happenings with this political responsibility at the core.

Rosa comments on Dulcinéia's urban interventions:

> We go to the street with the cardboard books, always with the *catadores*. This demonstrates an active artistic posture, of being present in

Figure 4.12. Sandwich board urban writing intervention; courtesy of Lúcia Rosa

public space, and not locked up in a white cube. We want to be troublesome, to force the visibility of something that people pretend every day not to see, to speak about inequalities. When we're in the street, we concern ourselves with developing a work with the public, with the population. This is the point. The exchange, the contact with the passerby, provokes ruptures in people's daily routines. To break automatisms. (Morris)

One of the group's most recognized street interventions is an interactive writing experience. Wearing a sandwich board with blank cardboard books attached to it, one of their members wanders through pedestrian and car traffic with a megaphone, inviting passersby to help compose the books (see figure 4.12). They use sandwich boards to display books for sale as well; cardboard not only binds the books but also serves as a physical support, a moveable shop, for their distribution in public space. The wearable A-frame signs, primarily used to advertise a business, are not an arbitrary mode of intervention, but an ironic gesture because the signs and the books are made out of the same material and remind spectators and potential customers that both the message and the commodity are reused refuse. The interveners refashion garbage to sell garbage. By giving the recyclers protagonistic roles, the group's activities make them visible.

Dulcinéia's most elaborate, sustained, and contestatory intervention took on the politics of the recent housing crisis due to urban redevelopment in Rio de Janeiro. In 2012 Rosa began collaborating with marginal communities in favelas that were being displaced by building and development related to Brazil's hosting of the 2014 World Cup and the 2016 summer Olympic games. She traveled regularly to Rio to work with members of Pedra Lisa, an extremely vulnerable favela community on one side of Morro da Providência, where they made books that were written and illustrated by members of the community and that directly addressed the housing threat.

The results of this project were shown in one of the inaugural exhibits of the new Museo de Arte de Rio in 2013. The museum, housed in Don João VI's former palace, was part of the "revitalization" of Rio's port area during the fervor of preparation for the upcoming international sports events. One of the most controversial and disruptive elements was the construction of the *teleférico*, a cable car, in Providência that eliminated the only public space in the community. The opening of the *teleférico* in July 2014 coincided with the razing of homes, which was justified by official designation of the neighborhood as an "area of risk."

Copies of the four books published by Dulcinéia that were based on their community interventions in Pedra Lisa—*ProvidênciaS, Soluções providenciais, De lá pra cá, de cá pra lá*, and *Nós, daqui*—were distributed to museum visitors. In the production of each of these books, the collective empowered members of the community as photographers, chroniclers, writers, and local experts to communicate their own stories of resistance and resilience in the face of political threats to destroy their homes. Residents then participated in bookmaking and painting workshops in the neighborhood, where they produced and decorated the books outside in the same precarious circumstances that the books document.

The Morro da Providência is significant as the site of the first favela in Brazil, built at the end of the nineteenth century. One of the Dulcinéia books produced with the residents mentions the origins of Pedra Lisa: "A long time ago, a huge rock fell on top of the houses and killed the residents living there. This is why the place is called Pedra Lisa. Later people began building new houses around the rock" (*Soluções providenciais* 36). One of the residents interviewed, Roberto Carlos, identifies with Morro da Providência not only as his home but as part of his family history, because several relatives on his father's side were survivors of the Canudos war: "My father was, you could say, one of the founders of Morro da Providência" (*ProvidênciaS* 21).

ProvidênciaS, the first publication of this series of books focusing on the favela, includes photographs, memoirs, and interviews with members of the community regarding the housing crisis. Two persistent complaints throughout the book are that politicians don't pay attention to the community except in an election cycle, when they promise "the sun, the moon, and the stars" (22), and that officials are threatening to destroy homes on the basis of hasty and inaccurate evaluations of the risks to residents. Many contributors pointed out that in an effort to show that the city was taking action, officials were quick to affirm that Pedra Lisa was an "area of risk." Resident Roberto Carlos claims that he supports renovations and improvements to the community, but that "they improve only the facade and the same garbage continues. . . . The same thing keeps happening" (18). The real estate speculation threatens to drive up land values and push people out. Carlos comments that "progress is not made for the people. Progress is made for real estate speculation" (16).

What especially comes through in *ProvidênciaS* is the raw poetic emotion transmitted in the community members' comments and reflections. A quote from one of the residents printed in a large font on the top of a page expresses residents' vulnerability and fear at the threat of losing their homes: "I don't want my house to go away" (10). Tereza Oliveira, a sixty-three-year-old widow, spoke out at a community meeting: "I prefer to have everyone living together, close, and in the future, these shanties will be passed down from their parents. People like to stick together, and don't want to go far away" (25). A sense of generations, of history, and of familiarity links these people to their surroundings: "You don't want to leave the place where you're born" (11). Another contributor speaks for the whole community: "We're suffering a lot from this because it's very difficult to be sent somewhere where we don't know anyone. People identify with each other for years and years, and then they have to go somewhere else" (29).

Through these multiple voices, the book documents how community leaders and legal and housing rights activists formed local associations to resist the move and to protest the threats. Along with fighting the authorities on razing homes, these solidarity organizations worked to strengthen the cultural and historical ties within the community. Another community member, Eron César Santos, points out that for twenty years favelas were associated with violence, but after a few years of "pacification" efforts and urban development policies "the password came to be 'culture'" (*ProvidênciaS* 5). Camila Soares, an activist and community leader who represents a samba school in the favela, mentions that the writer Joaquim Machado de Assis's house is located in the favela and insists on recognition for the community's cultural contributions and legacy: "There's a lack of valorization of our culture and our history. The places established in the region should be in conversation with the question of local history. That is what constructed our national identity, and built up our self-esteem so that people could speak up and participate in the political process" (36). *ProvidênciaS* represents a collective project in every sense: the multiple voices and images on its pages and the many hands that made and painted the books, all produced in the favela. This dramatic text reveals animated conversations with community members of all ages, including children, and features their local expressions, passion, frustration, and anger.

One of the other books Dulcinéia Catadora made in and about the favela, *Soluções providenciais*, celebrates the ingenuity of and creative architectural solutions implemented by residents of Pedra Lisa. Their own words, photographs, and drawings reveal tactics for managing the physical and spatial challenges of living in this precarious geography, which the preface calls "housing difficulties" (3). Some of the tactics are practical solutions to problems: to keep small children from falling off stairs without a railing, they attach a net along the open side of the stairway (14–15); to increase safety near doorways without doors or windows without glass, they install metal grating or reused wood (12–13, 16–17); makeshift benches provide places to rest along the steep ascent in the neighborhood; plastic containers collect rainwater; and electrical wires shared among households expand access to electricity. Other solutions address aesthetics and recreation: contributors suggest ways to maintain some greenery in the neighborhood and to secure places for children to play.

An entire section is devoted to chicken coops and details their construction out of discarded materials, recognizing that "everyone needs a place" (64, 67–80). According to the architect Pedro Rivera, the chicken coop section—with photographs and stories of children playing with chickens, children's drawings of maps of the chicken coops (74–75), and a creative story about chickens written collectively by children with guidance from a member of Dulcinéia (Lacerda, "A galinha feia" [The ugly chicken] 79)—is " a chronicle itself of Morro de Providência," an analogy for favela construction in general (Rivera 5). The materials the children repurpose for the chicken coop are the same materials used for building houses: "old closet doors, rusted metal bars, fabric, drawers, plastic boxes, everything that children find thrown out in the streets and neighborhoods is collected" (*Soluções providenciais* 71).

In the introduction to *Soluções providenciais*, Rivera calls these solutions "a combination of simplicity and subtlety applied to their everyday universe" (5). In the book's concluding essay, architect Marcos Rosa calls these tactics examples of "radical pragmatism" that rely on familiar architectural elements but reassigns them to perform new functions (83). While he praises the community's grassroots ingenuity, collective action, and adaptability, he warns against romanticizing these makeshift solutions. "The solutions have their origins in local space rather than in the meeting rooms of office buildings, . . . with decisions made during a process of reading and getting to know the space, out of exchanges and contact" (84). He recognizes these "pioneering forms" of place-based community knowledge building (86), but the results are far from adequate, practically or aesthetically. He points to a "necessary revision of obsolete planning and urban design practices" that are too often applied to these challenging communities (86).

By telling the story collectively of housing struggles in a vulnerable community, these cartonera books celebrate Pedra Lisa, its history, its culture, and its human and material dimensions. The parallels between the books and the favela housing itself—in their materials and their artisanal construction—reveals a dynamic overlapping of method and results, of process and product. With this project, Dulcinéia gave community members, even children, the roles of illustrators, writers, photographers, and bookmakers, and it featured community leaders' voices in interviews. Suddenly those whose voices had been silenced and whose roles had been invisible came to occupy positions of authority, dignity, and respect. Founder Lúcia Rosa describes the work of Dulcinéia Catadora, not only in the favela but in general, as a "way of fighting against invisibility" (personal interview). The group seeks to make the invisible visible by transforming marginal citizens into dignified local experts, published poets, and recognized visual artists.

From the Street and Back Again

Despite the contradictions of cartonera publishing collectives—the books' appeal to a mostly middle-class and academic audience, their limited circulation, the groups' multifaceted reliance on both artisanal handmade crafts and digital dissemination through social media and websites—the street as their material origin and imagined destination remains constant. While a few cartonera publishing collectives have emerged in rural areas, Celis Carbajal says that "the majority are indeed very identified with the urban, with the neighborhood. . . . The urban is their context[;] in one way or another, they are all associated with the street" (personal interview, my translation). She links this urban situatedness to many of the collectives' performative elements, which include public readings or performances of their books in the street or in spaces such as markets, public transportation, and public libraries, and in connection with public art such as graffiti. As Epplin comments regarding Eloísa Cartonera, in reference to Cucurto's novel *Hasta quitarle Panamá a los yanquis* (Until We Take Panama Back from the Yankees), "The act of reading is allied to dancing, the production of books to the production of transient, passing encounters. . . . These books and these encounters have rough, barely defined edges: they bleed into the texture and rhythms of the city around them" (*Late Book Culture* 68). To varying degrees and with varying intensity, all of the cartonera publishers work within this blending of reading and urban life, of materials and imagination, of literary creation and local intervention in public space.[22]

At the same time that the Eloísa cooperative established an organic farm outside the city, they were enhancing their urban presence as well. In 2013 they bought a newspaper kiosk on Avenida Corrientes in the center of downtown Buenos Aires (see figures 4.13, 4.14, and 4.15). To complement their studio in La Boca, they now sell books, paint covers, and host readings directly on the street at the kiosk. They consider it an "intermediary" space between their studio and street vending: "The difference is that at the studio people come to see us specially, while at the kiosk they run into us and learn about our world, and we learn about the world of the street" (Cucurto and Gómez, personal e-mail communication, my translation). Cucurto and Gómez commented on making their books more accessible and attracting new readers: "We learn about other worlds: the world of the city, of informal street sellers. There's a whole lumpen world that comes over that

Figure 4.13. Eloísa Cartonera kiosk, Buenos Aires; photo courtesy of Washington Cucurto and María Gómez

Figure 4.14. Eloísa Cartonera kiosk, Buenos Aires; author photo

Figure 4.15. Mural painted on Eloísa Cartonera kiosk, Buenos Aires; photo courtesy of Washington Cucurto and María Gómez

lives in the street, and that finds great affinity with us. Lots of people approach, happy to hug us, glad that we're downtown, more accessible. When we paint books everyone comes over, and many times we've stopped traffic on the street because of the number of people that gather around the kiosk" (personal e-mail communication, my translation).

The kiosk occupies a traditional and central literary location, on an avenue known for its many bookstores as well as for sidewalk vendors of used books. In the bookstore guide *El libro de los libros*, published by the Buenos Aires municipal government in 2009, which contains maps and lists of bookstores organized by neighborhood, an entire chapter is devoted to Avenida Corrientes (97–108). Cucurto nods to Avenida Corrientes as a literary and print media destination in his poem "Estaba yo leyendo a Enrique Lhin" [*sic*] (I was reading Enrique Lhin):

La tarde de Corrientes estaba hermosa	[The afternoon on Corrientes was beautiful
las librerías llenas de ofertas, los bares	the bookstores were packed with sales, the bars
llenos de chicas lindas, los puestos de diarios	full of pretty girls, the newspaper stands
con miles de revistas	with thousands of magazines]
	(*La cartonerita* 12)

The Eloísa kiosk stands out for its alternative merchandise of brightly painted book covers, but it also blends into the downtown ambience of news media and bookselling. Some critics view the establishment of Eloísa's newsstand, particularly given its location, as an uncharacteristically commercial move, contradictory to the pushback against neoliberal consumerism that cartonera publishing seems to espouse.[23] However, this interpretation misses the mark by ignoring Eloísa's aim toward economic sustainability and by underestimating the significance of their urban outreach. Perhaps rooted in an expectation that cartonera publishing eschew all commercial goals (see, for example, an oft-cited essay by Jesús Cano Reyes on cartonera publishers, which claims that they "eschew any lucrative aim"), this is an idealized and inaccurate assumption. In the case of Eloísa Cartonera in particular, bookmaking and bookselling is a business, and the cooperative sustains itself by selling its published work.

Combining alternative publishing and conventional bookselling can be a creative marketing strategy rather than a contradiction. Cala Buendía mentions newsstands among "nontraditional venues" for bookselling that emerged in the 1990s in Argentina, and condemns them as a neoliberal move toward the commodification of literature (113–114). However, this critique ignores the historical and traditional role of newsstands in the lettered urbanism of the River Plate region, where novels appeared serialized in newspapers from the 1880s on, and where newsstands sold popular literature, such as romance novels, collectors' editions of classics, and comic books.[24] Rather than an unconventional strategy, selling cartonera books at newsstands in Argentina is a return to a traditional venue for distributing literature alongside or included in other print media.

Along with selling more books, Eloísa's kiosk furthers the group's interrelated aims of reaching new readers and intervening in urban space: "We've managed to do what we've always hoped for: getting closer to readers, disseminating more widely, and being downtown, a strategic place where so many people circulate" (Cucurto and Gómez, personal e-mail communication, my translation). Cucurto and Gómez insist that the kiosk is more than a sales operation: "the stand is destined to be a major place of cultural encounters, of exchange and possibilities for distributing work by young writers. This is our aim and our dream" (personal e-mail communication, my translation). As a space for poetry readings, open mic evenings, and book painting sessions, the kiosk extends the Eloísa project into the urban center and broadens its collective scope.

Metacartón: Stories That Craft Books and Books That Graph Their Own Story

Eloísa's downtown kiosk underscores one of two main objectives that Epplin identifies in cartonera publishing: to "act as a mobile stage for collective existence, integrating itself into . . . the space of the neighborhood or of the entire city" (*Late Book Culture* 63). That outward, centrifugal force is accompanied by a second premise related to the inner workings of the books themselves, requiring "that the book can and should retain and exhibit the traces of the labor that formed it" (*Late Book Culture* 63).[25] Cartonera publishing is known for its overt way of revealing its process in its products. In a metatextual move, some fiction published by cartonera presses even includes characters and episodes involved with cardboard book publishing. Cucurto's novels provide the best-known examples, for they frequently dramatize cartonera publishing, often in exaggerated carnavalesque scenes, such as those in *Cosa de negros, El curandero del amor, Las aventuras del Sr. Maíz*, and *La culpa es de Francia* (*It's a Black Thing, The Love Healer, The Adventures of Mr. Maize*, and *It's France's Fault*). His poetry also makes reference to the cartonera enterprise in poems such as "La fotocopiadora" (The Photocopier) and "La cartonerita" (The Little Cardboard Picker). The latter is a love poem:

De una cartonerita	[With a little cardboard picker
yo me enamoré,	I fell in love
la seguí cerquita	I followed her closely
sin saber por qué	without knowing why
por Coronel Díaz	along Coronel Díaz Street
hasta Santa Fe.	until Santa Fe Avenue.
. . .	. . .
juntando cartones	gathering boxes
trastos, botellitas	pots, little bottles
iba solita	she went by herself
con su carrito	with her little cart
de cachivachitos.	of this and that.] (*Veinte pungas* 39)

Although the poem does not directly mention cardboard books, its urban itinerary follows the attractive garbage picker and makes a stop to photocopy a book. This musically rhythmic poem of short lines and a loose rhyme scheme links urban space and reading. Brief details scattered throughout the poem trace the meandering speaker through the city until the *cartonerita* boards a truck with "una prole de cartoneritos" (a gang of little garbage pickers) (40). The friend who accompanied him disappears into the subway, and he is left alone, reading:

Yo me volví solo	[I returned alone
sin saber por qué	without knowing why
caminé diez cuadras	I walked ten blocks
leyendo sin querer	reading distractedly
a Juan Julián José.	Juan Julián José.] (40–41)[26]

The invented author's name punctuates the last stanza with alliteration and end-line rhyme. As the poem concludes with the act of reading, the image of the desired *cartonerita* becomes a fiction.

Less studied examples of this self-reflexive turn include cartonera books that tell the story of cardboard pickers and of cartonera publishing itself in documentary and testimonial modes. Dulcinéia's *Catador* (D'Angelo) and Amapola Cartonera's *El regateo, la ñapa y la vaca* (Baena Echeverry et al.) and *Libro contable* (Amapola Cartonera) incorporate interviews, photographs, drawings, maps, games, graffiti, and some lyric verse in books that reveal their own production both inside and out.

It is not surprising that Dulcinéia produced a book written by the *catadores* who are members of the Cooperativa do Glicério. The São Paulo co-op was founded in 2006 where the largest concentration of Brazilian garbage pickers works, and the book recounts their history and their function environmentally, politically, and socially. A collection of "stories, memories, and images" that includes interviews, photographs, and essays, the book continues Dulcinéia's hybrid style of texts and images (D'Angelo 7). The result is a sort of album or scrapbook reminiscent of Julio Cortázar's visual-verbal "almanacs" (Dávila). The voices of the cooperative members, in dialogue as they tell their very personal stories, occupy the majority of the book and dignify and communicate appreciation for their work: "The role of garbage pickers is very important for society. Not only for collecting and sorting, but for environmental and social issues. A cooperative is a group of people who discuss and resolve things together" (20). Along with providing recycling and garbage collection services, the cooperative is a societal model for discussion and problem solving.

Catador celebrates the labor of the *catadores* in a broad context of environmental sustainability and cultural development. It includes among its authors a rap artist and a graffiti painter. These outsiders, recognized as cultural workers in their own right, legitimize the co-op members' work, particularly their political and institutional organizing. Graffiti artist Mundano staged an urban art intervention with decorated recycling carts that formed a demonstration. The parade of colorful carts stopped at the police station, where the demonstrators read a manifesto defending the rights of the *catadores*. In his text in the book, Mundano expresses his pride in the gains the group has made: "I was happy to see the group organizing itself more and more as a cooperative and also establishing itself as a cultural center" (26).

Catador prints the lyrics to rapper Fábio Prestes's "Cata as Dores de Papel" (22–23), along with the YouTube link for the performance.[27] The song acknowledges the difficult work of the *catadores* amid traffic and pollution, in heat and cold. The physical materials enter into the lyrics, whose wordplay creates ironic images:

Eu visito os lixos eu limpo a cidade	[I visit garbage, I clean the city
Estou apenas empurrando uma oportunidade	I'm just pushing an opportunity
Nas ruas eu sou pelos carros amassado	In the streets I am crushed by the cars
Pareço o papelão que no meu carro foi jogado.	I look like the cardboard thrown into my cart.] (22)

The poem describes the paradox of cleaning up the city by literally moving through garbage. Not only is the cardboard picker invisible, in this fragment he practically turns into the cardboard that he collects. The piece concludes with images of the ground ("terra," "asfalto") and takes a metafictional turn with the mention of a book:

de leste a oeste do sul para o norte	[from east to west, from south to north
para carregar 300 quilos têm que ser muito forte	in order to carry 300 kilos you have to be very strong

no sol na chuva na terra ou no asfalto	under sun rain in the dirt or on asphalt
eu vou cumprir a meta e vender a preço alto	I will meet my goal and sell at the highest price
aprendi hoje a ser criativo na tristeza	I learned today to be creative in my sadness
minha vida eu reciclei e vi meu libro na mesa	I recycle my life and I see my book on the table
quem dera se fosse todo dia assim	who says every day can't be like this
que minhas palavras trouxessem vocês perto de mim	that my words will bring you all close to me] (23)

The president of the co-op, Bispo, articulates his social and cultural aspirations for the recycling cooperative: "I hope the cooperative moves forward, that they get a truck as well as social technology, a nicer space not just for sorting materials but for families to spend time there, a space for culture, for putting on shows. I think Cooperglicério could be not only a collection space but also a cultural and leisure space for families" (D'Angelo 18–19). He challenges the co-op to go beyond recycling materials, which he says the government and city administrations already handle. Bispo identifies a human dimension, involving families and social organizing, as well as aesthetic and cultural dimensions, to the co-op: "The point is not just to recycle. . . . From cardboard you can make a book cover for example, . . . encourage cultural and artistic production with the materials collected in the cooperatives" (28).

A cartonera book that grafts the local urban scene right onto its pages is *El regateo, la ñapa y la vaca* (Bartering, a Bonus, and a Cow; Baena Echeverry et al.), published by Amapola Cartonera in Bogotá. Amapola's central mission to bridge the urban and the rural uses cartonera books to demonstrate the interconnected resources and means of accessibility between rural agricultural producers and the marketing and distribution of their products in the city. The title suggests the bartering, haggling, tips, and tricks of buying and selling in produce markets.

This interactive and playful book is a childlike coloring and activity book, "where each one leaves his or her personal mark" (7). The first two-page spread after the introduction is a map of Bogotá's Siete de Agosto neighborhood, where the cartonera collective has its studio (8–

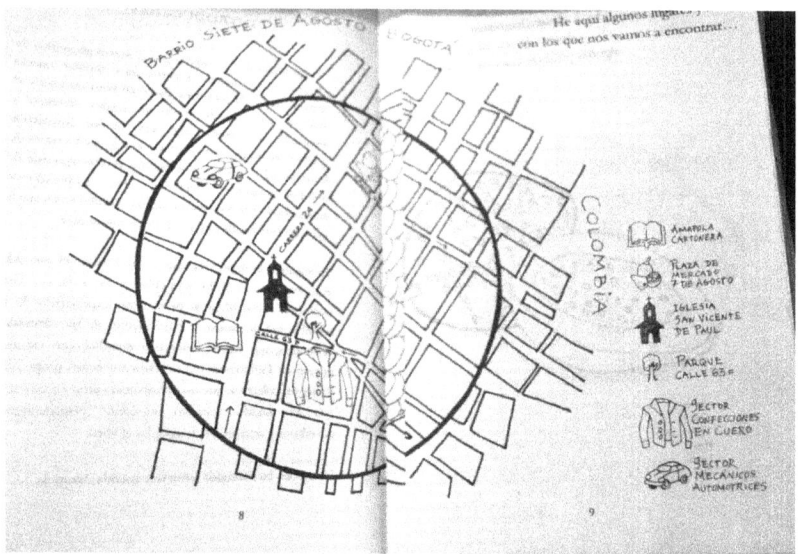

Figure 4.16. Map in Amapola Cartonera's *El regateo, la ñapa y la vaca*; © Amapola Cartonera; author photo; courtesy of Amapola Cartonera

9; see figure 4.16). Simple iconic drawings on the map as well as along the right side of the page, in a sort of legend, indicate a church, a park, an auto mechanic's shop, and a market; a drawing of an open book represents the cartonera shop. Instructions invite the reader to identify the places marked on the map: "here are some places and things that we are going to find" (9). Another page contains a word search with terms that pertain to the urban cartonera context—*Amapola, Calle 63, Bogotá*—hand-drawn inside the outline of a guava fruit, as if the words were its seeds ("Who would have thought? Inside the guava are some cartonera key words" [10]; see figure 4.17). This group considers cartonera books "a fun and alternative way to learn more about urban phenomena, in an unusual contact with rural life through selling" (7).

Amapola's book *Libro contable* (Accounting book) (printed on many of their covers as "Li3ro cont4ble"; see figure 4.18) is part of a multimedia project that includes narrative, photography, documentary video, and artwork. The book is the result of an "art and nature creation" grant from the municipal government's Instituto Distrital de las Artes (IDARTES). The title exploits the verb *contar*'s double meaning in Spanish: to narrate and to count. With the noun *libro* alongside *contable*, the title's polysemy slides between the redundant "book that tells a story" and the simultaneous meaning of an accounting ledger. To underscore the latter meaning, several pages of the book reproduce rows and columns of products and their prices. A brief statement at the end of the book confirms the group's persistent interest in exploring the commercial intersections of the rural and the urban, un-

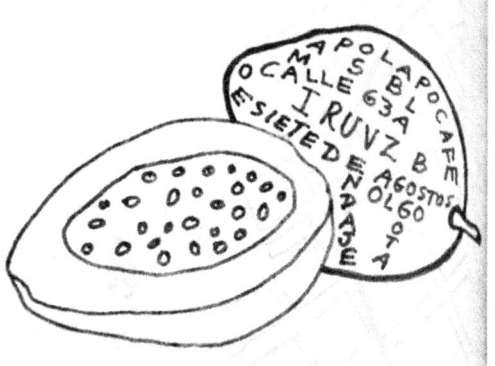

Figure 4.17. Amapola Cartonera's *El regateo, la ñapa y la vaca*; © Amapola Cartonera; author photo; courtesy of Amapola Cartonera

Figure 4.18. Amapola Cartonera's *Libro contable*; author photo

derscored by the letters exchanged for numerals in the painted titles: "*Libro Contable* consists of a proposed interactive artistic action that involves visual arts, audiovisual arts, and literature, through which we aim to explore and problematize the relationships and conflicts between urban contexts and domesticated nature that manifest themselves as food for city dwellers within a relationship of commercial exchange" (Amapola Cartonera 70).

Before it is found on the street, cardboard is used to pack and move goods; in this case, it transports produce from rural farms to city markets. The members of Amapola acted as "intermediaries" (14) for the fruit grown and harvested in the countryside and eventually sold in cities. The project began when participants identified "a precarious item of exchange available in rural areas near Bogotá"—fruit that spoils because of a lack of cost-effective exchange and transportation networks—and resulted in a complex participatory experience of documentation, bartering, and bookmaking (13).

Amapola members contacted a community of growers in La Virgen in the town of Quipile, spent a month with them as they harvested fruit, purchased the entire harvest, and brought it to Bogotá neighborhoods to distribute, particularly Siete de Agosto, where Amapola has its studio. Rather than sell the fruit, they peddled it in carts through the streets of Bogotá in exchange for residents' used cardboard. They thus acquired material for making their books via performative localized bartering, "a bartering process that went from the fruit growers to the publishers—cardboard pickers, who now work as 'book growers'" (14). The books, along with documentary film footage, interviews, photographs, and artwork, were exhibited in museums and cultural centers in the village as well as in Bogotá.[28] The project did not conclude with the finished book and audiovisual exhibits; copies of the book were bartered for more cardboard, fueling future Amapola projects. This interactive effort, with its title that references both accounting and recounting, places as much emphasis on participation and investigation as on artistic and literary production.

Toward the end of *Libro contable*, a two-page spread titled "Libro cartonero" (Cardboard Book) (68–69) includes a poem and photographs of Amapola's cardboard bookmaking. Something of a conclusion to the book and a milestone of the project, six five-line stanzas chant the glories of cartonera books by narrating their material origins, offering "a material reading of reading" (Masiello, "Reading" 203). Focusing on cardboard itself, the poem tells the story of its beginnings in the "bosques talados," their "árboles floridos," "el oxígeno de cada hora," and "su lentitud" (forests felled, flowering trees, oxygen available around the clock, their slow pace), in the long process that eventually turns paper and cardboard into a book that winds its way to readers. The poem includes a nod to the utopian future of the cartonera book, despite its rough, unfinished format ("Su corrugada piel no admite lástimas . . . si su belleza está en las utopías engendradas" [Their corrugated skin doesn't allow for regrets . . . since their beauty lies in the utopias they generate] [69]). The last stanza brings the poem's self-reflexivity full circle in a mention of "este libro" (this book):

> Este libro se lee con las yemas de los dedos
> para sentir las luces traídas por sus ritmos
> emancipados de las oscuras montañas de carbón,
> usadas de escalera para huir al cielo
> imaginándose las rutas de recuperar los sueños.
> [This book is read with the fingertips
> to feel the lights that come through its rhythms
> liberated from the dark mountains of coal,
> used as a stairway to escape to heaven
> imagining the paths to regaining our dreams.] (69)

At the end of the poem it is not just any cartonera book, or even all cartonera books generically, but this one, the one in our hands, that provides a path to recapturing our dreams. The utopian aspirations take the cardboard from the baseness of the street to heavenly heights, all the while celebrating the book and the materials of which it consists as a physical object.

The last pages of the book are devoted to drawings and photographs related to the project. The final two-page spread (n.p.) is a collage of photographs and drawings of signs and produce in markets, with examples of sales offers, special deals, and prices per kilo (see figure 4.19). On the right side of the spread, superimposed over the market signs, a tower of alternating fruits and books draws the viewer's eye. Climbing and leaning to the right, like mounds of stacked tomatoes or mangoes in a market stall, this precarious balance of round produce and rectangular books seems to reach out to the reader as a market client or customer. Inviting us to snatch an orange or grab a book, this final graphic reminds us that books are also commodities,

Figure 4.19. Collage in *Libro contable*; © Amapola Cartonera; author photo; courtesy of Amapola Cartonera

and that just like produce, they are sold or exchanged according to market value.

From Fruit to Fiction, or Selling but Not Selling Out

Amapola dramatizes Bogotá's fruit and vegetable markets as a meeting place of the urban and the rural where cardboard bookmaking becomes the product of alternative exchanges, which the group considers an "intercambio de saberes" (exchange of knowledges) (Amapola Cartonera 16). Beyond valorizing the work of *cartoneros* and *catadores* and often employing them, cartonera publishing celebrates knowledge exchanges. Amapola's documentary films that are part of the *Libro contable* project reveal the expertise of agricultural producers, and Dulcinéia's *Soluções providenciais* honors the construction ingenuity of favela residents. Amapola's focus on fruit and vegetable distribution as a way to privilege a local knowledge base reminds us that Cucurto's first job was as a produce handler in a grocery store and that Eloísa's first studio sold fruits and vegetables alongside books. Often referenced in Cucurto's autobiographical statements and fictionalized in his stories and novels, his work as a produce stocker positions his self-referential protagonist[29] as a working-class neighborhood guy who creates literature out of the *popular* (what he pejoratively calls middle-class "good literature," which he denigrates but ironically also produces).[30]

Even as a fictional character, Cucurto is a writer and cartonera publisher who straddles working-class daily life and high cultural production (also known as literature).[31] As Ofelia Ros comments, Cucurto "invites readers to enter into a world that is right there next to them, but that they know little about and perceive as distant, foreign and threatening" (27). The two worlds of popular fiction and high art fiction collide in much of cartonera publishing, where established writers (often referred to in analyses of cartonera literature as *consagrados*) brush up against new, young writers and artists, where *cartoneros* and *catadores* become bookmakers and local experts, and where rural agricultural workers and urban street vendors collaborate.[32] Here we see what Francine Masiello calls the rediscovery of *lo popular* in Argentine cultural production and consumption, where "the [literary] text produces a material relationship with the reader" ("Reading" 207). The subtitle of Cucurto's novel *Las aventuras del Sr. Maíz, el héroe atrapado entre dos mundos* (The Adventures of Mr. Maize, the Hero Trapped between Two Worlds) hints at dichotomies beyond the fictional scenarios of produce handler and cumbia king.

Just as Cucurto's narrative dismisses literary expertise to value play, imagination, and dreams—"un mundo en el cual no se necesite saber escribir, sino sólo soñar, imaginar, fantasear" (a world in which one doesn't need to know how to write, only how to dream, to imagine, to fantasize) (*El amor es mucho más* 2)—cartonera publishers build "social sculptures," "spaces where relationships and exchanges are woven" (Bienal de São Paulo 66, also quoted in Amapola Cartonera 12). Cartonera books urge readers to join in the process as "accomplices": "¡La lectura es una travesura cómplice, esta página es el nacimiento de una hermandad de Uds. conmigo . . . y ojalá con el mundo!" (Reading is a complicit trick; this page is the birth of brotherhood between all of you and me . . . and hopefully with the world!) (Cucurto, *Sr. Maíz* 65–66). Even if less explicitly than Cucurto's narrator/protagonist, who addresses his readers directly, cartonera books promote a collective, inclusive way of reading that calls for breaking down the barriers among the author, the narrator, and the readers.

This chapter proposed three characteristics that Eloísa Cartonera, Sarita Cartonera, Dulcinéia Catadora, and Amapola Cartonera share:

place-based activism, public outreach, and material self-reflection. The analysis of these groups' projects and products has demonstrated their commitment to collective reading in public space via new uses for and conceptions of literature that expand its scope, range, and impact. Of the four groups this chapter discusses, Sarita Cartonera no longer exists. However, duration is not a measure of success. Nor does evaluating the impact of a cartonera project rely on the usual numbers of a bottom line: the number of authors published or copies sold. Rather, success is evaluated on the basis of a qualitative assessment in relation to the publisher's interrelated goals. Sarita's founder, Saldarriaga, counts the personal triumphs of some of its members as a marker of success. She offers the example of Pepe, who was on the verge of dropping out of high school. Thanks to the support of the collective, he stayed the course and ended up landing a job with a major publisher. While he worked with Sarita, Vargas Luna was long frustrated by the hierarchies between the cardboard pickers and the artists and editors, which "we were never able to completely undo" (personal interview, my translation). But when a children's art program in Lima invited the *cartoneros* associated with Sarita to lead a bookmaking workshop, Vargas Luna sensed a welcome reversal in their status: "That moment when they recognized them as artists was key" (personal interview, my translation).

All of these projects reveal how bookmaking is part of a larger set of goals. Cartonera publishing is not only about the books. Cucurto and his cartonera colleagues across Latin America and abroad call for "a reformulation of the hegemonic cultural parameters that position literature as an expression of 'high culture' and books as the most elevated objects" (Ros 35). In Cucurto's poem "La fotocopiadora," a sort of ode to the copy machine,[33] which is the basis of most cartonera publishing, he takes apart the book once again to draw attention to the process. The first-person speaker in this poem personifies the photocopier through his own transformational resurrection:

Mañana cuando me muera	[Tomorrow when I die
dejaré de ser negro	I'll no longer be black
y al ratito (por sobre mi negritud)	and in a bit (thanks to my blackness)
volveré al mundo convertido en una fotocopiadora.	I'll return to the world transformed into a photocopier.] (*Como un paraguayo ebrio* 21)

Dismantling the work (in the sense of oeuvre, as Roland Barthes suggests in "From Work to Text"), and dismissing the author (as in Michel Foucault's "What Is an Author?"), this poem unravels the romantic ideals of art, exposing the machinations of book production so they are reduced to the absurd. When the poem is stripped down to its verbal material, all that matters is language in its powers of seduction, association, movement, and practicality:

> Yo solo quiero invitar a la palabra
> que el lenguaje no sea
> carriles de insultos en la boca
> de las personas
>
> ¡Que el lenguaje sea una flor como Paquita
> espiando subida al muro!
>
> ¡Que el lenguaje sea novia no inabordable
> porque no tenés coche!

> [I just want to invite words
> so that language is not just
> ditches of insults
> in people's mouths.
>
> Let language be a flower like Paquita
> spying from the top of a wall!
>
> Let language be the girlfriend
> who is unattainable
> because you don't have a car!] (22)[34]

Just as Cucurto dissolves the work and the author, often the cartonera books themselves are dismissed, relegated to the sidelines, or mocked, put to the service of other goals.

Similar to Cucurto in his praise of language, Raimundo Carrero celebrates language and happiness in his book *O paraíso de pão e manteiga*, published by Dulcinéia, because communication, words themselves, are his source of happiness:

> Isso, não perca a felicidade. Daria um bom título de livro. Com certeza, um bom livro. Aliás, não um bom livro, no máximo um bom título. Sim, porque o livro não interessa, essas coisas de livro não têm importância, basta juntar palavras e aí já está tudo resolvido, sobretudo se é para não perder a felicidade.
> [That doesn't bring happiness. It would provide a good book title. Certainly, a good book. In fact, not even a good book, at best a good title. Yes, because books are not what matter, all this book stuff is not important, it's enough to put words together and there everything is resolved, especially if it's to hold on to happiness.] (6)

When he comes across a phrase that he thinks would make a great book title, Carrero decides that the book itself is not necessary; rather, just putting words together will ensure happiness.

Many observers and even some of the cartonera publishers themselves note that the revolutionary aesthetic Cucurto calls for has not truly democratized literature or entirely transformed consumer practices around books, that its impact has been more symbolic than concrete: it "seems to exert more influence over the modes of cultural production and reflection than over consumption and consumers" (Vargas Luna, "La rumba" 126). These collective projects nevertheless have drawn attention to "the need to construct citizenship as well as the mechanisms of cultural consumption" (Vargas Luna, "La rumba" 124).

There seems to be no unified, overarching method for defining, cataloguing, and archiving cartonera books because no mutually agreed upon set of characteristics or conditions identify these objects. How could there be, with nearly one hundred independent cartonera publishers spread around the world? The lack of consensus around categorization points to an indeterminacy that complicates assigning value. But this complication is precisely what cartonera publishing generates: a questioning of codes, a shifting of hierarchies, and a reconsideration of commodity practices. Because cartonera projects promise much more than books, the books they produce embody an array of experiences, places, materials, and means of circulation. As objects, these books bound in reused and hand-painted cardboard are not the groups' end result but rather the starting point for conversations and interaction, catalysts for participation and exchange.

CHAPTER 5

Books That Bite: Libraries of Banned Books in Argentina

Books. The word censorship is inserted between the words towers and cubes. Elephant and space. grey. kingdom. bomb. Silence seeps between the lines of these texts. But these texts escape since their meanings cannot be fixed.
MATÍAS MANUELE ON THE BANNED CHILDREN'S BOOK *LA LÍNEA*, BY BEATRIZ DOUMERC AND AYAX BARNES, MUSEO DEL LIBRO Y DE LA LENGUA

In his photographic installation *Los condenados de la tierra* (The Wretched of the Earth), Marcelo Brodsky displayed the remains of four books that were buried during the Argentine dictatorship out of fear of political reprisal, then unearthed after the return to democracy twenty years later. Fragments of the books rest in dirt in a wooden box divided into four sections, a sort of coffin for the resurrected volumes (see figure 5.1). Despite nearly twenty years of exposure to moisture and worms, the unearthed books were still partially readable. The installation, including a video, has been exhibited in Argentina and internationally.[1]

One of the venues for the installation was the Buenos Aires International Book Fair in 2000, sponsored by the Mexican publishers Fondo de Cultura Económica and Siglo XXI, which had published some of the disinterred books; the publishers' logos appear clearly on the books' fragments. Brodsky said in an interview that he was motivated to "tell the story with visual elements" (*V7inter*, my translation), in this case through "recuperated" books that after being silenced have come back to life. The materiality of the books, underscored by the earth beneath them and the wooden case surrounding them, gives them a corporeal dimension. Hiding these books rather than destroying them re-

Figure 5.1. *Los condenados de la tierra* installation; © Marcelo Brodsky; courtesy of Marcelo Brodsky

veals their readers' hope that the books would have a chance of being resurrected in the future. In fact, the books "benefited from dignified burial, a privilege that many of the dictatorship's victims did not have" (Brodsky et al., *Nexo* 77). Their owner, Nélida Valdez, who buried them in 1976, explains, "I was thankful that the books were occupying that space rather than us" (*Nexo* 79, my translation).[2]

Practices of reading under dictatorship tell a frightening story, tales of books shared under great risk, stolen in military raids on suspected subversives, hidden, and—as dramatized in Brodsky's work—buried. Most of these books have been republished and have been sold and circulated freely since the return to democracy; Argentina libraries and exhibitions of banned books, however, commemorate this dark period of dictatorship. In transitions from repressive regimes to democracy, metaphors that involve books and reading are often used to express moving forward, and in some cases even to insist on forgetting the past: "turning the page," "closing the book," and "ending one chapter to begin another" (Richard 31). These libraries and collections use books precisely to remember the past and to bring it into the present by recovering and reopening volumes that had been forcibly closed. Libraries of banned books differ importantly from the numerous memory parks and monuments erected in the Southern Cone. They avoid the monumentalizing tendency of memory markers and bypass the commoditized "memory market" of published testimonials and other physical forms of remembrance (see Payne and Bilbija). Instead, they celebrate the end of censorship by transforming that experience into public reading spaces and events.

The libraries discussed in this chapter offer modest, unadorned spaces that invite readers to explore, discuss, and commune with previously banned books at no charge. Some of these collections travel to bring books to readers in public spaces such as schools, museums, and cultural centers. This chapter explores how previously prohibited books are put to the service of commemorating the violence and censorship of dictatorship by engaging participants not only as readers but as participatory citizens. The tours, workshops, arts activities, public readings, and performances programmed around banned books host opportunities for reflective, introspective, critical thinking about authoritarianism, freedom of speech, and the values of an open and free press in the context of the transition to democracy. Participants are encouraged not only to read, but even more to interact aesthetically, performatively, and critically with these materials as the physical remains and ideological residue of censorship. This engagement is staged in a group setting, sometimes in spaces that were once clandestine torture centers established and run by the junta and that are now open to the public. By housing collections of previously censored books—which had been invisible, silenced, hidden, buried—the spaces help resuscitate these objects as they are displayed and recirculated.[3] Thus the physical place surrounding these collections, together with the materiality of the books as objects, denounce censorship by reenacting the books' (and metaphorically human beings') disappearance and by celebrating their reappearance.

Two of the collections are housed in former centers of detention and torture: Olimpo in Buenos Aires and the Archivo Provincial de la Memoria in Córdoba. Another collection at La Grieta, a neighborhood cultural center in La Plata, primarily comprises children's and young adult literature, and organizes temporary traveling exhibits of censored books in public spaces that engage readers of all ages. These exhibits restore the books not only with readings but also by animating them with role-playing, creative movement, music, and other artistic interventions. Collectively reading these books in public activates them through what Diana Taylor calls "acts of transfer": "doubling, replication, and proliferation . . . [that] preserve[s] rather than erase[s] the antecedents" (*Archive* 46).

Public programming with prohibited books also asks participants to reconstruct the books' itineraries, to examine the history of censorship, and to celebrate freedom of expression. Leaders ask young readers to imagine the conditions and criteria of censorship in an effort to teach recent history and to prevent future repression, in the spirit of "nunca más" (never again).[4] At the same time, adults who were children during the dictatorship reencounter favorite books. While public readings may open old wounds by recalling this aspect of repression, they also fill in memory gaps in personal histories. Resuscitating these books recognizes that "the systematic disappearance of people's bodies parallels the project of the systematic disappearance of symbols, discourses, images, and traditions" (Invernizzi and Gociol 23). All of these examples from Argentina pry open the closed book of repressed reading through collective interaction in public space.[5]

Renovated Spaces for Recuperated Books: Archivo Provincial de la Memoria and Olimpo

In the Museo del Libro y de la Lengua, located right next to the National Library in Buenos Aires, a permanent exhibit on censorship during the dictatorship displays a few censored volumes, including children's books by Laura Devetach, Beatriz Doumerc, and Ayax Barnes. The picture books are framed in large display cases with quotes from the censorship decrees condemning them, and comments from critics, writers, and historians. One of them is Devetach's picture book *La torre de cubos*, a book she considers a "kidnapped child" because all copies were removed from libraries and schools (Carreras) (see figure 5.2). The decree attacking *La torre de cubos* faults the book for its "confusing symbolism, ideological-social questioning, inappropriate aesthetics, *unlimited fantasy*, lack of spiritual and transcendent stimuli." It says that the book "criticizes the organization of labor, private property, and the principles of authority facing social, racial, and economic groups from a completely materialist perspective, . . . [and] questions family life" (emphasis added).

Unlimited fantasy became the key phrase for the regime's clamping down on the imagination through censorship, and it now serves as a slogan, resignified for reembracing creative expression. The phrase adorns the mural on the main wall in the activity room at the Archivo Provincial de la Memoria in Córdoba (see figure 5.3). Surrounding a large conference table and chairs for visitors, display cases built into

Figure 5.2. Censorship decree, Museo del Libro y de la Lengua, Buenos Aires; author photo; courtesy of Museo del Libro y de la Lengua

Figure 5.3. Mural at the Archivo Provincial de la Memoria, Córdoba; photo by Selma Cohen; courtesy of Selma Cohen and the Archivo Provincial de la Memoria

the other walls exhibit copies of banned books: prohibited children's books, school textbooks, literature by homosexual writers, and political and historical works deemed subversive. This room hosts most of the center's activities—workshops for visiting school groups, lectures, and readings that often feature the Archivo's collection of banned books. Through its space and the programming, the Archivo celebrates books that do indeed contain "unlimited fantasy."

Both the Biblioteca de Libros Prohibidos at the Archivo Provincial de la Memoria in Córdoba and the Biblioteca Pública y Popular Carlos Fuentealba, located at the Garage Olimpo in Buenos Aires, are housed in former centers of detention and torture that operated during the dictatorship.[6] These centers were restored (*recuperados*) thanks to the organizing of survivors and neighbors, and supported by provincial and municipal memory organizations—Buenos Aires's Instituto Espacio para la Memoria and the province of Córdoba's Comisión Provincial de la Memoria, respectively—that formed in the early 2000s[7] to convert these spaces so that "where there was death and torture, today there is life" (Fresneda 4). As Elizabeth Jelin and Victoria Langland explain in the introduction to their book on monuments and memorials in the Southern Cone, these are "physical public spaces, recognized by the State and legitimate authority, which implies processes of political struggle by those who carry these initiatives forward" (2). Ksenija Bilbija and Leigh Payne consider such recuperated torture centers "memoryscapes" that offer "a physical space and an opportunity for mourning, grieving, and reflecting on the losses from state terrorism" (7).

Dedicating space in these two centers to house formerly banned books preserves the memory of prohibited pages and denounces the military regime's surveillance of reading. Collections of books for display and use in former centers of detention and torture memorialize their prohibition by constituting a canon of dangerous reading in buildings that served as scenarios of repression. The archival function of these reconfigured spaces is multifaceted, and they amplify their impact not only by housing documentation—including records from the regime and testimonies of victims—but by doing so amid physical remnants of the regime's detention and torture practices.[8]

The Archivo Provincial de la Memoria, located in downtown Córdoba, was originally called the Departamento de Informaciones under provincial police jurisdiction. Informally referred to as "D2," it served as a clandestine center for arrests, torture, and extermination from 1969 to 1983. Housed in the historic city hall on the Pasaje Santa Catalina next to the cathedral, the center was at its most active in de-

Figure 5.4. Archivo Provincial de la Memoria: broken wall; photo by Selma Cohen; courtesy of Selma Cohen and the Archivo Provincial de la Memoria

tention and torture of prisoners who were considered subversives between 1974 and 1979, just before and in the early years of the last dictatorship. In the 1970s alone D2 detained some one thousand prisoners (Said 57).

The Archivo was established in 2006 and moved into the former D2. It was the first memory site in the province of Córdoba. The center falls under the jurisdiction of the Comisión Provincial de la Memoria, which in turn depends on the provincial Ministerio de Justicia y Derechos Humanos. The military regime had significantly modified the space of the center, erecting walls to hide precisely how the space was used for clandestine detention and making it difficult to identify where the detainees were held, interrogated, and tortured. As a recently published catalog of all the Argentine memory sites notes about the Archivo, "the building resembles a labyrinth: it has numerous rooms of varied dimensions and six internal patios" (Said 57). In 2007, surviving detainees were invited to the center to help break down the walls that had been erected to hide its use.[9] Some of the walls remain broken, unfinished, to serve as reminders of what they were intended to hide, of the horror contained within their boundaries (see figure 5.4).

In her article on the architectural repurposing of memory sites in Argentina and Chile, Karen Bishop questions "the purpose of rebuilding disappearance" in former centers of torture and disappearance (566). She points out that "both architecture and memory are concerned . . . with the incomplete, the open, and the relational" (557). The reconstruction of any former clandestine center of detention and torture, such as the Archivo or Olimpo, embodies "the questions that call for its reconstruction in the first place" (557). Plans for the recuperation of the Casino building on the former Escuela Superior de Mecánica Armada (ESMA) campus in Buenos Aires, where thousands of prisoners were held, tortured, and disappeared, had to consider whether to restore the building to the condition it was in when it was used for this horrific purpose, or to leave in place the changes that the military implemented in order to hide its activities there. Various proposals for reopening the space as a memory center had to determine what physical state would best serve the goals of memory: "Its original condition was one of invisibility and disavowal. The effort here then is to (determine whether or not to) take apart that which covered up this invisibility in order to render it visible, viewable, and visitable and to make chartable over time the perfection of invisibility" (Bishop 566).

Visitors to the Archivo walk through the restored structure, its rooms assigned different functions related to preserving the memory of those detained and disappeared. In the Museo de Sitio building, where victims were held and tortured, testimonies and photos retell their stories. "The walls of this memory site still contain the marks of horror: on the inside of two cells that have been conserved intact, there are inscriptions by the detained during their captivity" (Said 57). The facade of the building constitutes a public memorial in the form of a permanent mural that lists the names of all the victims of state violence who passed through D2; the inscribed names trace the shape of huge fingerprints (see figure 5.5). The site was decreed a "national historic place" in 2015.

Most of the Archivo's programming is related to the "pedagogía de la memoria" (memory pedagogy), a continually evolving methodology for education and commemoration of the historical past as well as for addressing contemporary human rights issues and proposing a more just and inclusive societal future. The center hosts guided tours, workshops, educational programs, and events related to human rights. The politics of memory is a constant presence, along with awareness of the political act of recuperating historical sites that participated in repres-

Figure 5.5. Archivo Provincial de la Memoria: facade; photo by Selma Cohen; courtesy of Selma Cohen and the Archivo Provincial de la Memoria

sion, detention, torture, and disappearance. The Archivo's programs and workshops offer a creative, participatory process for building a knowledge base that reconstructs history. A statement on the center's website defines its mission: "The processes of memory construction are a laboratory of ideas and resources for imagining and reconstructing that are produced in a country around the uses of the past, what is remembered, what is silenced and forgetting the past in the present. A result of the interaction and construction between individuals' subjectivity and collective, social, political, religious, and legal norms, memory work builds social identities, articulating not only ties of belonging but also relationships of differentiation." The center hosts school groups three times a week for "Encuentros de Memorias" (Memory Encounters), whose activities encourage the students to take an active role in creating history. All the visits conclude in the "Sala de vidas para ser contadas" (Lives Recounted Room), where an exhibit of photographs and testimonials of the center's victims memorializes their lives.

Nearly every guided tour, school visit, and cultural event at the Archivo Provincial de la Memoria includes activities related to the Biblioteca de Libros Prohibidos. The library was established in 2007 when the center first began to collect and display banned books and to put them to use in programs with adults and children. The collection was founded with a few books, then grew thanks to word of mouth and eventually a public call for donations. Once the collection was under way, staff from the center hunted for books in used bookstores and at publishers' sales; now the library has some three hundred books. Those who come to the Archivo to donate books are invited to write an entry in a notebook to "tell the story of all the vicissitudes that the books have gone through: their hidden destiny, their modes of resistance, their recuperation" (Boero, my translation). The planning, exhibition, and activities work to animate the books, consciously avoiding turning them into "museum pieces" (Boero, my translation). Rather than being a fixed memorial that focuses on the past, the library seeks to bridge that past with the present and to exploit the books' stories as tools for confronting contemporary issues:

> We try to have these books dialogue with forms of censorship or prohibition in our contemporary world (especially in terms of prejudices, vulnerable or questioned rights, inherited practices from the period of the dictatorship that have not been denaturalized or undone in some institutions like schools, for example). To encourage dialogue, recuperation, and attention to the present. To make sure they don't become museum pieces but rather materials that burst into the culture of the present and enrich it. (Boero, my translation)

Visiting student groups read a selection of the banned children's books and discuss the censorship decrees, always with an emphasis on current societal issues, "intending to focus on the meanings of prohibition and on continuities and ruptures with the present" (Boero, my translation).

The Archivo's memory mission echoes analogous efforts in Chile during its postdictatorship period to avoid turning memory work into a return to the past. Rather, as Nelly Richard explains, memory work can be "a back and forth between the niches of memory that doesn't stop at precise points, that moves along a critical multidirectionality of alternatives without consensus, . . . a memory-subject capable of formulating constructive and productive links between the past and the present" (32). Another workshop activity at the Archivo reviews the military regime's document from 1978 called "How do you detect a subversive in the school environment?" The activity serves to initiate discussion on otherness, fear, and the ways in which the media disseminates societal and cultural messages of acceptance or rejection. As staff member Virginia "Vicky" Rozza comments, in this way "we think about who constructs the other, how that construction is produced, and what the spaces of circulation are" ("Los Sitios").[10]

In the workshops with children, after reading aloud a banned children's book, the staff circulates documents such as the censorship decree banning the book they have just read. Even if the young visitors are not able to read the document themselves, the official nature of the page with its seals and signatures gives the censorship ruling a level of materiality: "It's important to have the document in your hands, to call it a 'document' and a 'censorship decree.' We don't need to resort to facile diminutives to help them understand. . . . In this way it will not be an abstract concept but rather something that they've touched themselves" (Rozza, "Los Sitios"). The visitors touch, hear, and interact with the material objects, from the banned books to the government documents, thus actively experiencing them.

The library visits often use stories by Elsa Bornemann, such as "El caso Gaspar," from her collection *Un elefante ocupa mucho espacio*, about a door-to-door salesperson who tires of walking around on his feet and decides to train himself to walk on his hands. People call him crazy, but he finds the world quite amusing when he views it upside down. The police consider him a subversive, and crime increases all over the city because the police are distracted with the "Gaspar case" (see figure 5.13, later in the chapter).

In one of the workshops, presenters read this story to second graders and asked why the regime banned the book. The students' comprehension was evident in their thoughtful responses. They mentioned Gaspar's transgression and society's fear of doing things differently. One student noticed that "the military loved order"; another pointed out that "if you walk the right way, the police don't arrest you." The student who determined that the book was censored "so that children wouldn't imagine odd things" identified the regime's fear of "unlimited fantasy," the slogan of resistance that adorns the mural. A brainstorming session followed in which the students generated their own "inside out" or "upside down" ideas. One child mentioned raining up, another suggested that adults nap while kids play, another cheered for meals with lots of French fries and only a little bit of salad, and another rooted for cars driving on the sidewalk while kids play in the street. Upset by this disorder, one of the kids said, "That can't be!" to which a classmate replied, "We're imagining." Reassured by the reminder of the role of the imagination, the first child responded: "Oh, then okay, it's all right" (Rozza, "Los Sitios").

All of these collections of banned books both remind readers and participants of censorship and raise awareness of human rights broadly. They work toward reversing the various repressive habits and attitudes that persist from the dictatorship years despite the return to democracy. Under the slogan "Leer nos torna rebeldes" (Reading makes us rebels), a remark by Heinrich Böll, the Archivo library's major event, the "Ronda de lectura" (Reading Round), offers an annual two-day festival of books, art, music, dance, and exhibits. Invited writers present readings, and children's book author Laura Devetach has been a featured speaker at the event.

The Ronda does not limit its programming to books that were banned during the dictatorship; it draws attention to other forms of oppression as well. For example, in 2015 the Ronda featured Camila Sosa Villada, a local transsexual writer and actress, thereby focusing on freedom of gender expression. Her readings and discussions served to "frame and inscribe Camila's writing in that lineage of writers whose relevance keeps popping up by dialoging with current literature" (Boero, my translation). The library's exhibit of books banned because of gender nonconformity, called "Destellos de Luz y Resistencia" (Flashes of Light and Resistance), both had historical significance in the context of the dictatorship and offered homage to writers and artists who have fought for gender justice. Highlighting gender discrimination underscored the former military regime's persecution of LGBTQ citizens, who were categorized as subversives, and its censorship of LGBTQ writers and books about sexual diversity. It also recognized the continuing struggle for freedom of gender expression and sexual preference in Latin America.

In contrast to the Archivo complex in Córdoba, the Olimpo center was not always controlled by police or the military. Located in the Floresta neighborhood of Buenos Aires at Ramón Falcón 4250, the center was originally a tram station and then became a bus terminal. It was occupied by the military for seven months, from August 1978 to January 1979, a period during which eighty-nine people were imprisoned, tortured, or disappeared.[11] Upon the return to democracy in 1983, the space became a local police station. Then in 2005 the center was recuperated under the umbrella organization Instituto Espacio para la Memoria. When the site was scheduled for recuperation it was turned over to an independent Mesa de Trabajo y Consenso, a sort of advisory board, consisting of survivors, victims' family members, and representatives from neighborhood organizations, that determines the specific plans and programming for the center. During my visit there in 2011, the center had seven employees: anthropologists, sociologists, and workshop and tour leaders. By 2016 the staff had increased to twelve employees working in education, communications, and research, and four in preservation and maintenance.

One of the first steps in transforming the complex into a memory center involved identifying the site for the neighborhood, with banners and murals on the exterior to inform residents and visitors of the building's history. Once the site was no longer used for detention and torture, the military tore down cell walls and cleaned out objects and furniture, eliminating most signs of imprisonment and torture. For the reconstruction of the center, the leaders "began with the materiality of the space" (Joncquel, my translation). Unlike decision makers for Córdoba's Archivo, the Olimpo advisory board decided to leave the center as it was when it was turned over to them. A detailed floor plan mapped the various spatial zones (areas of forced labor, interrogation and torture rooms, cells, lavatories, offices). Thorough interviews and archeological and forensic research guided the recuperation of the center, and cells and other spaces in the structure were marked with tape along the floor rather than rebuilt. The objective was to "try to avoid adding more terror and fear to a place that has already suffered its dose of terror" (Joncquel, my translation).

As Bilbija and Payne comment about "memoryscapes," "locating the place of horror seems more important than re-creating the experience of horror" (29). One of the workshop leaders described Olimpo as "a space for education, for memory construction, for exhibits, for debate" (Joncquel, my translation). Along with guided tours and workshops for adults and children, the center has hosted film screenings, symposia related to historical memory, press conferences, art exhibits, knitting and crocheting workshops, book launches, and storytelling with senior citizens. While some of the activities involve the history and victims of Olimpo, most of them explore the wider issues of memory politics and human rights.[12]

The Biblioteca Pública y Popular Carlos Fuentealba, Olimpo's library of banned books, was established in 2007 and occupies a cou-

Figure 5.6. Sign for Olimpo library; the decorative *fileteado* (filigree) is a traditional art form in Argentina from the early twentieth century; author photo; courtesy of Olimpo

ple of rooms in the center (see figure 5.6). Surprisingly, the library is not named for a victim of Olimpo or the dictatorship, but for a teacher and labor activist from Neuquén. Fuentealba was killed by police in a teacher union protest during a labor strike in 2007. Dedicating the library in his memory exemplifies the center's interest in human rights in general, beyond the context of the dictatorship.

The books on the shelves of this modest library, numbering over four thousand volumes, include banned children's books and works by Karl Marx, Manuel Puig, Mao Zedong, Osvaldo Bayer, and Rodolfo Walsh. The stacks at Olimpo, which began as an exhibit called "El retorno de lo prohibido" (The Return of the Banned), now labeled "Prohibido bajo terrorismo de estado" (Banned under State Terrorism), are part of the public memorializing gesture of the recuperated center and remind visitors that reading can be a practice of resistance (see figures 5.7a and 5.7b). These books also circulate in workshops for school groups and senior citizens who visit the center, as the staff works "toward dissemination and development of critical thinking" (Cerruti, *Ex centro*, 2010 edition 63).[13] By providing material evidence

Figures 5.7a and b.
Shelves of banned books at Olimpo; author photos; courtesy of Olimpo

of repression, as Susana Draper elaborates, these objects represent "the incomplete character of the void. . . . Each book will relate its own story on censorship" (169).

A broad concept of censorship guides the Olimpo library and its activities. The Olimpo catalog enumerates five modes of censorship that the center strives to feature: national dictatorial decrees against individual books; other decrees; censorship directed at publishers; authors, publishers, and booksellers who were detained, assassinated, or disappeared; and testimonies of self-censorship. While the Olimpo publication defines censorship as an everyday practice that impacted all social relations and modes of communication (emotions or actions people hide, power dynamics that limited certain gestures, speech, or behaviors), during the dictatorship censorship was part of a systematic cultural policy "that strove to destroy and—if only partially—succeeded in destroying social solidarity" (Cerruti, *Ex centro*, 2010 edition, 66). As many studies of censorship in the context of the Argentine dictatorship point out, the regime's attack on arts and culture was as calculating as its implementation of detention, interrogation, torture, and disappearance of citizens (Cerruti, *Ex centro*, 2010 edition, 66).

The library at Olimpo serves as a tool, a "catalyst for questions and reflection" for groups that visit the center (Cerruti, *Ex centro*, 2010 edition, 70). Most visits consist of three parts: a video presentation, a tour of the facility, and discussion. The documentary video that introduces the visit includes interviews with neighbors and survivors of detention at Olimpo, and information about victims who were disappeared. The video also reviews the recuperation of the site and its current functions. Guided tours of the facility vary according to the age of the participants; young children do not visit the areas of detention. For teens and adults, the tour in these areas of the site stresses human rights and forms of resistance more generally. Paola Hernández calls these guided tours "performative narratives" (76) that verbally fill in the gaps for visitors regarding physical details related to the compound's use as a center for detention and torture, particularly because the military removed most structural signs of this function. With young visitors, reading censored children's books leads to discussions of how and why the regime implemented these limits on human rights through literature and the arts. Adolescent students participate in workshops in which they split into smaller groups to examine a selection of banned books from the library. The students are then asked to identify the origins and rationales for the censorship of each title.

Libraries of Banned Books **207**

Figure 5.8. "Life albums" in memory of Olimpo victims; author photo; courtesy of Olimpo

Most of the visits conclude in the Sala de Vidas (Room of Lives), an inviting respite from the difficulty of touring the site. A wall of windows lets in sunlight, and each pane frames a black and white portrait of one of Olimpo's detained or disappeared. Brightly colored cushions are on the floor, and low tables display albums decorated with cloth and embroidery by neighbors and victims' families (see figure 5.8). Each "life album" tells the story of one of these individuals, including details about the dates and circumstances of their detention, elaborated by photographs, stories, poems, and remembrances of other moments in their lives. The visitors sit informally on the cushions and browse through the albums while refreshments are served. The vivid, blown-up portraits on the windows, faces that are among the first things visitors see when they look up from the entrance, harbor them at the end of their visit, as if the pictured detainees were reading the banned books in the library too.

Indeed, some of the detainees did read forbidden books. A small circulating library reached the prisoners in their cells, thanks to other prisoners who gathered books confiscated from recent detainees or from ransacked homes and delivered them to fellow prisoners on a cart. An Olimpo survivor wondered, "How could there be a library in the dungeon?" The secret library, "organized quietly and passionately by a buddy," reconnected the detainees with their previous lives outside the center. The books formed "a bridge to our dreams, to our story. . . . It is comforting to see a buddy in his cell reading, because at that moment he's not suffering, his mind flies with the book and escapes his captivity, he escapes; we may get out of here, but we'll remain together through sharing the freedom of those books" (Cerruti, *Ex centro*, 2010 edition, 65). Olimpo's library of banned books, therefore, continues the practice of reading as resistance at this very site.

Draper points out the unfinished, inconclusive nature of the Olimpo center: "The entire process of the Olimpo transformation reveals a commitment to the present rather than a museification of the past. . . . [Visitors] are confronted by the haunting incompleteness that characterizes these ruinous spaces" (169–170). Olimpo's physical complex maintains the empty areas where prisoners' cells and interrogation and torture rooms were located. There are no plaques or printed explanations on the walls, only tape along the floor demarcating the spaces. According to Bilbija and Payne, experiencing the open wound of violence and loss is intentional in these memory spaces and their programming. "They seek to represent the openness of the wounds—the enduring sense of loss, fear, and distrust—so as to catalyze action and to ward against comfort and complacency" (8). When I visited the center in 2011, areas designated for vocational training held classes in industrial baking and mechanics, and one room served as the office for a community radio station. Although the center's staff has increased in size in the last few years, and Olimpo now offers tours and workshops to a growing number of visitors, the center remains a work in progress. The library area has been damaged by roof leaks, and a construction proposal is currently under consideration to expand the center to include a more prominent area for the library (Joncquel).

Politics aggravate the precarious circumstances of Olimpo and all the memory sites. The projects were mostly established under the two Kirchner presidencies (2003–2015) and boosted by their human rights policies, which included legal action on overlooked crimes from the dictatorship period. As I write this, President Mauricio Macri's term, which began in December 2015, has implemented obstructionist policies regarding all the memory sites and projects. From his first months in office, Macri made a number of decisions that weakened or jeopardized these initiatives.[14]

Exploring banned books at Olimpo, in the very space where political prisoners were tortured and from which many were disappeared, adds an extra layer of materiality to visitors' experiences with these objects that is fundamental to the programming around memory and space. Although the collection does not generally travel, the center occasionally collaborates with other venues, using a selection of titles from the library as a display. At the Buenos Aires Book Fair in 2008, Olimpo participated in the Instituto Espacio para la Memoria's stand with a questionnaire asking visitors to comment on "the relationship between people and books during the dictatorship" (Cerruti, *Ex centro*, 2010 edition, 64). Their anecdotes about their forms of resistance and self-censorship contributed to the center's research on banned books.

In the most high profile example of this off-site exhibition, the Olimpo library was featured at the Argentine stand at the international book fair in Frankfurt, Germany, in 2010, when Argentina was the country of honor. With the slogan "Culture on the Move," the 2,500-square-meter exhibit received 250,000 visitors. The pavilion was designed by the architect Atilio Pentimalli with intersecting hexagonal rooms modeled on the description of the library in Jorge Luis Borges's story "La biblioteca de Babel." An emphasis on human rights was one of the stand's organizing themes, and the exhibit included banned and burned books. This exhibit included one hundred titles chosen for new translations into German, with Rodolfo Walsh's *Operación masacre* to be among the first (Friera).[15] Columns in the stand were covered with images of a selection of banned books from the Olimpo collection, including examples from all of the areas of censorship that the library delineates: titles that were specifically prohibited, books by disappeared authors and publishers, and books from publishers whose books were burned (see figure 5.9). The catalog expresses the center's pride at the international recognition of the Olimpo center at the book fair, where the library was an emblem of all the memory work the group is engaged in: "We feel that the presence of these books in Frankfurt brings recognition to the Library and to all the work that we have been developing in the Recuperation Program. . . . This site should denounce not only our friends' physical extermination but also

Figure 5.9. Olimpo's banned books at the 2010 Frankfurt book fair; © Agencia EFE; courtesy of EFE

all the forms of State Terrorism in our country" (Cerruti, *Ex centro*, 2010 edition, 65).

Banned Books on the Move: Libros que Muerden

While the memory centers dedicate space to banned books and invite visitors to read and interact with them, another group in Argentina takes collected banned books on the road. Reading activities in public space in Latin American cities often exploit transit, movement, and circulation. Previously prohibited books have come out of hiding, have survived being burned and buried, and are on the move as part of their newfound freedom. In traveling exhibits, mobile reading programs, performances, and workshops, the books reach new readers with the stories of their own trajectories as banned books added to the stories inside their covers.

In 2013, a series of programs and events celebrated the thirtieth anniversary of the end of the dictatorship, under the banner "Thirty Years of Argentine Democracy." One of these anniversary programs included the production of ten prizewinning documentaries. The contest sponsored by the Centro de Producción e Investigación Audiovisual, Radio y Televisión Argentina and the national Secretaría de

Cultura received 170 proposals; the ten winners were offered grants allowing them to complete their films.

One of the films celebrates a beloved elementary school teacher, Paulino Guarido, who continued to read banned children's books to his students in a town in Greater Buenos Aires, despite having been kidnapped and imprisoned with his pregnant wife early in the dictatorship years. Guarido was released after eleven days; his wife and child never reappeared. When he returned to his teaching position, Guarido was determined to continue reading imaginative stories with his students even if they had been banned, so he covered the books with paper, gave them alternative titles, and never revealed the authors' names so the students could write essays, draw pictures, and work on projects related to the books without anyone alerting the authorities. This was his form of resistance, a method of revolutionary struggle at a time when "the most beautiful books were banned and burned along with burning the whole society" (Guarido in Carreras). One of Guarido's former first-grade students, Luján Di Pasca, now an elementary teacher herself, helps organize a class reunion with their teacher. The former students, adults with their own families, reveal their vivid memories of Guarido's reading and the literary imagination and social values that have stayed with them, and Guarido realizes "in a marvelous and brutal way" that it was worth the risk (Carreras). For Di Pasca, reading stories "opens the window to the imagination, to curiosity, it transports you, and that's freedom. Stories are freedom" (Carreras).

The film concludes as Di Pasca and her first-grade class take a field trip to a community library where there is a temporary exhibit of banned children's books. After the students spend some time browsing through the original editions of the banned books, Guarido reads to them from one of Devetach's most beloved titles, *La planta de Bartolo*, one of the books that he had disguised and read to his own first-grade class. The exhibit and public reading program were offered by Libros que Muerden (Books that Bite), a collection of banned children's literature in La Plata that has been traveling around the country since 2006.

Libros que Muerden is an initiative of La Grieta, an arts and culture collective in La Plata, in Buenos Aires province, that since 2006 has been collecting children's and young adult books that were banned during the last Argentine dictatorship. Their library, Biblioteca Popular La Chicharra, is named after their small independent press Ediciones La Chicharra. The group emerged out of neighborhood activism in the 1990s in the Meridiano V district,[16] published a journal (also called *La Grieta*), and gradually expanded its activities to offer arts and literature workshops, public exhibits, and performances. While the library collection and the core activities of the center are directed to youth, the group also leads workshops in art, dance, theater, writing, and reading for adults and senior citizens.

For years La Grieta's activities functioned nomadically in and around the neighborhood, until in 2004 they settled into an abandoned cargo building that belonged to the provincial railroad company (see figure 5.10). Because the railroad line was no longer operating, the group managed to formally occupy the space and transform it into a cultural center for the neighborhood. The two-story brick building has a kitchen; an art studio; a stage for dance, theater, and gymnastics classes and performances; and rooms for reading and writing groups. The banned books collection is housed in an office and conference room. The transitory nature of the space, which originally served as a warehouse for goods being transported by train, suits the group well. As an essay in a catalog documenting a series of La Grieta's art shows points out: "There were products that came in from the country to the city. . . . In the warehouse, abandoned when the provincial train stopped operating, we worked toward creating a place for workshops and classes in art, objects and toys, film, radio, writing and thought, music, dance, theater, and aerial acrobatics, . . . where kids, adolescents, and adults would have a meeting place" (Colectivo La Grieta 147). Literature is at the heart of their projects and programming; as director Gabriela Pesclevi states, "We move around in the world of books. . . . My workshops always revolved around a book" (personal interview, my translation).

The philosophy and overall objectives of La Grieta provide a consistent foundation for all of their activities, including the library of banned books. The group embraces a sense of play, aims to restore human companionship and communication, and engages in continual questioning and debate. These core values and goals clearly respond to the postdictatorship moment and seek to overturn habits and attitudes left over from the period of repression. La Plata suffered the largest rate of disappearances in the country,[17] and the persistent culture of fear and repression lingering after the return to democracy overlapped with economic insecurity during the crisis that came to a head in 2001. "In a climate of mounting fear, few looked for collective

Figure 5.10. La Grieta logo; courtesy of La Grieta

responses. . . . Ties frayed, and even worse, many lost their will, their passion, and the skills to put them together" (Colectivo La Grieta 185). La Grieta's discourse, articulated in published catalogs, brochures, and personal interviews, insists on collective work that intervenes in public space: "meeting the other," "weaving a new texture," "reappropriating public space," and "re-creating the ties of a fragmented society" (Colectivo La Grieta 101, 119, 187). For La Grieta, literature and art are the tools for rebuilding a broken society plagued by alienation, isolation, and distrust.

Furthermore, literature and art, reading and exhibiting, go hand in hand at La Grieta. While accumulating books for the library and launching multimedia workshops, the group began to experiment with what they called *muestras ambulantes* (moveable exhibits): multidisciplinary art shows in alternative spaces throughout the neighborhood. Instead of being held in galleries and museums, these exhibits occupied local businesses, neighbors' garages, the street, and the sidewalk. There have been four of these moveable exhibits between 1995 and 2007, lasting from four days to two weeks.[18] All of the *muestras* included reading events and book exhibits, such as a pop-up book display, story reading for children, and books available for browsing in local businesses. The event Libros Animados, an early example of La Grieta's banned book workshops called Libros que Muerden, was hosted in a neighbor's garage. Its banner, posted in the street, announced the event as "a library to touch, browse, and open up worlds" (Colectivo La Grieta 80–81). Much more than an exhibit to look at,

Libros animados brought the books to life through play, dramatic games, and tactile experiences, strategies that the group puts into action with banned books as well. In fact, the phrase *Libros animados* figures as a sort of subtitle on the brochure for Libros que Muerden.

La Grieta's commitment to intervening in public space grows out of the group's street activism leading up to and following the economic crisis in 2001–2002. That relationship to activism in common public spaces also reflects the group's nomadic existence before the collective moved into the warehouse, and has persisted since they found a physical home there. As the multimedia *muestras ambulantes* demonstrate, "taking art into the neighborhood recalls art's quotidian character. Art is not an exceptional line of work but rather a daily practice" (Colectivo La Grieta 29). Reading literature, along with other arts experienced in the exhibits, is recognized as a practice of everyday life rather than a segmented, exceptional activity (Certeau). "It's not about bringing art to the people, but rather about putting the people into the art" (Colectivo La Grieta 91). Making use of garages, local businesses, plazas, and sidewalks encourages neighbors to rediscover their own surroundings, "with the blinds pulled up, the chair out on the sidewalk" (Colectivo La Grieta 165). La Grieta rejects the idea that art requires a ceremonial space, a museum or a gallery, to be appreciated; rather, "we take art intentionally from the center to the periphery and we move it into daily life" (Colectivo La Grieta 173). The epigraph for the catalog quotes Christian Ferrer praising the *muestras ambulantes* for their itinerant and mobile nature: "Never before had we known of a fragmented exhibit that circulated through the city, sidestepping those ecological preserves for painters called galleries. An exhibit that is intermittent and unbeatably public. A nomadic show" (Colectivo La Grieta 7).

La Grieta's library of banned books has also become "unbeatably public." The Biblioteca Popular La Chicharra, housed at La Grieta, began with eighteen books and has grown to some 350, mostly children's and young adult literature but also textbooks, encyclopedias, and other reference books that were banned during the country's last two dictatorships in the 1960s, 1970s, and 1980s. The group started to collect banned books in 2006, on the thirtieth anniversary of the coup that brought the last military dictatorship to power. Pesclevi, who teaches social work at the Universidad Nacional de La Plata, sees a close connection between retrieving lost and hidden books and the work the center does with a needy local population: "Why not redeem these books, and everything that happened to them, especially since we work with stigmatized populations?" (personal interview, my translation).[19]

In the context of historical commemoration of the beginning of the dictatorship, "the collection of books resonated with the recuperation of rights in Argentina" (Pesclevi, personal interview, my translation). Pesclevi referred to the collection as an archive and proudly showed the books' careful cataloging and storage in acid-free archival boxes (personal interview). As the members add to the collection, they also keep track of bibliographic items that are still missing, and they systematically track editorial series, titles by specific writers, and specific volumes of youth encyclopedias that were banned, doing so in an attempt to complete the archive with the very editions that were censored. Although the library has earned official recognition from the municipality and the province, La Grieta does not receive regular funding for its support.[20] Occasional grants help cover practical needs, such as funding from the Dutch company C&A in 2007 and 2008 that paid for air conditioning and for cabinets for the books. La Grieta also manages a small lending library of children's and young adult books (see figure 5.11).

During my visit to La Grieta in 2015, the more I asked members of the collective about their traveling presentations with banned books, the more they told me about the multimedia *muestras ambulantes*. In this insistence, they reoriented my queries toward a better understanding of the thinking behind and experience of the traveling book exhibits. The brochure for Libros que Muerden calls the programming around the traveling books "essentially itinerant." While the group is committed to the ongoing collection, what it values most is the movement and experience of the books with the public. Beyond the archival significance of collecting original editions of censored titles, the group exploits the books as *disparadores* (triggers) for discussion, play, and critical thinking.

The exhibits, public reading, workshops, and activities that La Grieta has mobilized with the banned book collection include events in other parts of Argentina as well as La Plata. The facilitators plan each exhibit installation and the accompanying activities in accordance with the space and its overall mission in order to have the greatest impact. Thus each show reimagines how previously censored books can prompt discussions about repression, experiences of exile, and freedom of expression. One of the exhibits, held at La Plata's famous

Figure 5.11. Shelf at La Grieta; author photo; courtesy of La Grieta

Museum of Natural Sciences, was scheduled to coincide with children's school vacations.[21] The group chose children's books related to animals and the natural world, used specimens from the museum in the visual part of the exhibit, brought animal toys and games, and created simple props and costumes for the children to use to role-play becoming different animals (see figures 5.12 and 5.13).

As Florencia Bossié affirms, "Each place that they arrive is transformed into a workshop, a moment of action, in which the stories pour out of the books with a suggestive, playful, vibrant, troubling tone. We're more interested in posing questions than stating certainties and, above all, allowing the readers to encounter them, because we think of books as brilliance, as trenches, as instruments for change."

According to Pesclevi, La Grieta members conceptualize literature "not as an escape but rather as the invention of worlds" (personal interview, my translation). Fiction particularly lends itself to their inventive, creative, performative approach. Manuel Negrín, a La Grieta

Figure 5.12. Poster for Libros que Muerden event; photo courtesy of La Grieta

Figure 5.13. Walrus role-playing activity; photo courtesy of La Grieta

member and workshop leader with the traveling exhibits, mentioned that they always begin by reading the books and telling the stories, not by a history of the books' censorship and how they were rediscovered, which he said would put everyone to sleep (personal interview, my translation). The imaginative qualities of the books, their language and images, take center stage; the history of the books as objects comes into play later. The performances that accompany reading banned books at La Grieta, Olimpo, and the Archivo also counter the dictatorial regime's military shows of force and terrorizing acts in public space, giving voice to previously silenced texts. As Taylor points out in *Disappearing Acts*, during the dictatorship, "everyone was performing. Everyone was trying to look the part that offered them security and relative invisibility (if they wanted to stay out of the fray) or access and information (if they were somehow involved)" (109). The programming in public of these collections of banned books overturns the regime's prohibition, repression, censorship, and silencing to reassert a healthy, expressive imaginative world.[22]

While the texts at the center of Libros que Muerden pertain to children's literature, the workshops and activities involve participants of all ages. The publicity for the events tends to underscore this, often mentioning "children and adults," and the sessions incorporate strategies to "incite reflection about censorship and the construction of collective memory" (poster for museum exhibit). In the same way that the multiarts exhibits in the neighborhood sought to break down the barriers between insiders and outsiders, between sacred exhibit spaces and everyday surroundings, the animated presentations that accompany the banned books exhibits work to connect adults and children, appealing to the youth audience and to the parents, grandparents, older siblings, and caregivers who are responsible for bringing the children, as well as to the adult professionals who are associated with the exhibit sites. For Verónica Barbera, an art teacher and La Grieta member who works with the traveling book exhibits and workshops, the most memorable part of the event is watching others experience the books. She notes a particular empathy among participants as they connect their own life stories with the collection and share anecdotes about their own households' books, such as volumes hidden between the slats of venetian blinds. "People participate, uncover, and reveal their own stories" she says (Barbera and Negrín, my translation). The organizers and workshop leaders themselves represent a broad generational span.

Pesclevi reveals an episode from her own childhood that is foundational to the work she is doing today with banned books. After school she and her friends often played with books, setting up a pretend bookstore on the sidewalk outside her house. At the beginning of the last dictatorship, a neighbor who would stop by and chat with the girls warned them that one of the books they had on display was prohibited (the Spanish version of *Uses and Abuses of Psychoanalysis*, by Lawrence Friedman), and suggested they keep it inside. Pesclevi was bewildered, and she never forgot this incomprehensible warning:

> I saved that book with the uneasiness of someone who doesn't understand what it's all about. For over thirty years it stayed with me like a symbol, like something that becomes precious and secret, that never got lost in spite of moves, hiatuses, silences, and it probably holds much more that I even knew at the time. The book in question has signified, on a personal level, a point of departure leading me to a way of looking at memory in which things speak, things describe us, and books are among those things. (*Libros que muerden* 289)

The traveling book exhibit helps others rediscover their own childhood books, reexamine why they were targeted by the censors, and work with their own memories of the period, all while encouraging children to construct new memories around beloved books and illustrations.

The book *Libros que muerden: Literatura infantil y juvenil censurada durante la última dictadura cívico-militar 1976–1983* (Books that Bite: Children's and Young Adult Literature Censored during the Last Civil-Military Dictatorship 1976–1983), edited by Pesclevi, was published in 2013 by the National Library. The title glosses the common Argentine expression "Books don't bite!," used to encourage children to read. Pesclevi's book accomplishes a number of important tasks as both an exhibit catalog and an annotated bibliography of censored youth literature. As a catalog, the book prints color photos of more than a hundred book covers included in La Grieta's library of banned books, along with examples from some of their pages, with text and illustrations (see figure 5.14). Organized into chapters devoted to authors, illustrators, publishers, textbooks, religious texts, and reference books, the volume concludes with a complete bibliography of the library's collection. Along with photographs and basic identification information of the authors and books highlighted, it prints censorship decrees, interviews with writers, photographs of book burnings, and

Figure 5.14. Pages from *Libros que muerden*; © Gabriela Pesclevi; author photo; courtesy of Gabriela Pesclevi

news clippings and posters from the period. The book chronicles specific cases of censorship, notorious book burnings, and histories of the most prestigious presses that were targeted by the regime to document the controversies surrounding youth literature under the dictatorship.

La Grieta members are proud that the book was published by the National Library, and they appreciate the demonstration of state support for their initiative, but they insist that the real work remains in collecting books and sharing them with the public. Libros que Muerden—the book and the traveling exhibits and programs—is both an archive and a repertoire, to gloss Taylor's meditation on these terms: the catalogue, the collected books, and the traveling participatory reading experiences gather and preserve books and also insist on performing them as a method for "learning, storing, and transmitting knowledge" (*The Archive and the Repertoire* 16). A review of the catalog echoes the group's effort to veer away from museification: the book "is not intended to highlight the exhibit, as if it were a rare specimen conserved in amber" (Huergo). Tapping on the book cover, Pesclevi affirmed the project as "an experience more than research. . . . Our project was to find, one book at a time, those that had been banned, and that's the most important story, not this book" (personal interview, my translation).

Despite Pesclevi's disclaimer, the book *Libros que muerden* does represent an impressive research effort and provides a reference point for both La Grieta's library and the wider topic of censorship, repression, and the history of publishing in Argentina. The volume's aesthetic is as carefully considered as its contents: "a strident aesthetic, like the aesthetic of children's books" (Huergo) seems to re-create the books it celebrates by relying on fonts, lettering, colors, and a collage effect to reproduce the effect of rereading them.

The Biblioteca Popular La Chicharra is named appropriately after the cicada, a noisy, chattering insect. In the library's name it refers to "a very chatty person," as well as to a whistling toy (Moliner vol. 1, p. 604). The library's traveling exhibits and workshops restore these books through public display and reading aloud, reversing the secrecy and silence of censorship. The workshops perform the books through movement, music, play, and animation, which draw the participants into an aesthetically and politically charged experience. Pesclevi elaborates on her own and La Grieta's conception of reading as an act that can be performed anywhere and that produces subjective interpersonal encounters:

> Reading disseminated in all possible forms.
> Reading as an act.
> Reading inside, alongside a thermos—in the rattling of the train to Buenos Aires.
> The reading lighthouse—refuge—gesture—tone—possibilities—uncertainties.
> Yesterday J. M. Coetzee came to mind, and I jotted down:
> If there's anything that literature is not . . .
> It is not objective.
> It is not impersonal.
> And so it went, although the definitions are not that interesting, the sketches scribbled out that
> can keep being rewritten, over and over again.
>   . . .
> Not a whit of the picturesque or the infantile.
> Garden and conflicts.
> The issue of language, of migration, of coming together with others.
> Excuses for talking about marginal things, about remote things, and about those that are right next to us. (Pesclevi, "La lectura")

Reading undoes censorship by resuscitating these books through acting, reacting, sketching, scribbling, reinventing, and embracing all their stories in new public places that are, as Pesclevi maps them, near, far, and in between.

Objects in Space: Urban Collections and Performative Resignification

The collections and exhibits of banned books mentioned here reveal public initiatives that remember censorship by using books as concrete material evidence. As the catalog essay on Olimpo states, exploring the process of repression and censorship demands "the need to understand the continuous relationship that exists between people and objects" (Cerruti, *Ex centro*, 2010 edition, 66). Elizabeth Grosz offers a pertinent view of the object as it connects with culture and space: "The thing is what we make of the world rather than simply what we find in the world, the way we are able to manage and regulate it according to our needs and purposes. . . . The thing is an outlined imposition we make on specific regions of the world so that these regions become comprehensible and facilitate our purposes and projects, even while limiting and localizing them" (170).

Grosz discusses "the Thing" as an entity that contributes to human attempts to situate ourselves in the world; without solid objects we cannot make sense of the space around us. Banned books are things that allow us to perceive their movement and change. These books that once circulated freely among readers, then had to be hidden or burned or buried, and finally reappeared to be collected in libraries trace a particular cartography that transcends their apparent static material objectivity.

Scholarship on material culture from a variety of fields complements Grosz's theory of things by taking into consideration their movement. In his definition of objects of consumption and the cultural politics of value, the anthropologist Arjun Appadurai insists on "things-in-motion." Transactions of exchange determine the value and the meaning of things according to their use and their trajectory (Appadurai, "Introduction" 5). In particular, the digression in the expected path of an object of consumption reveals how that object changes and challenges its preestablished order: "The diversion of commodities from their specified paths is always a sign of creativity or crisis, whether aesthetic or economic" (Appadurai, "Introduction" 26). In the case of Argentine banned books, that diversion signals both crisis and creativity: the crisis of political repression and the creative repurposing in the books' collection and recirculation.

In the cultural biography of the Latin American book, the story of banned books is an essential chapter. The cultural biography of an object, according to the anthropologist Igor Kopytoff, considers the object "a culturally constructed entity, imbued with culturally specific meanings, classified and reclassified within culturally constituted categories" (68). Banned books in Latin America fall into the category of used goods whose story is prized, "a use that is imagined, that is located in a historic past, and that is valued above 'new'" (Gregson and Crewe 8).[23] As they move among new readers after having been discarded, censured, hidden, and silenced, the books discussed here, whether housed in archival collections in recuperated memory sites or in temporary traveling exhibits, are continually resignified. When they are rediscovered, banned books reclaim their value and use as they are read aloud, publically reanimated, collectively brought back to life. They are resignified according to their spatial trajectories and as members of a gradually reconstituted set.[24]

The "materialization of memory" that is so significant in reconstructing the story of censorship rests not only on the books but also on the places where repression was carried out. The reopened prisons and torture centers become "zones of the past that have been lost and disappeared, locations that become key for performing different practices of reading and imagining those (political) pasts and the (dis)connections with the present" (Draper 9). While Draper's use of *reading* here is most likely metaphorical, referring to the semiotic process of decoding physical places and material objects for signs of the past, in the case of banned books that reading is both metaphorical and literal. The urban location of these libraries makes their initiatives all the more accessible to residents and visitors, turning them into truly public reading sites. In Paola Hernández's discussion of the former ESMA in Buenos Aires, she points out how cities "led the way in creating spaces in which to perform cultural memory" (68). The collections of banned books discussed here are rooted in urban space; they intersect with neighborhood identities and rely on local interaction and participation.

Particularly at Olimpo, where the garage functioned as a clandestine detention and torture center in the middle of a bustling Buenos Aires neighborhood, the arrests, interrogations, torture, and disappearances had a direct impact on the surrounding residents and businesses. Interviewing the neighbors about their memories and awareness of the center was one of the first strategies in recuperating the space, and installing signage and identification for the building were preliminary steps in adapting the space as a memory site. La Grieta in La Plata

Figure 5.15. Display of banners at the Archivo, Córdoba; photo by Selma Cohen; courtesy of Selma Cohen and the Archivo Provincial de la Memoria

evolved from an urban neighborhood association, and outreach to the neighborhood residents, schools, and businesses is its primary mission. The Archivo Provincial de la Memoria in Córdoba exploits its location in the center of town for various events and programs. For example, every Thursday at the Archivo a display of banners with photos of the disappeared crisscrosses the Pasaje Santa Catalina (see figure 5.15). The scheduling of this display is not arbitrary, but coincides with the Thursday demonstrations (*rondas*) by the Mothers of the Plaza de Mayo, which in Córdoba take place at the Plaza San Martín, directly across the street from the Archivo.[25] This ongoing weekly event at the entrance to the Archivo underscores for passersby "how visible and urban the space was" (Archivo website).

Rozza calls this physical archive a "testimonial topography, since the physical materiality of the Museum Site proposes other possible questions and approaches." A section of the Archivo's website documents the group's urban interventions, such as planting trees, engaging in *escraches* (demonstrations that publicly shame perpetrators of crimes against citizens), flying banners marking kidnapping sites, dramatically intervening during human rights trials, and using public art to remember state violence and commemorate the disappeared:

> These markers intended to materialize memory take on their force and meaning through spontaneity, in day-to-day life and improvisation that (re)constructs their forms. Forms that absorb the various expressions of those who intervene with a flower, a word, a letter, a tear, a smile. These initiatives of public marking aim to transform space into a place of memory. Place is the site where memory is expressed, exists, happens, forging a collective project for the future. (Archivo website)

Memory work, as all these collections underscore, links the past to the present and the future by opening the archive to programming that brings places, documents, and objects into conversation with the public. Collection of banned books and organization of programs around them at La Grieta, the Archivo, and Olimpo "are burdened with the complicated task of satisfying the needs of competing temporalities. . . . They treat materials—buildings, plots of land, landscapes—that exist in and express different temporal registers" (Bishop 564). The libraries are interactive, like the memory sites where some of them are housed, inviting "the visitor to participate and collaborate in the vast undertaking of collective remembrance" (P. Hernández 68).

Figure 5.16. Rayuela from the video *Los condenados de la tierra*; © Marcelo Brodsky; courtesy of Marcelo Brodsky

These libraries of banned books all incorporate their urban location as an integral part of their memory pedagogy. Closely related to their urban context, they share a commitment to circulation and participation either at their centers or through outreach to other public venues). As Pesclevi insisted regarding the published catalog *Libros que muerden*, it is the story of the books, the process of collecting, and reading them as a tool for memory work with a public audience that are the real goals. Publicly circulating, displaying, reading, and discussing these books re-creates communities of readers who participate in a joyful imaginative experience. The books are less monuments to repression than stimuli for play, fantasy, movement, and music. These collections launch the books from the shelf to the library circle, to the street, to the parade, and from the page to the banners and tours and scenes and games that make up festivals, exhibits, and workshops.

The sense of play that children's literature in particular generates is reminiscent of Julio Cortázar's *Rayuela*, his novel in which the reading process itself is playful, nonlinear, experimental, and imaginative, turning the reader into the text's accomplice. A hopscotch board visually guides the player's journey as she jumps from square to square, symbolic of the cosmic journey from earth to heaven. Brodsky's installation of unearthed books titled *Los condenados de la tierra* has a photographic component, a photo collage of the books, their covers decayed and their pages mangled, that recalls the fragmentation of a collection in process (see figure 5.16). "These texts rescued from oblivion can be read in many ways, like a Hopscotch extracted—with Julio's permission—from its tomb. These are silenced words that have re-emerged into the light and that try to hold onto their meaning. Finally legible, recomposed, resurrected from the earth after being abandoned, they are once again in search of readers" (Brodsky, *Nexo* 84–85).

The libraries of banned books at Olimpo, the Archivo Provincial de la Memoria, and La Grieta help find those readers. They are readers who will dance, play, dress up, shout, sing, march, and act—precisely the complicit readers Cortázar sought to encourage. The books that these libraries bring back to life, like the books that Brodsky honors in his installation and photographs, reach readers who not only read the past but actively engage with the present toward a future that welcomes unlimited fantasy.

CONCLUSION

Stories at the Intersection

We're not just living in any random time, and we need to grasp the current moment to think about where we are right now. We need to make way, join in, and attract voices with no strings attached, wild readings with no particular pedagogy. We're proposing zigzags, crossings, ravines, rhythms. Inhabit and habilitate. Mix, radiate, replicate.
GABRIELA PESCLEVI, PERSONAL E-MAIL COMMUNICATION

Reading allows us to get back on track when we need to, and to experience simultaneously a connection to others and the feeling of our own individuality.
MICHELE PETIT, *LEER EL MUNDO*

Three boys sit on mud-colored ground, knees bent, hunched over their open notebooks, pencils in hand, while a girl stands above them, her skinny legs emerging from a tattered dress, and reads to them from her open book. The girl's stance, one foot a bit in front of the other, indicates confidence; her head pops up against the dirty white background of the rough wall behind her, while the boys are all framed in the dark ground. She occupies her position firmly, rising into the narrow but brighter horizon. She knows how to read. The boy in the foreground, cross-legged and smudge-faced, gazes out from under the brim of his cap past the viewer; his eyes have a look of both bewilderment and concentration.

Juanito Laguna aprende a leer (Juanito Laguna Learns to Read) is one of Argentine painter Antonio Berni's Juanito Laguna series of mixed media works that combines traditional painterly materials with

Figure 6.1. *Juanito Laguna aprende a leer*; © Antonio Berni; used by permission of the Archivo Antonio Berni

garbage: cardboard, discarded metal, fragments of advertisements, signs, industrial logos, and newspapers (see figure 6.1). In this canvas, the collage provides texture and depth; others in the series further exploit the theme of reading with the inclusion of numbers, prices, commercial logos, and advertisements incorporated into the scenes. Berni dramatizes urban poverty in the Juanito Laguna collages, which are set in the *villa*, Buenos Aires's slums; he uses the very materials that residents rely on to build their makeshift homes. In *Juanito Laguna Learns to Read*, playing school in the street takes the place of the classroom. Fernando Degiovanni calls this work "an open air reading lesson" and points out how Berni's work vindicates all kinds of reading.

Berni takes cardboard and other discarded objects—he calls them "leftovers" (quoted in Perazzo 61)—and works them into his canvases in order to tell a story; in this case, a story about reading. The materials themselves become part of the tale, serving as the narrative backstory of use, refuse, and reuse. Similarly, cartonera publishers rely on reused cardboard for their covers, not only to contain the texts but also to visually tell the story of their own production. This transposition of ordinary materials in Latin American urban culture—where tin cans and bottle caps find their way to museum galleries, and cardboard binds the fiction and poetry of young writers—parallels the revalorization of reading as a common, daily activity and the rediscovery of the street as a space for cultural expression.

In the previous pages, I have traveled along streets, traversed plazas, ridden on high-speed buses and subways, browsed in libraries, and ventured into memory centers to explore the story of reading in Latin American public space. This concluding section pauses at the intersections where these programs' broad reach and common goals cross paths. A description of Bogotá's Libro al Viento could well apply to all the programs studied in this book. They all champion reading as an activity that "should be everyone's right and be accessible to all" and promote reading works of literature that are "resignified and appropriated in unexpected ways." The programs "offer literature at no charge to sectors of the population who are removed from the habitual artistic and cultural centers of the city, as well as to the general public, exposing them to works outside of the texts that they are accustomed to and that can therefore burst into their daily lives and open new meanings and horizons" (Libro al Viento's website). The surprising and unexpected reactions to these literary experiences occur in part due to their unconventional settings—often outside typical educational and cultural institutions. The programs resignify not only the written texts but also the everyday public spaces that the texts occupy and animate. As Gabriel Zaid elaborates in *Leer*, culture "manifests and reproduces itself live and out loud" in the conversations between written texts and readers who converse freely and in open spaces—not only in classrooms (113).

While the Latin American urban public reading programs discussed in the previous five chapters might appear as discrete initiatives, they share common cultural motivations and political circumstances. Whether sponsored by high-level municipal institutions or grassroots organizations, these programs all emerge as a response to a renewed engagement with the public, in terms of both readership and audience, and a sphere of civic space and interaction. Language is one of the key ingredients in the culture of the public, and recognizing its potential is "the first step in a project to win back and expand the common and its powers" (Hardt and Negri ix). Programming in public reading takes literary works from the realm of individual, private reading and resituates them where they can occupy and enliven communal urban places. Some examples of overlapping projects confirm that a wider conversation has been unfolding where literary reading extends the reach of the lettered city.

The connections among these programs, collections, events, and series cross national borders as well as programmatic lines. Similar initiatives reveal how major public reading events in one place can inspire others elsewhere. For example, the Buenos Aires *La ciudad contada* anthology of narratives by a group of international visiting writers, one of the culminating activities of that city's World Book Capital year, prompted a similar project in Bogotá's Libro al Viento series. The Colombian writer Antonio García Ángel, who was invited to participate in the Buenos Aires readings and anthology, subsequently became the literary editor of Libro al Viento in Bogotá. He organized his own event of visiting writers in Bogotá and edited the anthology *Bogotá contada*, a compilation of narratives based on the visitors' impressions of the city. The event and anthology were so successful that Libro al Viento hosted a second round, called *Bogotá contada 2.0*, with another anthology published in 2016. Always underscoring the local urban experience, these events also combined national and international writers in public readings and lectures, where the narrative impressions capture the familiarity of home turf as well as the perspective of writers newly discovering Buenos Aires's and Bogotá's charms and challenges.

Another transnational project was held in 2010 when the Olimpo former torture and detention center in Buenos Aires hosted a presentation by several independent publishers who announced a contest inviting letters about personal stories of exile and displacement. The contest was sponsored by an Argentine small press, Editorial Retazos, and the Bolivian cartonera group Yerba Mala. The book of winning letters, titled "Stories, Anecdotes, and a Thousand Things that You Don't Want to Only Be Kept in Your Memories, Because You Want Them to Be Free and to Help Others Who Want to Understand What Migration Means," would be coedited by the Argentine and Bolivian publishers (mentioned in Cerruti 2010, 71). Demonstrating the Olimpo center's commitment to hosting events that go beyond the issues of historical memory related to the dictatorship, this event honors testimonial writing and more recent memory work around Bolivian immigration to Argentina. The recognition of Yerba Mala Cartonera, one of the first wave of Latin American alternative cardboard publishers, in a repurposed Argentine memory center offers an example of contemporary writing and publishing whose topic and contributors are international. The project reaches out to a wide audience in a public setting where cooperation among the various groups enhances all of their missions.

Beyond shared literary and aesthetic sensibilities, all of these projects emerge out of common circumstances: a reaction against neoliberal policies and their consequences at the local, national, and regional levels, and in some cases, a contribution to ongoing political and social transitions after periods of violence and authoritarian rule. Much of the cross-pollination among public reading programs stems from the work of cartonera publishers, independent collectives that organized precisely to combat the results of multinational publishing consolidation. Although these groups are independent, they have maintained ties with one another informally because the alternative models inspire more groups, and the editors train one another and meet in person at independent book fairs and symposia.

One of the public reading intersections involves the cartonera publisher La Sofía Cartonera and the Córdoba memory center. At the Archivo Provincial de la Memoria, a handmade cardboard shelf decorated with markers announces the Latin American Cartonera Archive. La Sofía is the only cartonera group affiliated directly with a university (the Faculty of Philosophy and Humanities at the National University of Córdoba), and this project of cardboard bookmaking with regional collaboration pertains to one of the group's university-funded programs, Desacartonando la Cultura (Uncardboarding Culture), whose subtitle in English is Network of Cartonera Publishers for Regional Integration and Resignifying Latin American Memory. A selection of forty titles from different cartonera groups housed in a cardboard archive in the library of the Archivo Provincial de la Memoria creates common cause between alternative, eco-friendly publishing and historical memory work throughout the region. The inside cover of each of the books articulates the initiative's goals: "to contribute to critical reflection around the relationships between culture and democracy."

La Sofía's publications include local writers and titles with a focus on women's rights and sexuality, a topic that the Córdoba center also highlights in its programming. La Sofía's book *Sexo y trabajo* (Sex and Work), for example, offers historical background, legal advice, and testimonial accounts of sex workers in Argentina (Aravena and Maccioni). La Sofía Cartonera members have led bookmaking workshops in community libraries, elementary schools, and prisons. The connection between a memory site, its library of banned books, and the cartonera collection demonstrates the reach of these public reading initiatives. Rather than pursuing a narrow agenda, the various parties join together to support and reinvigorate the public through reading.

These relationships of mutual respect are more than alliances or passive gestures of recognition; alternative publishers and book collectors at memory centers make common cause through individual and collective perseverance.

Additional points of contact between cartonera publishing and other public reading efforts involve independent libraries and contributions to the field of cultural management. The Brazilian cardboard publisher Magnolia Cartonera in Curitiba produced a how-to book for establishing small, free, independent libraries titled *Ideias para bibliotecas livres* (Ideas for Free Libraries). The Facebook post announcing the book calls it "a practical manual that helps anyone who reads it transform the desire to create a free library or reading promotion activity into reality." The eighty-eight page book covers key elements in setting up an independent library, such as how to encourage book donations, work with recyclers, develop a sustainable structure, and maintain independence in the face of political and religious ideologies. The book is cosponsored by Bibliotecas do Brasil, a blog written by former public librarians who now promote reading in unconventional settings. The blog also announced a book by Daniele Carneiro titled *Guia prático para bibliotecas comunitárias* (Practical Guide for Community Libraries). The Brazilian group's commitment to cultural and political autonomy, one of the cornerstones of cartonera collectives, motivates many reading initiatives that work outside of conventional institutional frameworks.

Pairings between grassroots projects and high-level government agencies or municipal institutions are another fascinating intersection, in this case of scale. Although most of the projects explored here were either institutionally or municipally based or independently generated, many exchanges and collaborations blur structural lines. The independently proposed projects under Bogotá, un Libro Abierto that were funded by the city during the World Book Capital year are prime examples of independent initiatives that originated as *autogestionados* being supported and funded by a huge institution. Another example is the Córdoba group La Sofía Cartonera, an alternative publisher directly affiliated with a major public university that seeks public funding from prestigious granting agencies. In spite of La Sofía's academic affiliation, the group's goals and mission rest firmly in decentralizing civic engagement in cultural life. The group's books enumerate two principal goals, printed inside the book covers: "first, to assure the effective access, enjoyment, and availability of cultural goods; and second, to promote active citizen participation in the process of production and management of those goods, decentralizing creative endeavors and making them accessible to everyone." In the context of the lettered city that public reading challenges, enhances, and expands, the commitment to access and wide reach necessitates mutual reliance between large institutions and small grassroots initiatives.

These intersections among separate and independent programs connect public reading in different cities and countries and with varying levels of municipal support. Even when these programs' scale of outreach appears circumscribed, in keeping with their scope (ranging from extremely narrow and local in the case of a small library in an urban neighborhood to international in the case of Buenos Aires's World Book Capital campaign), close observation reveals shared elements that confirm how interrelated they are. In Alfons Martinell's overview of interactions in professional development in Latin American cultural management, he praises a dynamic field that benefits from modes and planning that draw from both the public and private sectors, and from a broad array of institutions, universities, and publishing houses (102–103). He concludes that cultural and multilateral cooperation leads to the most effective and far-reaching implementation "through the evolution of processes of coproduction, and not always for profit, [that] have created a climate of mutual trust" (103). Most of the examples I've outlined here are not so much coproduced projects but informal cooperative relationships, yet they demonstrate how the value of urban public reading motivates very different kinds of initiatives.

What unites these reading initiatives is the basic principal of freely circulating, noncommercial printed literary materials intervening in public space and accessible to all, which represents a shared response to the consequences of the region's political situations and economic policies. Public reading insists on extensive access and no- or low-cost materials, reflecting Michael Hardt and Antonio Negri's view that "capital is in crisis" (142). The politics of memory and the struggle toward reconciliation and peace also pervade many of these initiatives, where fragile peace accords and ongoing transitions from violence and authoritarian regimes have eroded civic interactions and cast a shadow over—or in some cases completely obstructed—cultural expression. The neoliberal economic policies over the last few decades, in many countries implemented under authoritarian regimes, exacerbated income inequality and abandoned the public and the local in favor of private and global investment. The disastrous effects on culture and public amenities prompted a reassessment, particularly in cities, and since 2000 the emergence of public reading initiatives throughout the region is part of that reaction. Political scientists, economists, and cultural critics have been suggesting for a decade that Latin America had entered a postneoliberal era, particularly in the wave of presidential elections that turned to the left (Evo Morales in Bolivia; the populist Peronists, the Kirchners, in Argentina; Hugo Chávez's Bolivarian Revolution in Venezuela; Ollanta Humala in Peru; Lula, followed by Dilma Rousseff, in Brazil; Michelle Bachelet in Chile). New alliances were forged among left-leaning leaders as they curbed the neoliberal zeal of previous administrations and began to refocus attention on the public sphere.

However, following this period of leftist national governments, more recent elections and political struggles in Latin America have signaled a return to neoliberal practices. Since Enrique Peña Nieto was elected president in Mexico in 2012, a new wave of presidential elections has put right-wing leaders in power, such as Mauricio Macri in Argentina in 2015 and Pedro Pablo Kuczynski in Peru in 2016. Further indications of the shifting political scene introduce a series of uncertainties for the future of cultural policy generally and urban public reading specifically. Corruption investigations into Bachelet's family in Chile and the impeachment of Rousseff in Brazil have generated tense internal political dramas that affect the whole region. Other uncertainties include the reestablishment of diplomatic relations between the United States and Cuba, and the political and economic crisis in Venezuela. At the time of this writing, it is unclear what these political panoramas spell for cultural policy nationally and regionally. At the municipal level, where the programs I have studied here are rooted, some mayoral administrations, such as Enrique Peñalosa's second term as mayor of Bogotá (2016–2019), continue to support public investment, but others have fallen in line with presidential trends. The complex relationship between the national and the municipal levels in terms of public policy for culture and the arts needs to be observed over the next few years before it is possible to reach any firm conclusions.

In Latin American urban centers since the new millennium, promoting literary reading through reinvesting in public space has been a high priority. But these recent political transitions have produced enormous uncertainty in the cultural sphere, and it's difficult to predict the future of public reading and of the organizations that initiate, host, and lead these activities. I asked La Grieta director Pesclevi what changes the group was facing since Macri was elected in Argentina in

December of 2015. Her response echoes a number of other Argentine groups' concerns about the future of the already limited public support for their memory spaces and programming. Pesclevi's worries stem not only from the current presidential administration, which promptly cut support from many memory initiatives across the country, but also from the municipal government. The center relies on funding from the city for use of the space, for the library, for utilities, and for student grants. The student grants had been funded, but the city was a full year behind in providing the library funds. The group is quite concerned about what the future holds and yet persists with planning, programming, and acts of solidarity with other groups. As Pesclevi comments:

> Since the end of 2015 we have been living in a climate of deep uncertainty and constant worry. We're worried about the continuation of some projects promoted by the former national government but also about the climate in our city, where we recently saw the violent repression of a workers' demonstration in Plaza Moreno.[1] We're in a state of alert. Our organizational model is to work collectively, so we organize as a neighborhood, through an assembly that we've always been part of. This way we can protest together, as an alternative collective for taking stock of the context. We keep on documenting our practices, training ourselves; it's a time of utmost dedication. We continue to work with young people; we continue to offer workshops in reading and writing for adults. Even though we live in a microclimate where we support each other and carry on, what's going on around us is not only noticeable but hostile and indecipherable. (personal communication, my translation)

Pesclevi's assessment of the national and municipal political climate indicates once again relationships across scale, registering how small, grassroots cultural programs feel the impact of political and economic change. Her comments also highlight one more public-reading intersection: the cooperation between a neighborhood assembly and a cultural center with a library of banned books.

Following the 2001 economic crisis in Argentina, local neighborhood associations supported small libraries and a host of reading and literary activities for their communities as part of the solidarity movement. Many of these assemblies also interconnected with historical memory activities related to the dictatorship. This relationship between the La Plata group and an assembly is not new, as La Grieta cultural center grew out of neighborhood organizing in the years leading to the crisis in Argentina. Collective literary reading initiatives do not operate in a vacuum but participate in local and national public debates and contribute to many other goals and activities—in the case of La Grieta, community organizing and historical memory work around censorship. Pesclevi and her group forge on, even in the face of precarious funding and threatening policies carried out around them.

In his celebrated work on reading in seventeenth- and eighteenth-century France, Roger Chartier notes that although only a small percentage of the population was literate, the printed word played a central role in the circulation of cultural models. This is why he chose to study print culture's "diffusion and effects, by crossing the history of objects with the history of their use, contrasting the strategies of publishers with the tactics of readers" (87). For Chartier, the study of reading illustrates the tensions between private and public life, particularly in cities, where, he notes, reading is "carried out in the sociability of the family, in lettered company, and in the street" (166).

Hardt and Negri also identify the city as a space for political and cultural encounters, and they define the metropolis as the "skeleton and spinal cord of the multitude, that is, the built environment that supports its activity, and the social environment that constitutes a repository and skill set of affects, social relations, habits, desires, knowledges, and cultural circuits" (249).[2] The primary role of the city, for these theorists, is to welcome diverse exchanges and interactions, to discourage harmful conflict, and to help rebuild trust and civic understanding following conflict:

> The politics of the metropolis is the organization of encounters. Its task is to promote joyful encounters, make them repeat, and minimize infelicitous encounters. This requires, first, an openness to alterity and the capacity to form relationships with others. . . . Second, and perhaps more important, it requires learning how to withdraw from conflictive, destructive relationships and to decompose the pernicious social bodies that result from them. . . . Finally, . . . this politics of the metropolis requires discovering how to transform conflictive encounters, as much as possible, into joyful and productive ones. (255)

Urban public reading in Latin America intervenes in public space to invite new interpersonal encounters, to rebuild civic trust, and also to provide "joyful and productive" experiences—to simply have fun.

Public reading prompts live conversations and interactions that directly rely on urban space: transportation infrastructure, the built environment, the diversity of people and neighborhoods, and municipal institutions. One of my favorite examples of joyful reactions to public reading was from a student who attended a lecture at a university where I presented some of this research. The young man approached me after my presentation and expressed incredulity at the notion that municipal governments would fund programs to give away tens of thousands of books on public transportation. I responded that in the case of Libro al Viento in Bogotá, the investment in the books is intended to create an atmosphere of interpersonal exchange that builds trust and promotes a healthier and friendlier civic environment. He still looked puzzled, so I tried to offer him a more concrete scenario. I asked him how he might react if he read a book on a bus or subway and the next week saw another passenger reading that same book. "Would you approach that person, say hello, mention that you just read the same book last week?" His face brightened, his eyes opened wide, and he said, "Now I get it! I could meet a girl!"

To create his fictional episodes with Juanito Laguna, Berni layered oil paint with fragments and objects—cloth, metal, cardboard, the detritus of urban industrial production—to produce textured material, a collage that resists the two-dimensionality of conventional fine art painting. And from his three-dimensional visual work, which included sculpture, he expanded his artistic repertoire to incorporate sound, light, movement, and dance. I have framed these concluding comments with Berni's work not only because it features reading but also for its multidimensionality. His scene of Juanito and his companions learning to read, or perhaps playing at learning to read, dramatizes the little group, each of them occupying a particular role in an interactive exercise. Similarly, the reading programs discussed in these chapters offer group experiences that create conversations.

Although these programs are anchored in print culture, they do not limit their activities to the two-dimensional page of a book; rather, they jump off the page and onto the street through urban public reading's multidimensionality and commitment to public space. They read aloud, circulate books on public transit, create libraries in unlikely spaces, decorate cardboard book covers with paint and collage, design murals, and perform children's literature that had once been silenced in order to bring it back to life, sometimes in the very spaces where lives were obliterated. Although the printed page provides the foundation and many of these initiatives do publish books, public reading insists on dialogues, group experiences, and encounters that are often performative and playful; they invite unexpected outcomes in unconventional spaces open to all. French anthropologist and reading specialist Michele Petit argues for both the intimate and collective benefits of reading. For Petit, imaginative literary experiences work like arrows that attack hesitation and resistance (*Leer el mundo* 126). She warns against the practice of "locking up readers in a room" and instead encourages an inviting opportunity through reading in order to "offer readers passageways, or better yet give them the chance to create their own passageways" (*Lecturas* 27).[3] These programs do not simply strive for more and more readers (although increasing readership is among their goals); they all propose qualitative outcomes whose achievement is difficult to measure, such as the enhancement of interpersonal interaction, intensified local belonging, and shared imaginative experiences. These chapters have investigated reading in urban public space to link these programs' reasons for being to enhancing individual readers' own experiences as well as to the geopolitics of recent and current urban challenges—political, environmental, economic, and architectural.

Juanito Laguna and his friends participate in an outdoor scene of reading and writing. They occupy a basic, unadorned space created out of layered materials found in the street. As the girl stands and reads from her book to the boys, the group forms an open circle. The scene leaves room for the viewer to wander in like another neighborhood kid and complete the circle. Like public reading available in open space, we are all invited to join in and listen to the story.

Notes

Introduction

1. Quotations from sources in Spanish and Portuguese will appear in English translation only. When a published translation is available, I supply a reference to the English translation of the work, with page numbers indicated. Otherwise the translations are mine. The exceptions to this practice are quoted literary passages that appear in the original Spanish or Portuguese, as well as in English translation. Quoted passages of interviews conducted in Spanish will indicate "my translation."

2. Juan Poblete offers an analogous definition of literary reading as "the social and institutional mechanisms by means of which specific texts *are used and socially deployed*" ("Reading as a Historical Practice" 179; Poblete's emphasis). Poblete is paraphrasing Tony Bennett.

3. Pascale Casanova links the emergence of literary language to the cumulative effect of revolts and revolutions that "create the conditions of a pure and autonomous literature, freed from considerations of political utility" (*The World Republic of Letters* 47).

4. While the field of New Literacy Studies has contributed enormously to broadening the definitions of reading and literacy in society, the concept of illiteracy has also benefited from a less judgmental and classist and more politicized and engaged approach. Abraham Acosta redefines illiteracy for Latin American studies as a cultural paradigm of modernization that "foregrounds the social contradictions [such as] subalternity and deculturation" (10). Rather than use the term to refer to the inability to read and write, Acosta relies on *illiteracy* "to express the condition of semiological excess and ungovernability that emerges from the critical disruption of the field of intelligibility within which traditional and resistant modes of reading are defined and positioned. . . . I read illiteracy as tracing the critical contradictions at play between ideologically opposed reading strategies, . . . textual anomalies that emerge between and amid competing ideological appropriations of cultural texts, subverting the very economy of reading that serves as their normative, interpretive matrix" (9). In his reinterpretation of illiteracy as a liberating,

egalitarian, and heterogeneous position, Acosta studies discourses of indigenous resistance such as José María Arguedas's fiction, the Zapatista movement in Chiapas, and Rigoberta Menchú's controversial testimonial work.

5. Sabine MacCormack points out that in the differing versions of this story, it's unclear whether the book was a Bible, a breviary, or some other Christian text. She also recognizes the role of the interpreter and the extreme lack of communication between the Inca and the friar.

6. Rama's book unleashed an ongoing conversation with his concept of the lettered city. Scholarship that reconsiders and critiques Rama's work, and in some cases strives to bring it up to date, resituates his analysis in the context of contemporary technology, geopolitics, and media studies. More than a handful of titles propose going "beyond the lettered city"; they emphasize the "not only lettered" city to account for global culture flows, electronic and online media, and intersections with the visual arts. See, for example, books by Ávaro Cuadra, Boris Muñoz and Silvia Spitta, Edmundo Paz Soldán and Debra Castillo, and Jean Franco as well as several chapters in Mabel Moraña's volume. Many other critics approach reconsidering the lettered city from feminist, indigenous, and racial perspectives.

7. Scholarship and cultural criticism on this period is extensive. See, for example, works by Beatriz Sarlo, Adolfo Prieto, Benedict Anderson, and Jorge Schwartz.

8. See Poblete, *Cambio cultural*, and Sarlo, *Imperio*.

9. The tradition of the reader in Cuban cigar-rolling factories that began in the 1860s also pertains to this oral practice. It continues to this day in Cuba and in some cigar-producing centers in Florida. See Tinajero.

10. Each of the campaigns highlighted only one event or initiative related to digital reading. In Bogotá, the annual international Seminar on Copyright, Culture, and Development, held in conjunction with the book fair, chose the theme, "Books and Their Transition from the Shelf to the Internet." In Buenos Aires, the program donated e-readers to public libraries at the end of the campaign. The several years' difference between the two campaigns explains to some degree the more tentative approach in Bogotá. While the e-readers in Buenos Aires directly promoted digital reading, the seminar in Bogotá served more of a preparatory role for publishers and book professionals to debate and analyze "the life cycle of the book and its new digital environment, . . . facing these new challenges that the digital web poses to writing and reading" (Melguizo and Posada 59).

11. *Popular* in Spanish refers to folk or community-based culture, which is generally informal because it emerges without state or institutional sponsorship, often via grassroots initiatives. In some contexts *popular* refers to rural or traditional cultural forms—of dress, dance, music, or crafts, for example. Popular education, as developed by Paulo Freire and other educational philosophers, contrasts with formal, state-run education and generally refers to rural community literacy programs.

12. Biblioteca de Santiago's outreach to the surrounding community and other parts of the city includes a bookmobile, a reading program for hospitals, library branches in the subway, activities to support the LGBTQ com-

munity, book lending in food markets, and prison programs. The library has also sponsored Gente y Cuentos reading groups in prisons and other alternative venues since 2015.

13. The Uruguayan program Cuento Contigo, for example, was originally called "MonteviLeo" and began in Montevideo.

14. The Cuban government abolished copyright in 1967, considering it an "imperialist notion," but reinstated it in 1977 (Kumaraswami and Kapcia 27 and 30). Because the government employed many writers, they did not have to rely on royalties. Not paying royalties or recognizing copyright for those years coincided with Cuba's common practice of pirating foreign books. Par Kumaraswami and Antoni Kapcia note that the book fair adopted more commercial goals in the mid-1990s during the Special Period (218).

15. The report was published in 2012; the appendix of statistics for more than a dozen book fairs in the region does not specify dates. I assume the information provided by each country pertains to the most recent book fair before publication (2011 or 2012).

16. For more on the book trade and the impact on writers during the Special Period, see Quiroga's chapter "Migrations of the Book" (115–143) and Kumaraswami and Kapcia's chapter 5, "1990s–2000: The years of crisis and reassessment" (132–177).

17. The annual Zócalo book fair started in 2000 and lasts for ten days in October. Sáiz coordinated the fair from 2006 to 2009.

18. Montalván Lamas puts the number of illiterate Cuban citizens at one million and semiliterates at more than one million before the Revolution. Miller claims that Nicaraguan illiteracy was at 40 percent before the Sandinista literacy campaign.

19. Quiroga also underscores the role of the Revolution and the literacy campaign, which "fostered the creation of a continental reading public that consumed the latest Cuban novels and kept abreast of Havana's dazzling literary life . . . [in a] successful struggle to demolish the borders of the lettered city itself" (122).

20. Several other rural reading programs have exhibited long-term commitment. The Grupo Mandrágora has been leading theater workshops for children and teens in rural areas of Tucumán, Argentina, since 1995. The group travels to different villages and leads a full day of activities based on a children's book that the participants read, role-play, set to music, and perform, using props and costumes they design themselves. Grupo Mandrágora also donates books to create children's libraries in churches and community centers where they offer their workshops. In rural areas of Colombia most affected by the violence, reading and creative writing programs involve children and teens. The Laboratorio del Espíritu offers poetry, music, and art classes to children in El Retiro, Antioquía, in a remodeled school that had been abandoned because of this violence. The award-winning Colombian poet Horacio Benavides leads creative writing workshops for children in schools in Cauca.

21. The announcement highlights the following possible areas of research: democratization of public services, cooperatives and nonprofits, public health, housing, media and popular communication, popular education, environmen-

tal protection and management, social movements, and the development of participatory public policy.

22. A 1989 meeting in Washington, DC, sponsored by the Institute for International Economics imposed a "structural adjustment" that promoted more global trade and free-market investment in Latin America. The resulting decisions and agreements, known as the Washington Consensus, were a culmination of policies and practices already in place for years in many Latin American countries.

23. The cities listed in the graphs in *Santiago imaginado* are Buenos Aires, Barcelona, Bogotá, Caracas, La Paz, Lima, Mexico City, Montevideo, Panama City, Quito, and Santiago (Ossa, Richard, and Téllez 150–155). In response to the question about leisure time, reading was the preferred activity in Buenos Aires, Bogotá, Caracas, Mexico City, Montevideo, Quito, and Santiago. A similar graph appears in the volume *Quito imaginado* with the addition of one more city, São Paulo (Aguirre, Carrión, and Kingman Garcés 202).

24. As indicated earlier, literary passages will be quoted in the original with English translation. Unless otherwise indicated with bibliographic references, the translations are my own.

25. Warner insists on this in his discussion of publics and counterpublics, where he titles a section of a chapter: "A public is a relation among strangers" (74–76).

26. A published translation of Reyes's essay offers the following for this statement: "the American mind is more accustomed to the open air; we do not have, there is no place among us for, ivory towers" (Reyes, *Position of America* 37). I have included my own translation to correct the use of "open air" instead of "air of the street" for "aire de la calle," along with several other nuances. The essay was originally published in the Argentine journal *Sur*.

Chapter 1: Campaigning for the Capital

1. The Biblioteca Manuel Gálvez on Avenida Córdoba in Buenos Aires housed, sorted, and prepared the donated books until the *Torre de Babel* was ready to be assembled. Each book was encased in a sealed, weatherproof plastic bag before being installed on the metal mesh of the curving tower's walls. The books were subsequently returned to this library for the permanent multilingual collection.

2. The UNESCO World Book Capitals after Madrid in 2001 were Alexandria, Egypt (2002); New Delhi, India (2003); Antwerp, Belgium (2004); Montreal, Canada (2005); Turin, Italy (2006); Bogotá, Colombia (2007); Amsterdam, Netherlands (2008); Beirut, Lebanon (2009); Ljubljana, Slovenia (2010); Buenos Aires, Argentina (2011); Yerevan, Armenia (2012); Bangkok, Thailand (2013); Port Harcourt, Nigeria (2014); Incheon, Korea (2015); Wroclaw, Poland (2016); and Conakry, Republic of Guinea (2017). The most recently announced is Athens, Greece, for 2018.

3. The mayoral offices in Bogotá have shifted the charge of this minis-

try over the years. The Municipal Institute for Culture and Tourism was renamed in 2006 and became the Ministry of Culture, Recreation, and Sports. The city's public libraries fall under this ministry's office of reading: www.culturarecreacionydeporte.gov.co/institucion.

4. Macri succeeded Fernández de Kirchner as president in 2015.

5. In the middle of 2015, the estimate of displaced persons was well over 6 million.

6. Colombia's libraries benefited from two more grants from the Bill and Melinda Gates Foundation, one for Medellín's public libraries in 2009 and another for Bogotá's libraries in 2011.

7. See Guerrero (174–193) for an overview of these impressive libraries.

8. This event took place on 6 May 2007.

9. During the World Book Capital year, twelve Libro al Viento books were printed, and the series received attention in the municipal Ministry of Culture's monthly newspaper, *Ciudad Viva*.

10. The anthology includes stories by Daniel Alarcón, Gabriela Alemán, Claudia Amengual, Yolanda Arroyo Pizarro, Álvaro Bisama, Rodrigo Blanco, Pablo Casacuberta, João Paulo Cuenca, Junot Díaz, Álvaro Enrigue, Gonzalo Garcés, Antonio García, Wendy Guerra, Eduardo Halfon, Rodrigo Hasbún, Claudia Hernández, John Jairo Junieles, Adriana Lisboa, Pedro Mairal, Fabrizio Mejía Madrid, Ronaldo Menéndez, Santiago Nazarian, Guadalupe Nettel, Andrés Neuman, José Pérez Reyes, Ena Lucía Portela, Pilar Quintana, Santiago Roncagliolo, Ricardo Silva, Verónica Stigger, Karla Suárez, Iván Thays, Antonio Ungar, Leonardo Valencia, Juan Gabriel Vásquez, Jorge Volpi, Carlos Wynter, Alejandro Zambra, and Slavko Zupcic.

11. Íngrid Betancourt Pulecio is a Colombian politician and activist who was kidnapped by the FARC in 2002 and held for over six years until her release in 2008. She has been a Colombian senator and was a presidential candidate at the time she was kidnapped. Betancourt's letter excerpted in *Cartas de la persistencia* was originally published in the weekly news magazine *Revista Semana* in 2007.

12. The Paraderos Paralibros Paraparques are small stands that hold 350 books, installed in parks as extensions of the public library system. Bogotá has had them since 1999, and there are currently fifty-one in the city's parks and over a hundred throughout Colombia. Facilitators from the neighborhood, trained by Fundalectura, open the stands twelve hours per week for community programs and lending.

13. See Rotker, González-Pérez, and Mahieux on the *crónica*. The online journal *Textos Híbridos* is also an excellent source for recent scholarship on the genre.

14. The Juan de Castellanos novel prize was awarded to the Argentine Ariel Magnus for *Muñecas*; honorable mention went to the Colombian Gonzalo España for his novel *La biblioteca*. In the same year España also published a book of literary essays, *Letras en el fuego: El libro en Bogotá*, which was not officially sponsored by the World Book Capital campaign. The book's closing essay, "2007 Lectura y felicidad" (2007 Reading and Happiness), makes reference to the UNESCO award (296).

15. The collection unsurprisingly includes a story that concerns the "Bogotazo," a foundational episode in twentieth-century Colombian history. "Aquel 9 de abril" (That April 9th) by Miguel Ángel Arévalo Duque, tells the story in the form of a fictionalized diary of the 1948 assassination of Jorge Eliécer Gaitán, a popular liberal leader and presidential candidate, which unleashed a series of riots in Bogotá and other cities (Mejía and González Uribe 171–188). The event is often referred to by its date. It is considered the beginning of La Violencia, a period of civil wars during the 1950s, and the root of the country's continuing violence. After several years of peace talks, a tentative agreement between the government and the rebels was reached, but it was voted down in a national referendum in 2015. A revised plan for peace was signed in 2016.

16. Program founder Sarah Hirschman outlines the important role of facilitators, "who will actually run the groups, read the stories, and help propel the discussion" (*People and Stories* 53). The program in the United States calls the facilitators coordinators. Hirschman admits her unease with the name *coordinator*, stating that "it is a poor term for the key role that this particular actor performs but we use it for lack of a better one" (53). I prefer the term *facilitator*, and in Spanish *facilitador* has been adopted as the term for the person who leads the groups in the program in Colombia.

17. The BULA grant to Gente y Cuentos–Colombia covered the costs for my trip to Bogotá, where I trained thirty facilitators, visited programs to offer feedback, and provided orientation to Vélez and her co-coordinators. The documentary video is available on YouTube at www.youtube.com/watch?v =ISRycSRojyU. The program continues to lead reading groups in diverse settings in Colombia. One of the organizers of the BULA grant initiated a new Gente y Cuentos group in Quito, Ecuador. See that group's Facebook site at www.facebook.com/PicnicDePalabrasEcuador/?fref=ts.

18. Jeremy Adelman's intellectual biography of Albert O. Hirschman, *Worldly Philosopher*, devotes a chapter to the "Colombian Years" (295–324).

19. Paulo Freire (1921–1997) was a Brazilian philosopher, educator, and literacy specialist. He is best known for his book *Pedagogy of the Oppressed*, first published in Portuguese in 1968. He was imprisoned and then exiled during the military dictatorship in Brazil in the 1960s. He returned to Brazil in 1980 and was appointed secretary of education for São Paulo in 1988. Freire's theories and methodologies for community education rooted in local knowledge have been extremely influential internationally.

20. Sarah Hirschman's book on the program has also been published in Spanish translation (*Gente y cuentos*). See also my "The Right to Imagine."

21. Here Senn echoes the Iberoamerican Reading Plan–Unlimited, an international agreement signed in 2004 by the ministers of culture and education of numerous countries in the region and supported by the Centro Regional para el Fomento del Libro en América Latina y el Caribe (Regional Center for Promoting the Book in Latin America and the Caribbean, CERLALC).

22. Minujín's best-known installations include the Parthenon of Books, a structure made of 30,000 banned books (the number honors the 30,000 victims of state violence under dictatorship), erected in the middle of Buenos Ai-

res's grand 9 de Julio Avenue to draw attention to censorship under the dictatorship just as the country returned to democratic rule in 1983. When the structure was disassembled, spectators were invited to take books with them; thousands were donated to libraries. Another famous example was her sculpture of Carlos Gardel at the 1981 Biennial in Medellín, Colombia. The seventeen-meter-high structure, made of wire mesh and cotton, was set on fire.

23. Casanova also paraphrases Patricia Clark Ferguson in enumerating the elements of a literary capital, beyond reading habits and the number of books published. These include "the number of publishers and bookstores, the number of writers whose portraits appear on banknotes and stamps, the number of streets named after famous writers, the space allotted to books in the press, . . . the time given over to books on television programs, . . . [and] the number of translations" (15–16).

24. Casanova's analysis of literary space avoids assuming "an immutable structure, fixed once and for all in its hierarchies and power relations." Rather, she reveals these positions as "a source of incessant struggle, of challenges to authority and legitimacy, of rebellions, insubordination, and, ultimately, revolutions that alter the balance of literary power and rearrange existing hierarchies" (175).

25. Delgado's precise words were "nos viene como anillo al dedo" ("it fits like a ring on our finger") (personal interview, my translation).

26. Along with planning the annual international book fair, Fundación el Libro is the umbrella organization that includes the Sociedad Argentina de Escritores (SADE), the Cámara Argentina del Libro (CAL), the Cámara Argentina de Publicaciones (CAP), the Sector de Libros y Revistas de la Cámara Española de Comercio, the Federación Argentina de la Industria Gráfica y Afines (FAIGA), and the Federación Argentina de Librerías, Papelerías y Afines (FALPA).

27. See chapter 2 of my *Writing Paris* for a discussion of this and other stories by Cortázar that feature Paris. The other texts by Cortázar in the anthology include "La isla a mediodía" and "Conducta en los velorios"; those by Perec include "Ellis Island," "El arte y la manera de abordar a su jefe de sector para pedir un aumento," and "Un hombre que duerme."

28. Here I cite the World Book Capital edition of *Veinte poemas*.

29. Among the other events honoring Borges, the exhibit "Atlas de Borges," with photographs of Borges's travels with his wife, María Kodama, traveled to Milan and Prague. A children's theater production of Borges's work was held during the July school vacation, and Buenos Aires hosted a biennial symposium on Borges and Kafka in April 2012.

30. The program invited international writers Alejandro Zambra (Chile), Yuri Herrera (Mexico), Elvira Navarro (Spain), Wilmer Urrelo Zárate (Bolivia), Natalia Mardero (Uruguay), Gabriela Alemán (Ecuador), Carlos Yushimito (Peru), Eunice Shade (Mexico), and Antonio García Ángel (Colombia). The three Argentine writers who served as hosts and contributed to the volume are Juan Terranova, Oliverio Coelho, and Matías Capelli. Zambra's narrative is not included in the e-book but was available on the program's website.

31. For the video, see www.youtube.com/watch?v=6wcq-hsoTJk.

32. Melicchio's first novel, *Letra en la sombra* (A Letter in the Shade), tells the story of a teenage book thief in Buenos Aires. The Ministry of Culture recognized the novel by including its first chapter in a "best new novels of 2009" collection prepared for the Frankfurt book fair that year (edited by Delgado). Both *Letra en la sombra* and *Crónica* tell stories about reading under crisis; the protagonist in the novel and the participants in Melicchio's program look to books and reading for solutions to or escapes from various forms of hardship. See my "Spaces for Reading" for discussion of the novel in relation to urban used book markets in Latin America.

Chapter 2: Reading on Wheels

1. In the early decades of the twentieth century, a significant number of Latin American *vanguardista* writers highlighted public transportation, as in Manuel Gutierrez Nájera's *Novela del tranvía*, Lugones's *Luna ciudadana*, Mario Ferreira's *El hombre que se comió un autobus*, and poetry by Alfonsina Storni. Among the work of visual artists, Brazilian Tarsila do Amaral's is emblematic of 1920s industrialization in the region. Her most renowned painting, *E.F.C.B. (Estrada de Ferro Central do Brasil)* (1924) depicts iron railway bridges encroaching on a tropical landscape. The importance of the tram is the subject of Georg Leidenberger's historical study of transportation technology in Mexico City, where he considers the tram the "metonym of the city in transformation" (11).

2. The poem "Pedestre," a fragment from which is an epigraph for this chapter, and its sketch particularly embody Girondo's surreal juxtaposition of forms. The innovations of automobiles, trams, ironwork, and street lamps, all reflected on an angle in the lamp's convex glass, seem to slide and override, and perhaps ride over, the pedestrians.

3. Many critics have mentioned that for decades Girondo was relatively obscure until he was rediscovered in recent years. The next edition of *Veinte poemas* was published in 1966 by Centro Editor de América Latina in Buenos Aires, and the collection was reedited in 1981. In 2011, a facsimile edition of *Veinte poemas* appeared in Chile, with the drawings in color. Several other Girondo anthologies have appeared, such as the 1989 edition of *Veinte poemas* published by Visor in Madrid. Girondo's complete works were not published until Raúl Antelo's critical edition appeared in 1999.

4. This edition measures eleven by eighteen centimeters, identical in size to the original "edición tranviaria," but the drawings are in color. Buenos Aires's World Book Capital campaign sponsored other events related to reading on public transportation, such as a program in partnership with several bus lines called ¡Un Libro Es un Viaje, Viajá con un Libro! (A Book is a Trip, Travel with a Book!).

5. According to a 2013 Amnesty International report released on the fortieth anniversary of the Pinochet coup, between 1973 and 1990 3,216 people were killed or disappeared in Chile, and 38,254 were victims of political imprisonment or torture ("Chile: 40 Years On"). Other sources confirm these numbers.

6. Bogotá's TransMilenio introduced special elevated lanes, while some of the other BRT systems, including those in Mexico City and Buenos Aires, operate at street level.

7. The numerous awards include the Stockholm Partnerships for Sustainable Cities award (considered the "Nobel prize" for mobility) in 2003, the Transport Research Board's Sustainable Transport award in 2005, and the Venice Biennal's gold lion award for Best City in 2006. Jean-Paul Vélez also mentions "best practice" awards for TransMilenio in 2002 and 2004 ("Transit and Spatial Battles").

8. Rachel Berney cites twenty-six cities that have copied the TransMilenio system (28).

9. Vélez's 2007 MA thesis in urban planning on the TransMilenio takes an interdisciplinary approach to the planning, implementation, and results of Bogotá's BRT. He contrasts what he calls a modernist vision for the city in the early 2000s (particularly from Enrique Peñalosa's policies and "grandiose ideas" [18]) with the reigning neoliberal paradigm. Vélez finds that "Peñalosa adds on a classic modernist discourse of social justice to projects that are not likely to effect truly radical social change. . . . In this time of neoliberal globalization any form of direct intervention once associated with modernism has been replaced by the transformative might of the market. . . . While TransMilenio was indeed a project to improve transport conditions in the city, we must also be very aware of the many ways it moved government powers to activate new forms of capital accumulation in and through Bogotá" (*Third Millennium Modernity* 43).

10. Parrochia Beguin is an architect and urban planner whose long career spans the dictatorship and the postdictatorship. Among many distinctions, he was awarded the Premio Nacional de Urbanismo in 1996.

11. The term *micro* is Santiago slang for buses in general; it appears in many of the Santiago en 100 Palabras stories, including one quoted below.

12. The butt of jokes and sharp political attacks, the new buses were mocked on a political satire site that launched the contest Transantiago en 100 Palabras, a spoof on the short story contest (see Aravena).

13. According to Juan C. Muñoz, Marco Batarce, and Darío Hidalgo, the percentage of Santiago buses that satisfied the EURO III environmental standard rose from 53 percent in 2007 to 92 percent in 2012 (185).

14. Labbé considers the Metro "a semi-public space" and in the postdictatorship still associates the Metro with neoliberal policies and an atmosphere of control and exclusion (Schwartz, "La Literatura" 169).

15. Santiago's is the first Latin American subway system to establish library branches in the stations; the initiative has been copied in several other major urban centers, including São Paulo, Medellín, Mexico City, and Bogotá.

16. Another program of books that circulate on public transportation is Medellín's Palabras Rodantes (Rolling Words), an initiative inspired by Bogotá's Libro al Viento. Since 2006, some seventy titles in small paperback format have been distributed on the subway system, where they are made available on designated shelves for passengers to read and return at the end of the ride. The program is cosponsored by the Metro, the internet provider UNE, and the public social service and benefits organization Comfama, and its launch co-

incided with the year that BiblioMetro branches of the public library system opened in the larger subway stations. This chapter does not elaborate on Palabras Rodantes because the program did not coincide with a major innovation in public transportation (the Metro has been operating since 1995). Nevertheless, the reading program follows a number of cultural and infrastructural improvements in the city to fight violence and crime. The most notable of these innovations is the 2004 opening of the cable car line to the Santo Domingo neighborhood, Medellín's poorest and most troubled *comuna* (district). One of the line's stops is adjacent to the Biblioteca España, which opened in 2007: an impressive public library and cultural center that towers over the city and is an emblem of Medellín's dramatic rebirth after the very violent 1990s.

17. Ana Roda Fornaguera worked for Bogotá's municipal Ministry of Culture at the time she initiated Libro al Viento and directed the program. She was director of Colombia's National Library from 2008 to 2013 and is currently Bogotá's municipal director of public libraries.

18. Libro al Viento was inspired by the Mexico City program Para Leer de Boleto en el Metro (Reading on the Run in the Metro), initiated by Paloma Sáiz in 2004. Sáiz worked for the municipal secretary of culture at the time and convinced the subway company to cooperate with the venture. Shelves were installed in subway stations along Line 3 to display the anthologies, and staff were hired to distribute them. The first anthology published, in a print run of 250,000 copies, included writers who live in Mexico City, and all of the selections touched on some aspect of city life. The program has suffered changes and interruptions due to the politics of changing municipal administrations. In 2010, Sáiz launched Brigada para Leer en Libertad (Brigade for the Freedom to Read), a nonprofit that also publishes books to distribute free to the public. Its books on historical events and social struggle and its literary titles are given out at events held in public space with a reading or panel discussion on the topic. By the end of 2015, Brigada had published 129 titles with print runs of a thousand copies.

19. The number of copies in each edition has varied over the years on the basis of funding and sponsorship. The early years sponsored by TransMilenio saw the largest editions. More recently, fifteen thousand copies of each title are printed.

20. See idartes.gov.co/publicaciones?field_pu_tags_tid=2&field_pu_fecha_value%5Bvalue%5D%5Byear%5D= and www.banrepcultural.org/category/colecciones/libro-al-viento for free downloads.

21. A similar project with public readings and a published collection of texts was among the concluding events of the Buenos Aires World Book Capital campaign. The 2012 anthology titled *La ciudad contada: Buenos Aires en la mirada de la nueva narrativa hispanoamericana* includes works by two of the writers who participated in the Bogotá visit and book, Gabriela Alemán and Carlos Yushimito, as well as by the Libro al Viento director and editor of *Bogotá contada*, Antonio García Ángel.

22. Jaime Garzón was a journalist and peace activist who was allegedly killed by paramilitary forces in 1999.

23. A photo of the actual statue appears in the book with the explanation:

"In the original sculpture, the hand is holding a conch shell for scooping water. In our logo for *Bogotá contada* she holds a book" (55).

24. The second volume, also edited by García Ángel, includes selections by Élmer Mendoza (Mexico), Wendy Guerra (Cuba), Rodrigo Hasbún (Chile), Alberto Barrera Tyszka (Venezuela), Luis Fayad (Colombia), Juan Bonilla (Spain), Pablo Casacuberta (Uruguay), Diego Zúñiga (Chile), and Gabriela Wiener (Peru) (*Bogotá contada 2.0*).

25. According to the questionnaires, recognition of the program's promotion of solidarity and civic culture grew between 2005 and 2006 from 78.5 percent to 87.8 percent (39).

26. A similar challenge faced Mexico's Para Leer de Boleto en el Metro. In February 2011, when the eleventh anthology for circulation on the subway was published in an edition of 250,000 copies, the directors of the program changed the rules: in order to acquire one of the anthologies, subway riders had to donate a book of their own in exchange. The program has suffered interruptions but reappears sporadically. In January 2015 the program reemerged with a new anthology cosponsored by the cosmetics company Sophie. Staff members were posted in subway stations to distribute books and remind passengers to return them at their destination. The day of the book launch, a journalist commented on the program's objectives: "the idea of capturing new readers, as well as incentivizing the culture of giving back and solidarity," where returning the books is integrated as an explicit goal (Paul 3). The program's anthologies were available as downloadable files on the municipal Ministry of Culture's site when the program was officially sponsored by the city. Some of the more recent anthologies are available for download at http://brigadaparaleerenlibertad.com/descargas/.

27. The contest has evolved over the years from awarding first, second, and third prizes and honorable mentions to including a senior citizens prize, a teen prize, and a children's prize, as well as an audience favorite through online voting on a selection of submitted stories.

28. Since 2012, the free books have been published annually. The volume quoted here, "*10 años de Santiago en 100 Palabras*," is a special large-format book edited by Ignacio Arnold, Carmen García, and Silvia Dümmer in 2010 to commemorate the program's tenth anniversary. This book prints a selection of stories from the beginning of the contest to the present, with lively illustrations and short essays by Santiago writers and intellectuals about the impact of the contest on the city.

29. See Griffin's *The Labor of Literature* (141–147) on the complexity of Minera Escondida's role.

30. In citing the stories in the published books of Santiago en 100 Palabras, I have chosen to identify the book cited by its volume number in the parenthetical references.

31. I have eliminated the age and neighborhood references in the quoted stories here, as space does not allow for thorough analysis of this information. Ricardo Greene F. does consider this data for the complete corpus of stories submitted in 2005.

32. On the basis of my own reading, the number of stories featuring public

transportation in a major role in each volume is as follows: vol. 1: 20, vol. 2: 18, vol. 3: 16, vol. 4: 11, vol. 5: 8, vol. 6: 5, vol. 7: 12, vol. 8: 9, vol. 9: 6.

33. Labbé critiques the Metro's heavy hand in the contest and points out that there were "too many concessions to the Metro administration on the part of the organizers of Santiago en 100 Palabras" (169). For Labbé, the stories bear the mark of "that corporate aesthetic of the Metro that was directly evident in the conventional forms of the stories" (170).

34. Luis Campos Medina also studied a corpus of stories from the contest—the three hundred stories that were published in three of the biennial books—to analyze the social representation of Santiago that the contest generates. He admits that his corpus is "filtered" by the organizers, judges, and editors, since he does not have access to the submitted stories that were not chosen. Nevertheless, he still finds it "pertinent to develop an analysis that constitutes an initial approximation and can provide suggestive interpretations" regarding "the central aspects of the representations of the city in these stories" (104). Campos Medina does not single out transportation in the "thematic constellations" into which he divides his corpus (relationships, biography, day-to-day imaginaries, problems of urban living, the meaning of life, and commemorative or traditional aspects of the city [105]), but many of his examples do incorporate buses and the Metro.

35. Other stories by Cortázar that take place in the Paris Metro include "Cuello de gatito negro" and "El perseguidor." See my *Writing Paris* for a thorough discussion of Cortázar's fictional use of the Paris metro (49–59).

36. The literal translation of the title would be "blue envelope." I have chosen to translate it according to usage in English in this context.

37. *Napoleón* is a Chilean word for a metal tool like pliers, in this case to pry or break open the lock.

38. There is now an underground museum, Museo de los Tajamares, in Parque Balmaceda in Santiago.

39. In recent years the program has expanded beyond Santiago. It now hosts short story contests in other Chilean cities (Iquique, Antofagasta, Valparaíso, Concepción) and abroad in Puebla, Mexico; Budapest, Hungary; Warsaw, Poland; Bratislava, Slovakia; and most recently, Bogotá.

40. This first subway line in Buenos Aires opened in 1913. Several other Latin American cities modernized and expanded their public transportation services around the same time or even earlier, including Mexico City, whose first electric trams appeared in 1900 (see Leidenberger 75).

41. Programs such as Book Crossing, UNESCO's International Day of Bibliodiversity, Adopta un Libro in Venezuela, Movimiento Letras Voladoras in Mexico, Libro Libre Uruguay, and Movimiento Libro Libre Argentina promote book exchanges in public places.

Chapter 3: *Cacerolazos y bibliotecas*

1. "Warhol" is the first chapter in the novel's first edition, but in the revised edition (published by Eduvim in 2016), Abbate rearranged the chapter order, and "Warhol" became the third chapter.

2. See "Cronología de la crisis del 2001" at republica-economica.blogspot.com/2011/01/cronologia-de-la-crisis-del-2001.html. See also Rapoport (859–977).

3. See Botto on the contraction of publishing opportunities in Argentina in the 1990s.

4. Scorer here discusses works that depict Buenos Aires's metropolitan outskirts, such as Sergio Chejfec's novel *Boca de lobo*, musical examples of *rock barrial*, novels by Juan Diego Incardona, and several films (127–148).

5. One study indicates that there was an average of twenty-two protests per day in January, eleven in February, and four in March 2002 (www.nuevamayoria.com/invest/sociedad/cs0250402.htm). The same statistics appear in a 2006 source: www.ffyh.unc.edu.ar/alfilo/anteriores/34/investigacion.html.

6. I am grateful to the Princeton University Library's Latin American Ephemera Collection, whose holdings include original copies of the Argentine neighborhood association newsletters, posters, and flyers: libguides.princeton.edu/c.php?g=84286. Parenthetical citations throughout the chapter will reference newsletter titles, issues, and page numbers (where available); in the bibliography, the newsletters consulted appear in a special section with more complete information on their cataloging in the Princeton archive.

7. Most of the neighborhood associations emerged in Buenos Aires and the surrounding province (122 in the capital, 105 in the province); the others were in La Plata, Córdoba, and Santa Fe (Feijóo and Salas Oroño 25–26).

8. One of the slogans frequently heard during this period of solidarity organizing was "Piquete y cacerola, la lucha es una sola" (Picketing and banging on pots and pans, it's the same fight), referring to the common cause among classes. Maristella Svampa elaborates on the heterogeneous composition of the *asambleas*: "shop owners, employees, and professionals, from the public and the private realm, connected to administration, education, and healthcare; many of them impoverished, and some with a high level of job instability; add to that a group of unemployed people from different fields, along with young people with radical expectations, many of them engaged in political activism for the first time" (267). Much of the critical research on the solidarity movement following the crisis underscores this nearly unprecedented mix of classes that united in the struggle. Leonardo Pérez Esquivel, for example, notes the "intersectorial solidarity" within and among the *asambleas* (58).

9. Regarding the autonomy of each neighborhood association, Luis Mattini notes that "each association is a social knot that becomes the center of an autonomous unit that does not answer to any 'center of centers.' In other words, the interneighborhood organization is only a coordinating entity, not the center of the associations. If it were, then we would be repeating the vertical state structure that we are critiquing. The assemblies offer the opportunity to try out the horizontality of power" (Mattini 52). Svampa also highlights autonomy as the fundamental shared characteristic of the "uneven assembly experience" (271).

10. The Centro is located at Avenida Gral. Güemes 1411 in Buenos Aires, and is now an NGO.

11. *Murgas* are bands of musicians, drummers, dancers, and acrobats who perform in carnival celebrations in the street. *Murgas* originated in Spain and

were introduced by immigrants to Argentina in the nineteenth century. In Latin America *murgas* are most common in Argentina. Outlawed during the dictatorship, they reemerged after the return to democracy. One well-known *murga* is associated with the group H.I.J.O.S.; most of the groups are associated with specific neighborhoods. The active presence of *murga* performances and workshops following the economic crisis coincides naturally with the revitalization of the *asambleas* and neighborhood political organizing.

12. The stories and struggles of utilizing these spaces are long and varied. Many groups began through official channels, following city ordinances and requesting use of the buildings or lots through required municipal paperwork. Their requests were usually ignored, however. Most of the unofficial occupations followed frustrated attempts to gain legitimate access.

13. Space does not allow for a thorough analysis of the numerous Argentine factories taken over by workers during the crisis. I include the example from the Brukman newsletter to illustrate the connection between literary reading's role in occupations of abandoned buildings in urban neighborhoods and a similar initiative in an occupied factory. See also the well-known documentary film *The Take*, directed by Naomi Klein and Avi Lewis, about a closed automobile plant that workers turned into a cooperative.

14. www.conabip.gob.ar/.

15. The Mansilla mansion website contains more information ("Qué fue la Casona").

16. This group occupied the Banco Mayo building at Suarez 1244.

17. My thanks to Ksenija Bilbija for alerting me to *Libro que no muerde*. It is included in Valenzuela's collection *Cuentos completos y uno más*, and differs from her more conventional short stories in taking the form of brief vignettes, fragments, commentaries, and metafictional plays on words that she says "roamed all over the place" and "are supposed to work like little thinking machines" (30, 19).

18. Galeano's "Utopía," reprinted here as a poem, originally appeared as a prose piece titled "Ventana sobre la utopía" (Window on utopia) in his book *Las palabras andantes* (230).

Chapter 4: Recycled Reading and the Cartonera Collectives

1. My research in Latin America has allowed me to encounter numerous cartonera publishing groups. I have visited with them at independent publishers' book fairs, book launches, readings, performances, and bookmaking sessions. Some of these encounters and continuing conversations have been in the United States at academic symposia, including one that I organized at Rutgers University in 2009. I am grateful to the collectives' members for granting me interviews and for thoroughly enjoyable hours of painting covers and engaging in lively discussion.

2. See the University of Wisconsin–Madison library's website for comprehensive information on the growing presence of cartonera publishing: digital.library.wisc.edu/1711.dl/Arts.EloisaCart.

3. See Botto for a thorough discussion of neoliberalism's consequences for the book industry in Argentina. It is a case study representative of publishing in large urban areas in Latin America, where publishing and bookselling have traditionally had an impact on the rest of the region. Cala Buendía also provides an overview of the 1990s in Argentine publishing and the paradoxes and contradictions of transnational conglomerates existing alongside new independent publishers (108–115).

4. Botto devotes a section of her comprehensive article to Argentine independent presses, such as Beatriz Viterbo, Paradiso, Simurg, Adriana Hidalgo, Bajo la Luna, and Siesta (226–232).

5. Ksenija Bilbija similarly comments on how Eloísa Cartonera "challenges and contests the neo-liberal political and economic hegemony" in her seminal article "What's Left in the World of Books" (85).

6. Cucurto has become an international celebrity as an invited writer at book fairs and universities in the United States and Europe. Eloísa Cartonera has won international prizes such as the Prince Claus prize in 2012 and has been featured as a workshop at international art exhibits. The studio is a destination on tourist routes and for study-abroad students in Buenos Aires.

7. The initiative began informally as "Arte de tapa" (cover art), in which the three hand-decorated the covers of poetry books. Laguna's art gallery Belleza y Felicidad was something of a precursor to the cartonera publishing phenomenon, producing small handmade books out of random leftover materials and featuring queer writers. Laguna publishes her own literary work under the pseudonym Dalia Rosetti. See, for example, her *Durazno reverdeciente*, one of the first books published by Eloísa Cartonera. Other initiatives preceding the current wave of cartonera publishers include Chilean Pía Barros's Ergo Sum (see Griffin, *Labor of Literature*) and the production of Cuban handmade books by independent publisher Ediciones Vigía (see Jessica Gordon-Burroughs's dissertation and her article "Straight Pins, Gauze, and Linotypes").

8. The volume *Travesías de cartón* (Álvarez Oquendo and Madureira), a translation into Spanish from the original edition in Portuguese, *Travessias de cartão*, published in Mozambique in 2012, is a sort of companion volume to *Akademia cartonera*, which the editors of Travessias/Travesías call a "pioneering book" (Álvarez Oquendo and Madureira 7). Travessias/Travesías reprints some of the manifestos and articles that appear in *Akademia* and adds fifteen more manifestos by new groups in Europe and Latin America. The volume also includes a chronological list and map of the seventy-four known cartonera publishers active at the time of publication (66–68).

9. Two brief videos filmed in the Eloísa studio document their bookmaking process step by step. See www.youtube.com/watch?v=gR38SuJwnKw&feature=youtu.be and www.youtube.com/watch?v=WKKsGQU6f6Y&feature=youtu.be.

10. See also the article by Vila on the cartonera bookmaking process.

11. The annual Encuentro Cartoneras in Santiago is one example. The Chilean groups have been active in organizing other regional meetings and book exhibits as well. Many of the cartonera groups exhibit in independent

publishers' book fairs, such as La Furia del Libro in Santiago, the Feria de Libro Independiente in Caracas and Mexico City, and the Feria del Libro Independiente y Autogestiva in La Plata, Argentina.

12. See Cala Buendía (126–129) and Ruchansky for a thorough discussion of Eloísa's decision to register as a cooperative.

13. For more on Animita Cartonera, see Griffin, *Labor of Literature*.

14. Many of the cartonera books include some kind of graphic emblem or text on the inside front and back covers. The information they include is similar to a colophon, an added page at the beginning or the end of a book that identifies the publisher. I have chosen not to use the term *colophon* for a variety of reasons. First, *colophon* is associated with a more traditional kind of bibliographic description, and cartonera publishing consciously deviates from the conventional form of the book. Second, colophons are generally added pages, and in the case of cartonera books the information on the inside covers is printed or pasted directly on the cardboard. Finally, these handmade books do have a title page that generally indicates the publisher's name and the date; when the insides of the cardboard covers have printed information, it communicates more than the identity of the publisher.

15. See my "Spaces for Reading" and Daniel Alarcón's "Life among the Pirates" for more information on literary piracy in Peru.

16. In Peru there have been several organizations to promote solidarity and defend bibliodiversity within the publishing industry. The Alianza Peruana de Editores was founded in the early 2000s and brought together independent, autonomous, and university presses. Vargas Luna, one of the founders of Sarita Cartonera, served as its first president. In 2011 the association became Editores Independientes de Perú (Vargas Luna, personal interview).

17. Yerba Mala Cartonera in El Alto, Bolivia, includes a slightly revised version of this message on the back covers of their books: "For not despairing in traffic jams, for waiting for the TV ads to end, for putting up with demonstrations, for walking boldly without even realizing it, for dancing to cumbia rhythms on the bus, or just for when you simply feel like reading. A cartonera book, homemade, your best friend."

18. For the Harvard University Cultural Agents Initiative, see culturalagents.org/; for Pre-Texts, see www.pre-texts.org/.

19. James Scorer complements this aesthetic revalorization of cardboard with a legal and spatial one: "*Cartoneros* enacted changes in the value and understanding of rubbish and, in turn, in the legal and conceptual understanding of the street" (159).

20. Fascinating examples of Dulcinéia's publication of peripheral writers include *Um sarau da Cooperifa* (Rosa et al.), *Uma antologia bêbada: Fábulas da Mercearia* (Terron), and the three-volume series *Tribêbada: Contos escritos por freqüentadores da Mercearia São Pedro* (Assunção). The latter anthologies unite work by marginal poets who meet weekly at a bar called Mercearia São Pedro, which was once a small grocery store and still sells a few basic household items, as well as books, in honor of the history of the shop.

21. Scorer contends that *cartoneros* "not only created a debate over the nature of public space but also transformed it both in strict legislative terms

and insofar as they introduced a new set of rhythms and paths into the urban environment" (159).

22. The cartonera groups' flexibility and adaptability in their use of materials brings to mind Crembil and Lynch's definition of craft: "Craft is a type of applied knowledge about material, distinct from industrial and scientific knowledge. We must put aside the notion that craft is defined by a reliance on tradition, primitive methods, handiwork, a high degree of affect, or a feudal division of labor. The essence of craft work lies in its acceptance of variation, its incremental pursuit of mastery or virtuosity, its reliance upon embodied or tacit knowledge, and its acceptance of the fundamentally open-source dimension of work. Craft is adaptive behavior applied to non-routine, attentive, collective tasks of fabrication. Craft is haptic thinking" (49).

23. See, for example, Cala Buendía's interpretation: "A look at the way in which Eloísa and its products circulate in the public sphere reveals yet other contradictions and tensions that hint at how easy it is to slip right back into the same economic and political system that so favors the citizen-as-consumer paradigm and the correlative commodification of culture" (132).

24. The explosion of print media in Argentina and the press's role in literacy and nation building from the middle of the nineteenth century, and particularly between the 1880s and the 1930s, has been widely documented (see, for example, Anderson, Prieto, Acree). The development of newspapers and magazines went hand in hand with urban growth, modernization, and literacy and public education campaigns. In 1877 Argentina had a newspaper for every 15,700 citizens, a statistic comparable to that for Belgium in the same year (Prieto 34–35). Starting in 1879 the best-read *gauchesque* novels, such as *Juan Moreira*, by Eduardo Gutiérrez, were published serially in the daily *La Patria Argentina* before being printed as books. By the 1890s the newspaper *La Nación* printed fictional texts daily and eventually initiated a book series featuring novels (called Biblioteca *La Nación*) (Merbilhaá 34–35). Beatriz Sarlo analyzes the continuation of this publishing trend into the 1920s and 1930s; she identifies 1917–1925 as the apogee of weekly fiction supplements in Buenos Aires (*El imperio* 20; see also 33–38 on the role of the kiosk). In Argentina a growing "belief in the necessary alliance between newspapers and books provided the impetus for fiction publishing especially for decades" (Merbilhaá 32). Susana Zanetti underscores the importance of journalism in promoting literature in the late nineteenth century: "It's truly print journalism that multiplied the options in literary reading and took a lead role in forming new readers" (36). In his introduction to *Everyday Reading*, an impressive study of nineteenth-century print culture in Argentina and Uruguay, Acree points out that in both countries kiosks still "hawk newspapers, magazines, cheap histories, pulp fiction, and even reprints of 'classics'" (2).

25. Gabriel Wolfson similarly comments on current innovative editorial strategies of independent presses, such as those of the Mexican press Alias, where the text, the design, the paper, and the typography make the books "acts of reflection on, among other things, the very enterprise of publishing. . . . [These are] book-actions, speech acts that are also publishing acts" (24).

26. Cucurto's poem "La cartonerita" appears in various collections. The collection *La cartonerita* (Vox edition, 5–7) reprints it as the title poem in a slightly different version from the one cited above, extending the description of the collected refuse: "juntando cartones, / papeles, pedazos / de viejos diarios, / botellitas, plásticos" (gathering boxes, / paper, pieces / of old newspapers, / little bottles, plastic items) (5). This version omits the friend and the photocopying of the book.

27. The YouTube link listed in the book is no longer active, but the song is available at www.youtube.com/watch?v=T8IlAfwmMzE.

28. The members of Amapola held several events to present the book to the growers of La Virgen and the residents of Quipile. The project was exhibited at the Museo de Arte Contemporáneo Minuto de Dios in Bogotá. Short versions of some of the videos filmed during the project, produced by Deivis Cortés, are available on YouTube.

29. Two of Cucurto's novels, *Las aventuras del Sr. Maíz* and *El rey de la cumbia: Contra los fucking Estados Unidos de América* (The King of Cumbia: Against the Fucking United States of America), are structured around the semi-autobiographical protagonist's work as a produce handler in supermarkets, which is a source of pride modulated with absurd, exaggerated humor. Selma Cohen introduces Cucurto's extreme form of "autoficción": "Stretching beyond familiar limits, the concept of autofiction that some critics have defined as a creative operation that involves the creation of fictional authorship, Cucurto unleashes a complex mechanism of funhouse mirrors in which reality and fiction, the 'real author,' writers, names, pseudonyms, real people, and fictional characters are deliberately mixed to the point of impeding any clear, definitive distinction" (119–120).

30. A manifesto-like statement in *Las aventuras del Sr. Maíz* establishes a pantheon of Latin American writers against which Cucurto positions himself, all too aware that he is already becoming part of it: "Ataco y destruyo la buena literatura sin piedad. . . . Años después, pienso que en esa lista también entraría yo y no veo la hora de destruirme a mí mismo" (I attack and I destroy good literature mercilessly. . . . Years later, I think that I'd probably make it onto this list, and I can't wait to destroy myself) (41).

31. Cucurto published his first books with small independent presses such as Vox, as well as with Eloísa Cartonera. A few years later, he published the novel *Cosa de negros*, whose final episode fictionalizes cartonera publishing, with Interzona, a small independent press founded in 2002. Several of his more recent novels and poetry collections have been published with Emecé, a press that is part of the Spanish conglomerate Planeta, the same press that publishes Borges. Founding the first reused cardboard book publishing collective seems simultaneously to have launched his more conventional literary career.

32. Zanetti calls attention to this contemporary mixing of high and low culture, and encourages further study of "how the modalities of so-called high literature operate in popular urban literary production and how the latter comes to be converted into 'elite literature'" (33).

33. Photocopying in Latin America is also a common cultural practice, particularly among students and in the pirated book market.

34. "La fotocopiadora" was first published in *Como un paraguayo ebrio y celoso de su hermana* (Like a Drunk Paraguayan Who Lusts After His Sister). It is reprinted in the anthology *1999: Poemas de siempre*, a compilation of several earlier collections (131–132). A completely different poem with the same title, from *La fotocopiadora y otros poemas*, also appears in 1999 (75).

Chapter 5: Books That Bite

1. The three-minute video by Brodsky and Eduardo Feller is available at www.youtube.com/watch?v=X-oolT8XIOo.
2. Another example of conceptual art related to books and reading that celebrated the end of Argentina's last dictatorship is Marta Minujín's *Partenon de Libros* (Parthenon of Books). Installed on the iconic Avenida 9 de Julio in Buenos Aires, it was built of thirty thousand banned books, a number commemorating not only the immensity of the lack of freedom of expression but also symbolically the official number of disappeared victims of political violence.
3. Burying books was a common practice under the repressive regime.
4. "Nunca más" is the title of an Argentine presidential commission (Comisión Nacional sobre la Desaparición de Personas [CONADEP]; or National Commission on the Disappearance of Persons) and its resulting published report, which was produced after the return to democracy to document the cases of forced disappearance. Commissioned by President Raúl Alfonsín, the first president to assume power after the dictatorship, in 1983, the published report appeared in 1984. It has been a best-seller and has been in print continuously ever since then.
5. There are very limited initiatives related to collecting banned books in other Latin American countries. According to my research, Argentina has the most thorough and committed collections, several with permanent locations. There was a temporary exhibit of books banned during Brazil's long dictatorship (1964–1985) in São Paulo at the state-sponsored Oficina da Palavra in 1990. In Chile, where the memory market has been extremely active since the 1990s following the return to democracy, there is no library of banned books. Santiago's Museo de la Memoria y de los Derechos Humanos has a library and research center, but it is dedicated primarily to collecting testimonials and letters from political prisoners and the disappeared. A 2013 exhibit titled "Biblioteca recuperada: Libros quemados, escondidos y recuperados a 40 años del golpe" (Reclaimed Library: Burned, Hidden and Reclaimed Books 40 Years after the Coup) in Santiago at the Biblioteca Nicanor Parra of the Universidad Diego Portales displayed some eight hundred books lent for the exhibit. At the close of the exhibit, the books were returned to the various donors, in correspondence with the exhibit's "final objective," according to curator Ramón Castillo: "that the books return to where they came from: the shelf" (Brantmayer and Perez Retes). See Fernández and Rojas on censorship of the Universidad de Chile's libraries and librarians under Pinochet.
6. The Fundación Mempo Giardinelli, another former clandestine deten-

tion center in Resistencia in Argentina's Chaco province, also has a library, but it is not a collection of banned books. The organization has been housed in a former police station in the center of town since renovations were completed in 2008. The library's holdings, which began with the donation of writer and journalist Giardinelli's personal collection, now include over thirteen thousand volumes, and the library hosts many community reading programs, such as Abuelas Cuentacuentos (Grandmother Storytellers) and an annual international symposium on promoting reading. The foundation's slogan is "Leer abre los ojos" (Reading Opens our Eyes), and the organization supports public and school libraries in the region. Other recuperated former clandestine detention centers have libraries, but their collections do not consist of censored books. One such center is Virrey Cevallos in Buenos Aires, whose small library of donated books was established in 2013.

7. Established in 2002, the Instituto Espacio para la Memoria was charged with collecting and transmitting the history of state terrorism under the dictatorship. Its mission as stated in Municipal Law 961 concerns "saving and transmitting memory and history of the events that occurred during State Terrorism, . . . with the goal of promoting a deeper democratic system, the consolidation of human rights and the prevalence of shared values of life, liberty, and human dignity." The law is posted on the Buenos Aires city government's website: www2.cedom.gob.ar/es/legislacion/normas/leyes/ley961.html. Overseeing the transformation of the city's previously clandestine structures was one of the Instituto's responsibilities, and Olimpo was one of these sites. In May 2014 the Institute was dissolved when jurisdiction over the former torture and detention centers in Buenos Aires was transferred from the municipal to the federal government (Jorquera). This change provoked a controversy as to how the memory centers ought to be managed and who should manage them, with legislative votes divided along party lines. The Instituto was replaced with a national advisory board called Consejo Asesor en Políticas Públicas de la Memoria.

8. Paola Hernández points out that the Escuela Superior de Mecánica Armada in Buenos Aires, restored as a memory site in 2004, is similarly charged with archival significance. As the dictatorship's largest and most active detention and torture center, it will store testimonial evidence and will be the site "where testimonial evidence will take center stage, . . . giving ESMA the role of educator for future generations about past atrocities" (70–71).

9. Vicky Unruh's discussion of Cuban libraries depicted in fiction and film in the post-Soviet period reminds us that libraries are "ideologically charged cultural sphere[s]" (176). Although the historical and political contexts are very different, the informal Argentine libraries analyzed in chapter 3 and the libraries of banned books discussed here are certainly politically charged. Another similarity between tenement (*solar*) libraries in Cuba and libraries of banned books in Argentina is the role of the collection and the space as remnants. During the Special Period in Cuba, libraries had the task of "sifting through remnants in search of what might be salvaged for an unknown future" (Unruh 177), as do libraries of banned books, particularly in reconstituted memory centers.

10. Rozza is the coordinator of the Memory Pedagogy Section of the Archivo.

11. The recent book *Espacios de Memoria en la Argentina* states that Olimpo held some five hundred detainees during those months (Said 14).

12. The feature film *Garage Olimpo* (1999) is based loosely on experiences at the Olimpo center. It shows forced labor of the prisoners and death flights in which drugged prisoners were pushed from planes into the river. See Draper, Kaminsky, and Manzano for lucid analyses of this film.

13. The Instituto Espacio para la Memoria has published two editions of this book documenting the Olimpo center (2008 and 2010; the second edition does not print the date). The first edition devotes a chapter to the library titled "Biblioteca Pública y Popular 'Carlos Fuentealba,'" written by Ariel Korzin (65–72). The second edition revises and updates Korzin's text (63–66, with some information on the library on page 60 as well) and includes his name in a list of contributors (4), but does not specify which sections contributors have authored. I recognize Korzin here because the new version follows his original chapter very closely. All page references here are to the expanded second edition.

14. President Macri required that several historical memory websites be shut down, fired staff at some of the centers, and made incendiary statements revealing his skepticism regarding the work of these centers. Very soon after his inauguration, he began to implement a harder line, compared to policies under the Kirchners, in terms of funding and policies for memory spaces.

15. Walsh was a journalist and writer who was killed in 1977 and was one of the most high-profile victims of the dictatorship. *Operación masacre* (Operation Massacre), a narrative reconstruction and denunciation of the shooting of a group of political dissenters in the post-Peronist period, was originally published as a series of newspaper columns, and eventually appeared as a book in 1957. See a brief homage to Walsh by Miguel Bonasso in Invernizzi and Gociol (396–397).

16. The Asamblea Meridiano V was established in 2000, shortly before the economic and political collapse of 2001–2002, when many neighborhood solidarity groups emerged in Argentine cities.

17. In La Plata some two thousand people were disappeared. Among the many Argentine memory initiatives in public space, such as the *escraches*, a project called Paisajes de la Memoria (Landscapes for Memory) involves marking and then mapping specific sites of human rights violations during the dictatorship. According to the project's website, in the case of La Plata, "if we were to put a mark on every sidewalk on which someone was kidnapped or assassinated, not a single one would be unmarked" (paisajes.comisionporlamemoria.org/).

18. The first *muestra* was held from 24 May to 3 June 1995; the second took place from 24 November to 27 November 2005; the third was from 20 November to 3 December 2006; and the fourth occurred from 24 November to 8 December 2007 (Colectivo La Grieta 191–193).

19. An anecdote from my visit at the center confirms La Grieta's overlapping mission of arts and social services. During my interview with Pesclevi, as

we were looking at the book collection, she received a phone call informing her that a teenager had been picked up by the police for drinking alcohol on school property. The student was a regular participant in the center's arts and literature programs. Pesclevi excused herself to go meet the student at the police station and, along with her parent, intervene for her release.

20. During my interviews with members of La Grieta, only vague comments surfaced about their financial sustainability. The group advocated successfully for recognition from the city and the province, and the center receives a small subsidy; the city covers the cost of electricity.

21. The exhibit and programming at the museum were scheduled from 8 July to 2 August 2015.

22. Taylor calls the regime a "theater of operations" for "the theatricality, the medicalization, and the violence of the operation exercised simultaneously on social space and human bodies" (*Disappearing Acts* 96). She documents a "surreal" experience of reality as the junta denied the vigilance, censorship, and disappearances that people witnessed daily. "The make-believe world traditionally associated with theater became the official version of reality and was relentlessly transmitted through the media" (*Disappearing Acts* 98).

23. See my "Spaces for Reading" for a discussion of other examples of used books in Latin America, their commodification, and urban spatial presence.

24. Bilbija and Payne point out how "memory patrons," those interested in consuming artifacts of historically repressive periods, resemble collectors: "each good has value because it is part of a set. . . . Collectors value each piece. . . . They seek a complete collection, even if this is an impossible goal" (10). The collections of banned books will never be complete, but clearly the collectors are motivated by the idealized quest of recovering each and every item.

25. The Mothers of the Plaza de Mayo, who had affiliate groups in other cities, began protesting the disappearance of family members in front of the presidential palace in Buenos Aires in 1977. Even since the return to democracy, the group continues its weekly Thursday *rondas* around the plaza to commemorate the missing and demand "memory, truth, and justice." The Córdoba group demonstrates less regularly but still gathers to commemorate special anniversaries.

Conclusion

1. Pesclevi refers to the demonstration in La Plata on 8 January 2016, in the Plaza Moreno in front of City Hall. The demonstration was in response to the firing in December of 2,500 municipal workers. Hundreds of protesters gathered and were attacked by the police with tear gas and rubber bullets.

2. In Hardt and Negri's analysis of the role of the metropolis in what they propose as a new political commonwealth within the current biopolitical economy, they strive to undo traditional hierarchies and binaries, such as urban/rural and public/private: "The qualities traditionally associated with the

metropolis such as communication, unexpected encounters with social difference, access to the common, and the production of collective forms of life today increasingly characterize both urban and rural environments" (244).

3. Petit is known for her far-reaching sociological and anthropological research on literary reading practices among French youth. Her psychoanalytic approach in her earlier work combines with historical and political studies of reading in various contexts, including contexts of violence, repression, and political crisis, in her more recent work. She has lectured and served as a consultant throughout Latin America, invited by library associations, ministries of education, and organizations dedicated to youth development.

Works Cited

Abbate, Florencia. "Dulce fuerte grave/Sweet Strong Deep." *Escritores argentinos: Entrevistas/Argentine Writers: Interviews*, edited by María E. Romero, Julio Ariza, and Pablo Molina, translated by Luciano Camio, Patricia Rizzo Editora, 2005, pp. 72–89.
———. *El grito*. Emecé, 2004.
———. *El grito*. Eduvim, 2016.
Acosta, Abraham. *Thresholds of Illiteracy: Theory, Latin America, and the Crisis of Resistance*. Fordham University Press, 2014.
Acree, William G. *Everyday Reading: Print Culture and Collective Identity in the Río de la Plata, 1780–1910*. Vanderbilt University Press, 2011.
Adamo, Gabriela. Personal e-mail communication. 8 February 2016.
Adelman, Jeremy. *Worldly Philosopher: The Odyssey of Albert O. Hirschman*. Princeton University Press, 2013.
Aguirre, Milagros, Fernando Carrión, and Eduardo Kingman Garcés. *Quito imaginado*. Taurus/Flacso Ecuador, 2005.
Alarcón, Daniel. "Life among the Pirates." *Granta*, no. 109, 14 January 2010. granta.com/life-among-the-pirates/.
Alemán, Gabriela. "Buenos Aires Chroma Color." *La ciudad contada: Buenos Aires en la mirada de la nueva narrativa hispanoamericana*, edited by Maximiliano Tomas, Ministerio de Cultura del Gobierno de la Ciudad Autónoma de Buenos Aires, 2012, pp. 77–95.
Allard, Pablo. Untitled essay. *10 Años de Santiago en 100 Palabras (2001–2010)*, edited by Ignacio Arnold, Carmen García, and Sylvia Dümmer, Plagio, 2010, p. 131.
Almeyra, Guillermo. *La protesta social en la Argentina (1990–2004): Fábricas recuperadas, piquetes, cacerolazos, asambleas populares*. Continente, 2004.
Alonso, Rodrigo. "Minujín: revolcarse es vivir [Minujín: wallowing is life]." *Artinf*, vol. 23, nos. 103–104, 1999, p. 27.
Altamirano, Carlos, and Jorge Myers. *Historia de los intelectuales en América Latina*. Katz, 2008.
Álvarez, Luciano, editor. *Montevideo imaginado*. Taurus, 2004.

Álvarez Oquendo, Saylín, and Luis Madureira, editors. *Travesías de cartón: Aproximaciones al fenómeno de las editoriales cartoneras*. Kutsemba Cartão, 2012.

Álvarez Zapata, Didier. *Una región de lectores que crece: Análisis comparado de planes nacionales de lectura en Iberoamérica 2013*. CERLALC, 2014.

Amapola Cartonera. *Libro contable*. Amapola Cartonera, 2014.

Amnesty International. "Chile: 40 Years on from Pinochet's Coup, Impunity Must End." 10 September 2013. https://www.amnesty.org/en/latest/news/2013/09/chile-years-pinochet-s-coup-impunity-must-end/.

Anderson, Benedict R. O. *Imagined Communities: Reflections on the Origin and Spread of Nationalism*. Verso, 2006.

Anuario: Buenos Aires Capital Mundial del Libro 2011. Gobierno de la Ciudad de Buenos Aires, 2012.

Appadurai, Arjun. "Introduction: Commodities and the Politics of Value." *Social Life of Things: Commodities in Cultural Perspective*, edited by Arjun Appadurai, Cambridge University Press, 1986, pp. 3–63.

Aravena, Javier. "Transantiago en 100 Palabras." *192*, 8 May 2007. 192.cl/general/transantiago-en-100-palabras/.

Aravena, María E., and Franca Maccioni. *Sexo y trabajo: Textos sobre trabajo sexual en el contexto argentino actual*. La Sofía Cartonera, Facultad de Filosofía y Humanidades de la Universidad Nacional de Córdoba, 2013.

Archer, David, and Patrick Costello. *Literacy and Power: The Latin American Battleground*. Earthscan, 1990.

Argüelles, Juan D. *Leer bajo su propio riesgo: Mitos y realidades del hábito de leer*. Ediciones B, 2014.

———. Personal interview. Mexico City, 18 November 2015.

Arias, Eduardo, Luz M. Giraldo, and Mario Jursich Durán. *Cuentos en Bogotá*. IDARTES/TransMilenio, 2005.

Arnold, Ignacio, Carmen García, and Sylvia Dümmer, editors. *10 años de Santiago en 100 Palabras (2001–2010)*. Plagio, 2010.

Assunção, Ademir. *Tribêbada: Contos escritos por freqüentadores da Mercearia São Pedro*. Dulcinéia Catadora, 2009.

Ávila, Fredy. "Mercado de libros, libros en el mercado." *Ciudad Viva*, January 2007, p. 8.

Baena Echeverry, Carlos A., et al. *El regateo, la ñapa y la vaca*. Amapola Cartonera, 2013.

Barbera, Verónica, and Manuel Negrín. Personal interview. La Plata, Argentina, 3 June 2015.

Barbosa, Frederico. *SigniCidade*. Dulcinéia Catadora, 2009.

Barthes, Roland. "From Work to Text." *The Rustle of Language*, translated by Richard Howard, Farrar, Straus and Giroux, 1986, pp. 56–64.

Barton, David. *Literacy: An Introduction to the Ecology of Written Language*. Blackwell, 2007.

Bartra, Roger. "Los nuevos espacios públicos de la izquierda." *Reabrir espacios públicos: Políticas culturales y ciudadanía*, edited by Néstor García Canclini and Lourdes Arizpe S., Universidad Autónoma Metropolitana/Plaza y Valdés, 2004, pp. 331–344.

Bechis, Marco, et al., director. *Garage Olimpo*. Manga Films, 2004.
Bedoya de Flórez, Fabiola, and David F. Estrada Betancur. *Pedro Nel Gómez, muralista*. Universidad de Antioquia/Universidad Pontificia Bolivariana, 2003.
Berney, Rachel. "Pedagogical Urbanism: Creating Citizen Space in Bogota, Colombia." *Planning Theory*, vol. 10, no. 1, 2011, pp. 16–34.
Berni, Antonio. *Juanito Laguna aprende a leer*. Museo de Bellas Artes, 1961.
Bienal de São Paulo. *27a Bienal de São Paulo [Guide]*. Bienal de São Paulo, 2006.
Bilbija, Ksenija. "Fiction's Mysterious Ways: Eloisa Cartonera." *Review: Literatures and Arts of the Americas*, no. 88, 2014, pp. 13–20.
———. "What's Left in the World of Books: Washington Cucurto and the Eloisa Cartonera Project in Argentina." *Journal of Latin American Cultural Studies*, vol. 27, 2008, pp. 85–102.
Bilbija, Ksenija, and Paloma Celis Carbajal, editors. *Akademia Cartonera: A Primer of Latin American Cartonera Publishers = Un ABC de las editoriales cartoneras en América Latina*. Parallel Press/University of Wisconsin–Madison Libraries, 2009.
Bilbija, Ksenija, and Leigh A. Payne. "Introduction. Time is Money: The Memory Market in Latin America." *Accounting for Violence: Marketing Memory in Latin America*, edited by Ksenija Bilbija and Leigh A. Payne, Duke University Press, 2011, pp. 1–40.
Bishop, Karen E. "The Architectural History of Disappearance: Rebuilding Memory Sites in the Southern Cone." *Journal of the Society of Architectural Historians*, vol. 73, no. 4, 2014, pp. 556–578.
Blanco Calderón, Rodrigo. "Mi primera y última cena con Jaime Garzón." *Bogotá contada*, edited by Antonio García Ángel, IDARTES/Libro al Viento, 2013, pp. 42–54.
Bloodworth, Sandra, and William S. Ayres. *Along the Way: MTA Arts for Transit*. Monacelli, 2006.
Boero, María Soledad. Personal e-mail communication, 28 August 2015.
Bogotá un Libro Abierto. Advertisement. *Número*, number 54, September 2007, p. 61.
Bonasso, Miguel. "Homenaje a Rodolfo Walsh." *El golpe a los libros: Represión a la cultura durante la última dictadura militar*, Hernán Invernizzi and Judith Gociol, Eudeba, 2002, pp. 395–397.
Borja, Jordi. "La ciudad es el espacio público." *Espacio público y reconstrucción de ciudadanía*, edited by Patricia Ramírez Kuri and Miguel Angel Porrúa, Facultad Latinoamericana de Ciencias Sociales, 2003, pp. 59–87.
Boschi, Silvana. *El manto de plata*. Ministerio de Cultura de Buenos Aires, 2011.
Bossié, Florencia. "Un libro sobre los libros prohibidos: *Libros que muerden*." librosquemuerden-lagrieta.blogspot.com/2014/06/un-libro-sobre-los-libros-prohibidos.html#more.
Botto, Malena. "1990–2000: La concentración y la polarización de la industria editorial." *Editores y políticas editoriales en Argentina, 1880–2000*, edited by José L. Diego, Fondo de Cultura Económica, 2006, pp. 209–249.

Braedley, Susan, and Meg Luxton, editors. *Neoliberalism and Everyday Life*. McGill-Queen's University Press, 2010.
Brantmayer, Jorge, and André Perez Retes. "Biblioteca Recuperada UDP/Biblioteca Nicanor Parra." www.youtube.com/watch?v=8m-nlcENXXo.
Brodsky, Marcelo. *V7inter. Los condenados de la tierra*. Television interview. Televisión Pública Argentina, 11 May 2013. www.youtube.com/watch?v=morM-FixU9k.
Brodsky, Marcelo, and Eduardo Feller, directors. *Los condenados de la tierra*. 2001. www.youtube.com/watch?v=X-oolT8XIOo.
Brodsky, Marcelo, et al. *Nexo: Un ensayo fotográfico*. La Marca/Centro Cultural Recoleta, 2001.
Brouwer, Daniel C., and Robert Asen. *Public Modalities: Rhetoric, Culture, Media, and the Shape of Public Life*. University of Alabama Press, 2010.
Brum, Eliane. "A Terceira margem da rua." *Cátia, Simone e outras marvadas*, edited by Sebastião Nicomedes, Dulcinéia Catadora, 2007, pp. 6–7.
Bucchioni, Xenya. "Nossa proposta é artística e política." Interview with Lúcia Rosa, Circuito SESC de Artes, 22 April 2015. http://xenyabucchioni.com.br/circuito-sesc-das-artes-2015/.
Buendía Astudillo, Alexander. "Ciudad, espacio público y comunicación: Una reflexión en torno al discurso pedagógico de y sobre la ciudad." *Lo urbano en su complejidad: Una lectura desde América Latina*, edited by Marco Córdova Montúfar, FLASCO Ecuador/Ministerio de Cultura, 2008, pp. 257–266.
Busato, Susanna. "As tramas e as trilhas de cidade: Um exercicio para o olhar." *SigniCidade*, Frederico Barbosa, Dulcinéia Catadora, 2009, p. 3.
Caja de ideas: para darle vida al acervo Retomo la Palabra. CERLALC, 2009.
Cala Buendía, Felipe. *Cultural Producers and Social Change in Latin America*. Palgrave Macmillan, 2014.
Calhoun, Craig J., editor. *Habermas and the Public Sphere*. MIT Press, 1992.
Calloni, Stella. "Las asambleas populares: El susurro de la resurrección de un pueblo." *¿Qué son las asambleas populares?*, edited by Rafael Bielsa et al., Continente/Peña Lillo, 2002, pp. 16–21.
Campos Medina, Luis. "Representaciones de la ciudad en cien palabras: Narraciones breves y significaciones durables." *Revista Kütral*, vol. 2, no. 2, 2011, pp. 98–117.
Cano Reyes, Jesús. "¿Un nuevo *boom* latinoamericano? La explosión de las editoriales cartoneras." *Espéculo: Revista de estudios literarios*, no. 47, 2011. pendientedemigracion.ucm.es/info/especulo/numero47/boomlati.html.
Caram, Oscar. *Que se vaya todo: Asambleas, horizontes y resistencias: (un cruce de voces en el movimiento popular)*. Manuel Suárez Editor, 2002.
Cárcamo-Huechante, Luis E. *Tramas del mercado: Imaginación económica, cultura pública y literatura en el Chile de fines del siglo veinte*. Cuarto Propio, 2007.
Carneiro, Daniele. *Guia prático para bibliotecas comunitárias*. Magnolia Cartonera, 2016.

Caro Montoya, Juan D., director. *Crónica de un año feliz: Bogotá Capital Mundial del Libro 2007.* Secretaría Distrital de Cultura, Recreación y Deporte, 2007.
Carreras, Nicolás, director. *Prohibido no leer: Literatura infantil prohibida en la Dictadura.* 2013. www.youtube.com/watch?t=93&v=yhSnlOOybew and www.youtube.com/watch?v=5ITb7YKygz8.
Carrero, Raimundo. *O paraíso de pão e manteiga.* Translated by Katia B. de Mello-Gerlach, Dulcinéia Catadora, 2009.
Carvacho Duarte, Alberto E. "Plan regulador metropolitano de Santiago. Seremi 1994." *Juan Parrochia Beguin: Premio 1996: 6 planes para Santiago,* Antártica, 1996, pp. 61–68.
Casanova, Pascale. *The World Republic of Letters.* Harvard University Press, 2004.
Castro Castro, Ana P. "Un sombrero para la plaza." *Los que cuentan,* edited by Ana C. Mejía and Guillermo González Uribe, *Número*/Secretaría de Cultura, Recreación y Deporte, 2008, pp. 73–80.
Castro Osorio, Carolina. *Libro al Viento: Seguimiento y evaluación de impacto.* IDARTES, 2007.
Celis Carbajal, Paloma. "Las *cartoneras*: Editoriales alternativas que recorren el mundo." Interview by Saylín Álvarez, Madison, WI, July 2012.
———. Personal interview. Madison, Wisconsin, 26 March 2015.
Centro Latinoamericano de Economía Humana. *La construcción de conocimiento en cultura: Hacia la constitución de una red de profesionales y académicos de la cultura y centro de documentación.* Proyecto Vivi Cultura, Dirección Nacional de la Cultura, Ministerio de Cultura y Educación, 2010.
Centro Regional para el Fomento del Libro en América Latina y el Caribe (CERLALC). *El libro y la edición: Hacia una agenda de políticas públicas.* CERLALC, 2002.
Cepeda Buitrago, Yezid. "Con los pies en la tierra." *Los que cuentan,* edited by Ana C. Mejía and Guillermo González Uribe, *Número*/Secretaría de Cultura, Recreación y Deporte, 2008, pp. 81–92.
Cerruti, Isabel, coord. *Ex centro clandestino de detención, tortura y exterminio "Olimpo."* Instituto Espacio de la Memoria, 2008.
———, coord. *Ex centro clandestino de detención, tortura y exterminio "Olimpo."* Updated ed., Instituto Espacio de la Memoria, 2010.
Certeau, Michel de. *The Practice of Everyday Life.* Translated by Steven Rendall, University of California Press, 1984.
Chartier, Roger. *Lectures et lecteurs dans la France d'ancien régime.* Seuil, 1987.
Coelho, Oliverio. "Instrucciones para recordar una ciudad." *La ciudad contada: Buenos Aires en la mirada de la nueva narrativa hispanoamericana,* edited by Maximiliano Tomas, Ministerio de Cultura del Gobierno de la Ciudad Autónoma de Buenos Aires, 2012, pp. 97–106.
Cohen, Selma. *Los avatares del yo: Literatura argentina en primera persona a partir de 1990.* PhD dissertation, Rutgers University, 2012. ProQuest 3541067, 2012.

Colectivo La Grieta. *La muestra ambulante*. Universidad Nacional de La Plata, 2009.
Córdoba Martínez, Carlos. "Sara." *Los que cuentan*, edited by Ana C. Mejía and Guillermo González Uribe, *Número*/Secretaría de Cultura, Recreación y Deporte, 2008, pp. 139–146.
Cortázar, Julio. *Rayuela*. Sudamericana, 1963.
Costamagna, Alejandra. Untitled essay. *10 Años de Santiago en 100 Palabras (2001–2010)*, edited by Ignacio Arnold, Carmen García, and Sylvia Dümmer, Plagio, 2010, p. 189.
Coulin, Federico. Personal interview. Buenos Aires, 16 March 2012.
Crembil, Gustavo, and Peter Lynch. "No Resistance." *Journal of Architectural Education*, vol. 62, no. 4, 2009, pp. 48–55.
"Cronología de la crisis del 2001." República Económica. republica-economica.blogspot.com/2011/01/cronologia-de-la-crisis-del-2001.html.
Cuadra, Álvaro. *De la ciudad letrada a la ciudad virtual*. LOM, 2003.
Cucurto, Washington. *1999: Poemas de siempre, poemas nuevos y nuevas versiones*, illustrations by Pablo Martín. Eloísa Cartonera, 2007.
———. *El amor es mucho más que una novela de 500 páginas*. Eloísa Cartonera, 2009.
———. *Las aventuras del Sr. Maíz: El héroe atrapado entre dos mundos*. Interzona, 2005.
———. *La Cartonerita*. Ediciones VOX/Senda, 2003.
———. *Como un paraguayo ebrio y celoso de su hermana*. Vox, 2005.
———. *Cosa de negros*. Interzona, 2003.
———. *La culpa es de Francia*. Emecé, 2012.
———. *El curandero del amor*. Emecé, 2006.
———. *Hasta quitarle Panamá a los yanquis*. Eloísa Cartonera, 2005.
———. *El rey de la cumbia: Contra los fucking Estados Unidos de América*. Cuarto Propio, 2010.
———. *Veinte pungas contra un pasajero*. Vox, 2003.
Cucurto, Washington, and María Gómez. Personal e-mail communication. 18 December 2013.
———. Personal interview. Buenos Aires, 17 March 2012.
Cuervo G., Carolina. "Refugio en La Soledad." *Talleres de crónicas barriales: Antología*, edited by Maryluz Vallejo Mejía, Alcaldía de Bogotá/Archivo de Bogotá, 2007, pp. 105–109.
D'Angelo, Ana, editor. *Catador*. Dulcinéia Catadora, 2012.
Darrigrandi, Claudia, and Antonia Viu. "Introducción Dossier Culturas Lectoras en América Latina, siglos XX y XXI." *Revista de Humanidades* (Chile), no. 35, 2017, pp. 11–14.
Dávila, María d. L. *Desembarcos en el papel: La imagen en la literatura de Julio Cortázar*. Beatriz Viterbo, 2001.
Degiovanni, Fernando. "Lectores retratados: Visualidades de lo impreso en la cultura Argentina." Keynote address, Orbis Tertius Conference, La Plata, Argentina, 5 June 2015.
Delgado, Josefina, editor. *12 narradores argentinos 2009*. Ministerio de Cultura, 2009.

Delgado, Josefina. Personal interview. Buenos Aires, 3 May 2011.
Diez, Carola. Personal interview. Mexico City, 23 November 2015.
Dos Santos Piúba, Fabiano. "Las ferias del libro: Espacios de educación, cultura, economía y ciudadanía." *Las Ferias del Libro: Manual para expositores y visitantes profesionales*, Fernando Zapata López, CERLALC/UNESCO, 2012, pp. 45–54.
Draper, Susana. *Afterlives of Confinement: Spatial Transitions in Post-Dictatorship Latin America*. University of Pittsburgh Press, 2012.
Dulcinéia Catadora, editor. *De lá pra cá, de cá pra lá: Abrindo caminhos entre a Pedra Lisa e a cidade*. Dulcinéia Catadora, 2013.
———. *Nós, daqui: Documentos, fotos e relatos de moradores da Pedra Lisa*. Dulcinéia Catadora, 2013.
———. *ProvidênciaS*. Dulcinéia Catadora, 2012.
———. *Soluções providenciais*. Dulcinéia Catadora, 2013.
Duque López, Alberto. "Manzanita envenenada." *Los que cuentan*, edited by Ana C. Mejía and Guillermo González Uribe, *Número*/Secretaría de Cultura, Recreación y Deporte, 2008, pp. 127–138.
Epplin, Craig. *Late Book Culture in Argentina*. Continuum, 2014.
———. "New Media, Cardboard, and Community in Contemporary Buenos Aires." *Hispanic Review*, vol. 75, no. 4, 2007, pp. 385–398.
Esmoris, Manuel. "Cultura: Artes, patrimonio y tradiciones. Gestión cultural: una profesión de servicio." *Cuadernos del CLAEH*, vol. 32, no. 98, 2009, pp. 37–54.
España, Gonzalo. *La biblioteca*. Ediciones B, 2008.
———. *Letras en el fuego: el libro en Bogotá*. Panamericana, 2007.
Espinosa Caro, Julio. "Artevida y Amapola." *Hecho en Usaquén*. Amapola Cartonera, 2014, p. 65.
Faivre d'Arcier, Bruno. "Measuring the Performance of Urban Public Transport in Relation to Policy Objectives." *Research in Transportation Economics*, vol. 48, 2014, pp. 67–76.
Feijóo, Cristina, and Lucio Salas Oroño. "Las asambleas y el movimiento social." *¿Qué son las asambleas populares?*, edited by Rafael Bielsa et al., Continente/Peña Lillo, 2002, pp. 22–30.
Feinmann, José P. "Filosofía de la asamblea popular." *¿Qué son las asambleas populares?*, edited by Rafael Bielsa et al., Continente/Peña Lillo, 2002, pp. 31–33.
Fernández, José, and María A. Rojas. *El golpe al libro y a las bibliotecas de la Universidad de Chile: Limpieza y censura en el corazón de la universidad*. Universidad Tecnológica Metropolitana, 2015.
Fernández L'Hoeste, Héctor. "The TransMilenio Experience: Mass Transit in Bogotá and National Urban Identity." *Cultures of the City: Mediating Identities in Urban Latin/o America*, edited by Richard Young and Amanda Holmes, University of Pittsburgh Press, 2010, pp. 151–166.
Fiorito, Susana. "Las bibliotecas populares." *Monopolios artificiales sobre bienes intangibles*, Fundación Vía Libre, 2007. www.vialibre.org.ar/mabi/5-las-bibliotecas-populares.htm.
Foucault, Michel. "What Is an Author?" *Aesthetics, Method, and Epistemol-*

ogy, edited by James B. Faubion, translated by Robert Hurley et al., New Press, 1998, pp. 205–222.

Franco, Jean. *The Decline and Fall of the Lettered City: Latin America in the Cold War.* Harvard University Press, 2002.

Fraser, Ben. "Inaugural Editorial: Urban Cultural Studies—a Manifesto (Part I)." *Journal of Urban Cultural Studies*, vol. 1, no. 1, 2014, pp. 3–17.

Fresneda, Martín. "Prólogo." *Espacios de Memoria en la Argentina*, by Judith Said, Ciudad Autónoma de Buenos Aires: Ministerio de Justicia y Derechos de la Nación, Secretaría de Derechos Humanos, 2015, p. 4.

Friera, Silvina. "Preparándose para Alemania." *Página 12*, 7 May 2009. www.pagina12.com.ar/diario/suplementos/espectaculos/2-13779-2009-05-07.html.

Gainza, Carolina. "Escrituras electrónicas en América Latina: Producción literaria en el capitalismo informacional." PhD dissertation, University of Pittsburgh, 2012.

Galeano, Eduardo. *Las palabras andantes*. Chanchito, 1993.

García, Carmen. Personal interview. Santiago, Chile, 28 April 2011.

García Ángel, Antonio. "Persona grata/ Persona non grata." *La ciudad contada: Buenos Aires en la mirada de la nueva narrativa hispanoamericana*, edited by Maximiliano Tomas, Ministerio de Cultura del Gobierno de la Ciudad Autónoma de Buenos Aires, 2012, pp. 147–167.

———, editor. *Bogotá contada*. IDARTES/Libro al Viento, 2013.

———, editor. *Bogotá contada 2.0*. IDARTES/Libro al Viento, 2015.

———, editor. *Recetario santafereño*. IDARTES, 2013.

García Canclini, Néstor. *Art beyond Itself: Anthropology for a Society without a Story Line*. Translated by David L. Frye, Duke University Press, 2014.

———. *Consumers and Citizens: Globalization and Multicultural Conflicts*. Translated by George Yudice, University of Minnesota Press, 2001.

———. *Hybrid Cultures: Strategies for Entering and Leaving Modernity*. Translated by Christopher Chiappari and Silvia Lopez, University of Minnesota Press, 1995.

———, editor. *Imaginarios urbanos*. Eudeba, 1997.

García Canclini, Néstor, and Lourdes Arizpe S., editors. *Reabrir espacios públicos: Políticas culturales y ciudadanía*. Universidad Autónoma Metropolitana/Plaza y Valdés, 2004.

"Gente y Cuentos-Colombia." 2008. www.youtube.com/watch?v=ISRycSRojyU.

Gerencia de Literatura. Instituto Distrital de las Artes. *Protocolo del programa Libro al Viento*. Alcaldía Mayor de Bogotá, 2014.

Girondo, Oliverio. *Obra completa*. Edited by Raúl Antelo, Galaxia Gutenberg/Círculo de Lectores, 1999.

———. *Veinte poemas para ser leídos en el tranvía*. Ministerio de Cultura, Gobierno de la Ciudad de Buenos Aires, 2011.

———. *20 poemas para ser leídos en el tranvía*. Proa, 1925.

———. *Veinte poemas para ser leídos en el tranvía*. Coulouman H. Barthelemy, 1922.

———. *Veinte poemas para ser leídos en el tranvía*. Tajamar, 2011.

———. *Veinte poemas para ser leídos en el tranvía. Calcomanías. Espantapájaros.* Centro Editor de América Latina, 1966.
———. *Veinte poemas para ser leídos en el tranvía; Calcomanías; y Otros poemas.* Visor, 1989.
Girondo, Oliverio, and Jorge Schwartz. *Homenaje a Girondo.* Corregidor, 1987.
Godoy Barbosa, Oscar. "Susana y el sol." *Los que cuentan*, edited by Ana C. Mejía and Guillermo González Uribe, *Número*/Secretaría de Cultura, Recreación y Deporte, 2008, pp. 23–30.
González-Pérez, Aníbal. *Journalism and the Development of Spanish American Narrative.* Cambridge University Press, 1993.
Gooding, Mel, and Public Art Commissions Agency. "Public:Arts:Space." *Public—Art—Space: A Decade of Public Art Commissions Agency, 1987–1997*, Merrell Holberton, 1998, pp. 13–20.
Gordon-Burroughs, Jessica. "The Material Lives of Books: Politics of the Copy, the Canon, and the Reader in Cuba, Venezuela, and Chile (1960–present)." PhD dissertation, Columbia University, 2015.
———. "Red Wine and Gangrene: Subterranean Santiago." *Crítica Latinoamericana.* criticalatinoamericana.com/red-wine-and-gangrene-subterranean-santiago/.
———. "Straight Pins, Gauze, and Linotypes: The Cuban Post-Soviet Artists' 'Archival' Book." *Journal of Latin American Cultural Studies*, forthcoming.
Gorelik, Adrián. "A Metropolis in the Pampas: Buenos Aires 1890–1940." *Cruelty & Utopia: Cities and Landscapes of Latin America*, edited by Jean-François Lejeune, Princeton Architectural Press, pp. 146–159.
Greco, Martín. "El farol de Girondo." *Escritores del mundo*, 2011. www.escritoresdelmundo.com/2011/10/el-farol-de-girondo-por-martin-greco.html.
Greene F., Ricardo. *Mi Santiasco querido: Exploraciones del imaginario urbano en cien palabras.* Instituto de Estudios Urbanos y Territoriales, Santiago, 2006.
Gregson, Nicky, and Louise Crewe. *Second-Hand Cultures.* Berg, 2003.
Griffin, Jane. *The Labor of Literature: Democracy and Literary Culture in Modern Chile.* University of Massachusetts Press, 2016.
Grosz, E. A. *Architecture from the Outside: Essays on Virtual and Real Space.* MIT Press, 2001.
Guerrero, Arturo. *Bibliotecas de Bogotá.* Rocca, 2008.
Gumucio, Rafael. Untitled essay. *10 Años de Santiago en 100 Palabras (2001–2010)*, edited by Ignacio Arnold, Carmen García, and Sylvia Dümmer, Plagio, 2010, p. 125.
Habermas, Jürgen. *The Structural Transformation of the Public Sphere: An Inquiry into a Category of Bourgeois Society.* MIT Press, 1991.
"Hágase socio de las Biblioestaciones." *Ciudad Viva*, April 2008, p. 6.
Hardt, Michael, and Antonio Negri. *Commonwealth.* Belknap, 2009.
Harvey, David. *Rebel Cities: From the Right to the City to the Urban Revolution.* Verso, 2012.
Heffes, Gisela. *Políticas de la destrucción, poéticas de la preservación:*

Apuntes para una lectura (eco) crítica del medio ambiente en América Latina. Beatriz Viterbo, 2013.

Henkin, David M. *City Reading: Written Words and Public Spaces in Antebellum New York*. Columbia University Press, 1998.

Hernández, Paola. "The ESMA: From Torture Chambers to New Sites of Memory." *Imagining Human Rights in Twenty-First Century Theater: Global Perspectives*, edited by Florian Becker, Paola Hernández, and Brenda Werth, Palgrave, 2013, pp. 67–82.

Hernández, Raúl. Personal interview. New York, 15 May 2015.

Herrera Casilimas, Juan C. "Rayado de lo escondido." *Talleres de crónicas barriales: Antología*, edited by Maryluz Vallejo Mejía, Alcaldía de Bogotá/Archivo de Bogotá, 2007, pp. 197–200.

Hirschman, Sarah. *Gente y cuentos ¿A quién pertenece la literatura? Las comunidades encuentran su voz a través de los cuentos*. Translated by Julio Paredes Castro, Fondo de Cultura Económica, 2011.

——. *People and Stories Gente y Cuentos: Who Owns Literature? Communities Find Their Voice through Short Stories*. IUniverse, 2009.

Hoyos, Héctor M. "La paga." *Cuentos en Bogotá*, edited by Eduardo Arias, Luz M. Giraldo, and Mario Jursich Durán, IDARTES/TransMilenio, 2005, pp. 15–25.

Huergo, Damián. "Juguetes rabiosos." *Página 12*, 19 June 2014. www.pagina12.com.ar/diario/suplementos/libros/10-5344-2014-06-19.html.

Hurtado Tarazona, Adriana. *Portales de Transmilenio: Revitalización de espacios e integración social urbana*. Universidad de los Andes, Centro Interdisciplinario de Estudios sobre Desarrollo-CIDER, 2008.

Invernizzi, Hernán, and Judith Gociol. *Un golpe a los libros: Represión a la cultura durante la última dictadura militar*. Eudeba, 2003.

Jaramillo H., Bernardo. "Ferias, lectura y circulación del libro." *Las Ferias del Libro: Manual para expositores y visitantes profesionales*, Fernando Zapata López, CERLALC/UNESCO, 2012, pp. 39–43.

Jeftanovic, Andrea. Untitled essay. *10 Años de Santiago en 100 Palabras (2001–2010)*, edited by Ignacio Arnold, Carmen García, and Sylvia Dümmer, Plagio, 2010, p. 25.

Jelin, Elizabeth, and Victoria Langland, editors. *Monumentos, memoriales y marcas territoriales*. Siglo Veintiuno de Argentina, 2003.

Joncquel, Maryline. Personal interview. Buenos Aires, 19 March 2012.

Jorquera, Miguel. "El traspaso de los espacios de memoria." *Página 12*, 9 May 2014. www.pagina12.com.ar/diario/elpais/1-245843-2014-05-09.html.

Jovani, Sebastià. "(Vana) tentativa de agotamiento de un lugar colombiano." *Bogotá contada*, edited by Antonio García Ángel, IDARTES/Libro al Viento, 2013, pp. 108–117.

Kalman, Judy, and Brian V. Street. *Literacy and Numeracy in Latin America: Local Perspectives and Beyond*. Routledge, 2012.

Kaminsky, Amy. "Marco Bechis' *Garage Olimpo*: Cinema of Witness." *Jump Cut*, no. 48, 2006. www.ejumpcut.org/archive/jc48.2006/GarageOlimpo/text.html.

Kopytoff, Igor. "The Cultural Biography of Things: Commoditization as Pro-

cess." *Social Life of Things: Commodities in Cultural Perspective*, edited by Arjun Appadurai, Cambridge University Press, 1986, pp. 64–91.
Korzin, Ariel. "Biblioteca Pública y Popular 'Carlos Fuentealba.'" *Ex centro clandestino de detención, tortura y exterminio "Olimpo,"* coordinated by Isabel Cerruti, Instituto Espacio de la Memoria, 2008, pp. 65–72.
Krauze, Enrique. *Redeemers: Ideas and Power in Latin America.* Translated by Hank Heifetz and Natasha Wimmer, Harper, 2011.
Kudaibergen, Jania. "Las editoriales cartoneras y los procesos de empoderamiento en la industria creativa mexicana." *Cuadernos Americanos*, vol. 152, no. 2, 2015, pp. 127–146.
Kumaraswami, Par, and Antoni Kapcia. *Literary Culture in Cuba: Revolution, Nation-Building and the Book.* Manchester University Press, 2012.
Labbé, Carlos. "La literatura en el espacio público: Un diálogo con Carlos Labbé." Interview by Marcy Schwartz. *Confluencia*, vol. 30, no. 2, 2015, pp. 168–178.
Lacerda, Romina. "A galinha feia." *Soluções Providenciais*, edited by Dulcinéia Catadora, Dulcinéia Catadora, 2013, p. 77.
Ledesma, Eduardo. *Radical Poetry: Aesthetics, Politics, Technology, and the Ibero-American Avant-Gardes, 1900–2015.* SUNY Press, 2016.
"Leer . . . severo viaje." *Revista Leer . . . Severo Viaje*, issuu.com/erreachenegativo/docs/revistaleerseveroviaje.
Lefebvre, Henri. *The Production of Space.* Blackwell, 1991.
Leidenberger, Georg. *La historia viaja en tranvía: El transporte público y la cultura política de la ciudad de México.* Universidad Autónoma Metropolitana, 2011.
Lemebel, Pedro. "El Metro de Santiago (o 'esa azul radiante rapidez')." 25 May 2006. lemebel.blogspot.com/search?q=metro+Santiago.
Libro al Viento. Brochure. IDARTES, 2007.
Lombardi, Hernán. "Introducción." *La ciudad contada: Buenos Aires en la mirada de la nueva narrativa hispanoamericana*, edited by Maximiliano Tomas, Ministerio de Cultura del Gobierno de la Ciudad Autónoma de Buenos Aires, 2012, pp. 11–13.
———. "Palabras del Ministro de Cultura." *Julio Cortázar/Georges Perec: Versiones de la imaginación.* Ministerio de Cultura de Buenos Aires, 2012, pp. 8–11.
MacCormack, Sabine. "Atahualpa and the Book." *Dispositio*, vol. 14, nos. 36–38, 1989, pp. 141–168.
Magnolia Cartonera. *Ideias para bibliotecas livres—Um manual prático de autogestão independente.* Magnolia Cartonera, 2016.
Mahieux, Viviane. *Urban Chroniclers in Modern Latin America: The Shared Intimacy of Everyday Life.* University of Texas Press, 2011.
Manzano, Valeria. "*Garage Olimpo* o cómo proyectar el pasado sobre el presente (y vice-versa)." *El pasado que miramos: Memoria e imagen ante la historia reciente*, edited by Claudia Feld and Jessica Stites-Mor, Paidós, 2009, pp. 154–180.
Mardero, Natalia. "Ya no sé qué camino tomar." *La ciudad contada: Buenos Aires en la mirada de la nueva narrativa hispanoamericana*, edited

by Maximiliano Tomas, Ministerio de Cultura del Gobierno de la Ciudad Autónoma de Buenos Aires, 2012, pp. 39-49.

Mardones Z., Rodrigo. "Chile: Transantiago Reloaded." *Revista de Ciencia Política*, vol. 28, no. 1, 2008, pp. 103-119.

Martinell, Alfons. "Las interacciones en la profesionalización en gestión cultural." *Cuadernos del CLAEH*, vol. 32, no. 98, 2009, pp. 97-105.

Martínez Daniell, Sebastián. "Razones de la multitud letrada." *Ñ*, 7 May 2011, pp. 16-17.

Masiello, Francine. *The Art of Transition: Latin American Culture and Neoliberal Crisis*. Duke University Press, 2001.

———. "Reading for the People and Getting There First." *The Ethics of Latin American Literary Criticism: Reading Otherwise*, edited by Erin Graff Zivin, Palgrave Macmillan, 2007, pp. 201-216.

Massone Mezzano, Claudio. "Decreto 420: Planificación urbana 1979/1990." *Juan Parrochia Beguin: Premio 1996: 6 planes para Santiago*. Antártica, 1996, pp. 56-60.

Mattini, Luis. "La hora de las comunas." *¿Qué son las asambleas populares?*, edited by Rafael Bielsa et al., Continente/Peña Lillo, 2002, pp. 44-55.

Mejía, Ana C., and Guillermo González Uribe, editors. *Los que cuentan*. Número/Secretaría de Cultura, Recreación y Deporte, 2008.

Melguizo, Lina M., and María Candelaria Posada. *Crónica de un año feliz: Bogotá Capital Mundial del Libro 2007*. Secretaría Distrital de Cultura, Recreación y Deporte, 2007.

Melicchio, Pablo. *Crónica de los hombres que buscan un lugar*. Subsecretaría de Cultura/Ministerio de Cultura GCBA, 2011.

———. *Letra en la sombra*. Mondadori, 2008.

Merbilhaá, Margarita. "1900-1910. La época de organización del espacio editorial." *Editores y políticas editoriales en Argentina, 1880-2000*, edited by José L. Diego, Fondo de Cultura Económica, 2006, pp. 29-58.

Miller, Valerie Lee. *Between Struggle and Hope: The Nicaraguan Literacy Crusade*. Westview, 1985.

Mindlin, José. "The Book in Brazil: Libraries and Presses." Translated by Thomas L. Burns and Gláucia R. Gonçalves. *Literary Cultures of Latin America: A Comparative History*, 3 vols., edited by Mario Valdés and Djelal Kadir, Oxford University Press, 2004, vol. 2, pp. 23-27.

Minujín, Marta. Interview by Alicia de Arteaga. Feria Internacional del Libro, Buenos Aires, 1 May 2011.

———. *El Parthenon de Libros/Homenaje a la Democracia*. Installation, Buenos Aires, 1983.

———. *La Torre de Babel de Libros*. Installation, Buenos Aires, 2011.

Minujín, Marta, and Jorge L. Borges. *La Torre de Babel 2011/La biblioteca de Babel*, Ministerio de Cultura de Buenos Aires, 2011.

Mockus, Antanas, and Jimmy Corzo. *Cumplir para convivir: factores de conviviencia y tipos de jóvenes por su relación con normas y acuerdos*. Universidad Nacional de Colombia, 2003.

Moliner, María. *Diccionario de uso del español*. 2 vols. Gredos, 1987.

Montalván Lamas, Olga. "La campana de alfabetización: Su significado en

la revolución educacional." *Revista de la Biblioteca Nacional José Martí*, vol. 1, 1988, pp. 113–127.
Montt, Nahum. *Retomo la palabra: Relatos de violencia y reconciliación*. CERLALC, Alta Consejería para la Reintegración Social, 2010.
Moraña, Mabel, editor. *Ángel Rama y los estudios latinoamericanos*. Instituto Internacional de Literatura Iberoamericana, University of Pittsburgh, 2006.
Morris, Adam. "Recycling Literary Culture: A Conversation with Lúcia Rosa." *Public Books*, 18 June 2012. www.publicbooks.org/recycling-literary-culturea-conversation-with-lucia-rosa/.
Motoa Franco, Felipe. "El libro impreso vende 15 veces más que el electrónico." *El Tiempo*, 12 October 2015. www.eltiempo.com/bogota/libro-impreso-aumenta-sus-ventas/16400965.
Mühlschlegel, Ulrike, and Ricarda Musser. "De cómo la Donazela Teodora atravesó el mar, se casó con un cangaceiro y finalmente descubrió la cibernética en São Paulo: La literatura de cordel brasileña como medio de masas." *Iberoamericana*, vol. 2, no. 6, pp. 143–160.
Mujica H., María C. "Santiago en 100 palabras: Escenas y fragmentos de la memoria." *EURE*, vol. 31, no. 92, May 2005, pp. 123–130.
Muñoz, Boris, and Silvia Spitta, editors. *Más allá de la ciudad letrada: Crónicas y espacios urbanos*. Biblioteca de América, Instituto Internacional de Literatura Iberoamericana, University of Pittsburgh, 2003.
Muñoz, Juan C., Marco Batarce, and Darío Hidalgo. "Transantiago, Five Years after Its Launch." *Research in Transportation Economics*, vol. 48, 2014, pp. 184–193.
Muzart Fonseca dos Santos, Idelette. "Literatura de Cordel: Literature for Market and Voice." *Literary Cultures of Latin America: A Comparative History*, vol. 1, edited by Mario Valdés and Djelal Kadir, Oxford University Press, 2004, pp. 614–619.
Navarro, Elvira. "Buenos Aires: A tomar por el culo." *La ciudad contada: Buenos Aires en la mirada de la nueva narrativa hispanoamericana*, edited by Maximiliano Tomas, Ministerio de Cultura del Gobierno de la Ciudad Autónoma de Buenos Aires, 2012, pp. 169–184.
Nel Gómez, Pedro. *Homenaje a la Inteligencia Antioqueña*. Mural, Biblioteca Pública Piloto, Medellín, 1979.
Nicomedes, Sebastião, editor. *Cátia, Simone e outras marvadas*. Dulcinéia Catadora, 2007.
Ospina Pizano, María, ed. *Cartas de la persistencia*. Fundación Gilberto Alzate Avedaño/Banco de la República/Biblioteca Luis Ángel Arango, 2008.
Ossa, Carlos, Nelly Richard, and Armando Silva Téllez. *Santiago imaginado*. Convenio Andrés Bello/Universidad Nacional de Colombia, 2004.
"Para leer de boleto en el metro." televisa.esmas.com, May 2004.
Paredes Castro, Julio. "Introducción." *Pütchi Biyá Uai: Antología multilingüe de la literatura indígena contemporánea en Colombia*, edited by Miguel Rocha Vivas, Fundación Gilberto Alzate Avendaño, 2010, pp. 7–8.
———. Personal interview. Bogotá, Colombia, 3 November 2011.

Parise, Eduardo. "El tranvía, aquel fenómeno social." *Clarín*, 19 March 2012, p. 37.
Parrochia Beguin, Juan. *El futuro de ayer y el futuro de hoy*. Facultad de Arquitectura y Urbanismo, Universidad de Chile, 1987.
Paul, Carlos. "Comienza nueva etapa del programa Para leer de boleto en el Metro." *La Jornada*, 5 June 2007. www.jornada.unam.mx/2007/06/05/index.php?section=cultura&article=a05n1cul.
Paz Soldán, Edmundo, and Debra A. Castillo, editors. *Latin American Literature and Mass Media*. Garland, 2001.
Peñalosa, Enrique. *Conferencia de Enrique Peñalosa Londoño: (Alcalde Mayor de la ciudad de Bogotá, 1998–2001), en las ciudades de Caracas y Barquisimeto los días 16 y 17 de octubre de 2001*. Cuaderno 1, Fundación para la Cultura Urbana, 2003.
Perazzo, Nelly. "Berni's Objects from the 1960s." *Art Nexus*, no. 25, July 1997, pp. 60–64.
Pérez, Malena. "Una política cultural de doble subvención: Artistas y ciudadanos. Espectáculos de artes escénicas de calidad para habitantes en el interior del Uruguay." *Cuadernos del CLAEH*, vol. 32, no. 98, 2009, pp. 9–36.
Pérez Esquivel, Leonardo. "Cuando las cacerolas sonaron contra el neoliberalismo: Notas sobre las asambleas barriales." *¿Qué son las asambleas populares?*, edited by Rafael Bielsa et al., Continente/Peña Lillo, 2002, pp. 56–68.
Pérez Mejía, Ángela. "Epílogo." *Cartas de la persistencia*, edited by María Ospina Pizano, Fundación Gilberto Alzate Avedaño/Banco de la República/Biblioteca Luis Ángel Arango, 2008, 147–149.
Pesclevi, Gabriela. "La lectura." Facebook post, 3 September 2015.
———, editor. *Libros que muerden: Literatura infantil y juvenil censurada durante la última dictadura cívico-militar 1976–1983*. Biblioteca Nacional, 2013.
———. Personal interview. La Plata, Argentina, 3 June 2015.
Petit, Michèle. *Lecturas: Del espacio íntimo al espacio público*. Fondo de Cultura Económica, 2001.
———. *Leer el mundo: Experiencias actuales de transmisión cultural*. Translated by Vera Waksman. Fondo de Cultura Económica, 2015.
Pionér, P. "The Transantiago Project." *Public Transport International*, vol. 56, no. 5, 2007, pp. 44–46.
Poblete, Juan, editor. *Cambio cultural y lectura de periódicos en el siglo XIX en América Latina*. Special issue of *Revista Iberoamericana*, vol. 72, no. 214, 2006.
———. "Reading as a Historical Practice in Latin America: The First Colonial Period to the Nineteenth Century." *Literary Cultures of Latin America: A Comparative History*, vol. 1, edited by Mario Valdés and Djelal Kadir, Oxford University Press, 2004, pp. 178–192.
Prieto, Adolfo. *El discurso criollista en la formación de la Argentina moderna*. Sudamericana, 1988.
"Propuesta." Buenos Aires Capital Mundial del Libro. Ministry of Culture of Buenos Aires, 2009.

"Qué fue la Casona de Mansilla." *La Casona de Mansilla* website, 5 July 2011. lacasonademansilla.wordpress.com/2011/07/05/5/.

Quintana, Pilar. "Las guerras." *Bogotá contada*, edited by Antonio García Ángel, IDARTES/Libro al Viento, 2013, pp. 70–81.

Quiroga, José. *Cuban Palimpsests*. University of Minnesota Press, 2005.

Rabotnikof, Nora. "Izquierda y derecha: Visiones del mundo, opciones de gobierno e identidades políticas." *Reabrir espacios públicos: Políticas culturales y ciudadanía*, edited by Néstor García Canclini and Lourdes Arizpe S., Universidad Autónoma Metropolitana/Plaza y Valdés, 2004, pp. 307–330.

Rama, Ángel. *The Lettered City*. Translated by John C. Chasteen, Duke University Press, 1996.

Ramírez, Carlos. Personal interview. Bogotá, Colombia, 17 October 2014.

Ramírez Vallejo, Catalina. "En la Bogotá Positiva la promoción de la lectura seguirá siendo prioridad." *Ciudad Viva*, April 2008, p. 2.

Ramos Wettling, Ximena, and Tanya Núñez Grandón. Personal interview. Santiago, Chile, 25 April 2011.

Rapoport, Mario. *Historia económica, política y social de la Argentina (1880–2003)*. Ariel, 2006.

Rappaport, Joanne, and Thomas B. F. Cummins. *Beyond the Lettered City: Indigenous Literacies in the Andes*. Duke University Press, 2012.

Recart, María O. "Minera Escondida." *10 Años de Santiago en 100 Palabras (2001–2010)*, edited by Ignacio Arnold, Carmen García, and Sylvia Dümmer, Plagio, 2010, pp. 8–9.

Recoba, Diego. Personal interview. Montevideo, Uruguay, 6 May 2011.

Reyes, Alfonso. *The Position of America, and Other Essays*. Edited and translated by Harriet de Onís, Knopf, 1950.

———. *Última tule y otros ensayos*. Biblioteca Ayacucho, 1991.

Reyes, Álvaro Guillermo. "El hombre de la silla azul." *Cuentos en Bogotá*, edited by Eduardo Arias, Luz M. Giraldo, and Mario Jursich Durán, IDARTES/TransMilenio, 2005, pp. 106–118.

Richard, Nelly. *The Insubordination of Signs: Political Change, Cultural Transformation, and Poetics of the Crisis*. Duke University Press, 2004.

Rivas, Tomás. "Así funcionarán las bibliotecas con vagones del subte A." *La Nación*, 11 January 2013. www.lanacion.com.ar/1544813-asi-funcionaran-las-bibliotecas-con-vagones-del-subte-a.

Rivera, Carlos. *Transantiago: Humillación y negocio*. Ayun, 2008.

Rivera, Pedro. "Apresentação." *Soluções Providenciais*, edited by Dulcinéia Catadora, 2013, pp. 5–6.

Rocha Vivas, Miguel, ed. *Pütchi Biyá Uai: Antología multilingüe de la literatura indígena contemporánea en Colombia. Precursores*. Fundación Gilberto Alzate Avendaño, 2010.

———. *Pütchi Biyá Uai: Antología multilingüe de la literatura indígena contemporánea en Colombia. Puntos aparte*. Fundación Gilberto Alzate Avendaño, 2010.

Roda Fornaguera, Ana. *Bogotá Capital Mundial del Libro: Portafolio de Proyectos*. Fundalectura, 2007.

———. "Libro al Viento, un verdadero milagro al viento." *Ciudad Viva*, December 2007, section M, p. viii.
———. Personal interview. Bogotá, Colombia, 8 November 2011.
Rodrigues, Bárbara. "Qintiqartunira: Primorosas palabras." *Habla en Quechua: Como la estrella = Qichwapi rimay: quyllurshina = Speaking in Quechua: Like the Stars*, Genaro R. Quintero Bendezú et al., pp. 12–15.
Romero Rey, Sandro. "Capítulo final." *Los que cuentan*, edited by Ana C. Mejía and Guillermo González Uribe, *Número*/Secretaría de Cultura, Recreación y Deporte, 2008, pp. 147–160.
Ros, Ofelia. "Conflicto social, humor y lenguaje en la literatura y el proyecto editorial de Washington Cucurto." *Latin American Research Review*, vol. 50, no. 2, 2015, pp. 23–41.
Rosa, Allan da, et al. *Um sarau da Cooperifa: Coletánea de poemas recolhidos em 24.01.07, véspera do aniversário de São Paulo, no sarau da Cooperifa, poetas da periferia que se reúnem todas as quartas*. Dulcinéia Catadora/Eloísa Cartonera, 2007.
Rosa, Lúcia. Personal e-mail communication. 27 May 2015.
———. Personal interview. São Paulo, Brazil, 14 January 2013.
Rosa, Marcos. "Manuais para ação coletiva." *Soluções Providenciais*, Dulcinéia Catadora, 2013, pp. 81–86.
Rosetti, Dalia. *Durazno reverdeciente*. Eloísa Cartonera, 2003.
Rotker, Susana. *La invención de la crónica*. Letra Buena, 1992.
Rozza, Virginia "Vicky." "Los Sitios de Memoria, las prácticas pedagógicas y los libros prohibidos." Unpublished paper.
Ruchansky, Emilio. "Si no había recursos, se ponía ingenio." *Página 12*, 19 February 2013. www.pagina12.com.ar/diario/sociedad/3-214143-2013-02-19.html.
Sabato, Ernesto. *Cuatro hombres de pueblo*. Planeta, 2011.
Sáenz Quesada, María. "¿La cultura resiste?" *Reinventar la Argentina: Reflexiones sobre la crisis*, edited by Daniel A. Dessein, Sudamericana, 2003, pp. 145–147.
Said, Judith. *Espacios de Memoria en la Argentina*. Secretaría de Derechos Humanos, 2015. https://drive.google.com/file/d/0B2aU22zmzZagYlNMU1ifYnkocVk/view.
Saiz, Paloma, editor. *Para leer de boleto en el metro*, vol. 1. Fundación Cultural Metro, 2003.
———. Personal interview. Mexico City, 22 November 2015.
Saldarriaga, Milagros, and Tania Silva. Interview with Sarita Cartonera, by Lauren Pagel. Lima, Peru, June 2008. digital.library.wisc.edu/1711.dl/Arts.CartOH01.
Sánchez, Mery Yolanda. *El atajo: Novela*. Pontificia Universidad Javeriana, 2014.
Santiago en 100 palabras: Los mejores 100 cuentos I. Plagio, 2003.
Santiago en 100 palabras: Los mejores 100 cuentos II. Plagio, 2005.
Santiago en 100 palabras: Los mejores 100 cuentos III, edited by Alejandro Zambra and Ignacio Arnold, Plagio, 2007.
Santiago en 100 palabras: Los mejores 100 cuentos IV, edited by Ignacio Arnold and Carmen García, Plagio, 2009.

Santiago en 100 palabras: Los mejores 100 cuentos V, edited by Ignacio Arnold and Carmen García, Plagio, 2011.
Santiago en 100 palabras: Los mejores 100 cuentos VI, edited by Ignacio Arnold et al., Plagio, 2012.
Santiago en 100 palabras: Los mejores 100 cuentos VII, edited by Ignacio Arnold, Silvia Dümmer, and Carmen García, Plagio, 2013.
Santiago en 100 palabras: Los mejores 100 cuentos VIII. Plagio, 2014.
Santiago en 100 palabras: Los mejores 100 cuentos IX. Plagio, 2015.
Santiago en 100 palabras: Los mejores 100 cuentos X. Plagio, 2016.
Sarlo, Beatriz. *La imaginación técnica: sueños modernos de la cultura argentina*. Nueva Visión, 1992.
———. *El imperio de los sentimientos: Narraciones de circulación periódica en la Argentina, 1917–1927*. Siglo Veintiuno, 2011.
———. *Una modernidad periférica: Buenos Aires 1920 y 1930*. Nueva Visión, 1988.
Schmidt Quintero, Mariana, editor. *Retomo la palabra*. CERLALC, Alta Consejería para la Reintegración Social, 2009.
Schwartz, Jorge. *Vanguardia y cosmopolitismo en la década del veinte: Oliverio Girondo y Oswald de Andrade*. Beatriz Viterbo, 1993.
Schwartz, Marcy. "Beyond the Book: New Forms of Women's Writing." *Cambridge History of Latin American Women Writers*, edited by Monica Szurmuk and Ileana Rodríguez, Cambridge University Press, 2016, pp. 527–542.
———. *Invenciones urbanas: Ficción y ciudad latinoamericanas*. Corregidor, 2010.
———. "La literatura en el espacio público: un diálogo con Carlos Labbé." *Confluencia*, vol. 30, no. 2, 2015, pp. 168–178.
———. "The Right to Imagine: Reading in Community with People and Stories/Gente y Cuentos." *PMLA: Publications of the Modern Language Association of America*, vol. 126, no. 3, 2011, pp. 746–752.
———. "Spaces for Reading: A Cartography of Used Books in Urban Latin America." *Journal of Urban Cultural Studies*, vol. 1, no. 3, 2014, pp. 417–442.
———. *Writing Paris: Urban Topographies of Desire in Contemporary Latin American Fiction*. SUNY Press, 1999.
Scorer, James. *City in Common: Culture and Community in Buenos Aires*. SUNY Press, 2016.
Senn, Martha. "Bogotá, Capital Mundial del Libro 2007." *Ciudad Viva*, 7 July 2005, p. 2.
———. "Bogotá es un libro abierto." *Ciudad Viva*, 28 April 2007, p. 2.
Sevilla, Amparo. "El derecho al disfrute." *Reabrir espacios públicos: Políticas culturales y ciudadanía*, edited by Néstor García Canclini and Lourdes Arizpe S., Universidad Autónoma Metropolitana/Plaza y Valdés, 2004, pp. 189–202.
Sheridan, Dorothy, Brian V. Street, and David Bloome. *Writing Ourselves: Mass-Observation and Literacy Practices*. Hampton, 2000.
Silva, Armando. *Bogotá imaginada*. Convenio Andrés Bello/Universidad Nacional de Colombia/Taurus, 2003.

———. "Identidades urbanas en América Latina e identidades globales." Unpublished paper. www.contratiempohistoria.org/wp. . ./07/Ciudades-Imaginadas.doc.
Slater, Candace. *Stories on a String: The Brazilian Literatura de Cordel.* University of California Press, 1982.
Sommer, Doris. *The Work of Art in the World: Civic Agency and Public Humanities.* Duke University Press, 2014.
Sorensen, Diana. *Facundo and the Construction of Argentine Culture.* University of Texas Press, 1996.
Street, Brian V. *Social Literacies: Critical Approaches to Literacy in Development, Ethnography, and Education.* Longman, 1995.
Suescún, Nicolás, et al. *Un beso frío y otros cuentos bogotanos.* Instituto Distrital de Cultura y Turismo, 2005.
Sullawayta Cartonera. Facebook page. www.facebook.com/pg/Sullawayta.cartonera/about/?ref=page_internal.
Svampa, Maristella. *La sociedad excluyente: La Argentina bajo el signo del neoliberalismo.* Taurus, 2005.
Tamayo, Guido, editor. *B 39: Antología de cuento latinoamericano.* Ediciones B Colombia, 2007.
Tamayo Sánchez, Guido L. "Hay alguien en casa?" *Los que cuentan*, edited by Ana C. Mejía and Guillermo González Uribe, *Número*/Secretaría de Cultura, Recreación y Deporte, 2008, pp. 161–170.
Taylor, Diana. *The Archive and the Repertoire: Performing Cultural Memory in the Americas.* Duke University Press, 2003.
———. *Disappearing Acts: Spectacles of Gender and Nationalism in Argentina's "Dirty War."* Duke University Press, 1997.
Terranova, Juan. "La ciudad opaca." *La ciudad contada: Buenos Aires en la mirada de la nueva narrativa hispanoamericana*, edited by Maximiliano Tomas, Ministerio de Cultura del Gobierno de la Ciudad Autónoma de Buenos Aires, 2012, pp. 21–37.
Terron, Joca R. *Uma antologia bêbada: Fábulas da mercearia.* Dulcinéia Catadora, 2008.
Tinajero, Araceli. *El lector: A History of the Cigar Factory Reader.* University of Texas Press, 2010.
Tironi, Manuel. Untitled essay. *10 Años de Santiago en 100 Palabras (2001–2010)*, edited by Ignacio Arnold, Carmen García, and Sylvia Dümmer, Plagio, 2010, p. 32.
Toledo, Paulo de. *Concreróticos & outros versos.* Dulcinéia Catadora, 2012.
Tomas, Maximiliano, editor. *La ciudad contada: Buenos Aires en la mirada de la nueva narrativa hispanoamericana.* Ministerio de Cultura del Gobierno de la Ciudad Autónoma de Buenos Aires, 2012.
Tönnies, Ferdinand. *Community and Civil Society.* Translated by José Harris and Margaret Hollis, Cambridge University Press, 2001.
UNESCO. "The Pilot Public Library for Latin America in Medellin." 26 November 1954. unesdoc.unesco.org/images/0017/001794/179436eb.pdf.
Unruh, Vicky. "Unpacking the Libraries of Post-Soviet Cuba." *Revista de Estudios Hispánicos* 48, no. 2, June 2013, pp. 175–198.

Valderrama Pineda, Andrés. "How Do We Co-produce Urban Transport Systems and the City? The Case of Transmilenio and Bogotá." *Urban Assemblages: How Actor-Network Theory Changes Urban Studies*, edited by Ignacio Farías and Thomas Bender, Routledge, 2010, pp. 123–138.

Valenzuela, Luisa. "Libro que no muerde." *Cuentos completos y uno más*. Alfaguara, 2003, pp. 323–386.

Vallejo Mejía, Maryluz, editor. *Talleres de crónicas barriales: Antología*. Alcaldía de Bogotá/Archivo de Bogotá, 2007.

Vargas Luna, Jaime. Personal interview. Madison, Wisconsin, 26 March 2015.

———. "La rumba y el rumbo: Editoriales cartoneras y edición independiente en Latinoamérica." *Akademia Cartonera: A Primer of Latin American Cartonera Publishers = Un ABC de las editoriales cartoneras en América Latina*, edited by Ksenija Bilbija and Paloma Celis Carbajal, Parallel Press/ University of Wisconsin–Madison Libraries, 2009, pp. 111–129.

Vélez, Jean-Paul. "Third Millennium Modernity: TransMilenio and the Project for a New Bogotá." 2007. Master's thesis, University of California–Berkeley.

———. "Transit and Spatial Battles in Bogotá: Citizenship in the Face of Progress." Panel presentation, Latin American Studies Association XXVIII International Congress, 5–8 September 2007, Montreal, Canada.

Vila, Adrián. "¿Qué es una editorial cartonera?," *Libre Digital*, 21 August 2015. llibredigital.blogs.uoc.edu/es/que-cosa-es-una-editorial-cartonera/.

Walsh, Rodolfo. *Operación massacre*. Ediciones de la Flor, 1972.

Warner, Michael. *Publics and Counterpublics*. Zone Books, 2002.

Weil P, Andrés, et al. "La planificación urbana y el Transantiago." *CA: Revista Oficial del Colegio de Arquitectos de Chile*, no. 131, 2007, pp. 18–20.

Weintraub, Jeff A. "The Theory and Politics of the Public/Private Distinction." *Public and Private in Thought and Practice: Perspectives on a Grand Dichotomy*, edited by Jeff A. Weintraub and Krishan Kumar, University of Chicago Press, 1997, pp. 1–42.

Williams, Raymond. *The Country and the City*. Oxford University Press, 1973.

Wolfe, Alan. "Public and Private in Theory and Practice: Some Implications of an Uncertain Boundary." *Public and Private in Thought and Practice: Perspectives on a Grand Dichotomy*, edited by Jeff A. Weintraub and Krishan Kumar, University of Chicago Press, 1997, pp. 182–203.

Wolfson, Gabriel. "Dos o tres caminos—entre otros posibles—para entrar y salir de Alias." *Galleta China*, vol. 2, no. 6, 2011, pp. 20–24.

Wood, Alejandra. Untitled essay. *10 Años de Santiago en 100 Palabras (2001–2010)*, edited by Ignacio Arnold, Carmen García, and Sylvia Dümmer, Plagio, 2010, p. 104.

Wortman, Ana, editor. *Entre la política y la gestión de la cultura y el arte: Nuevos actores en la Argentina contemporánea*. Eudeba, 2009.

Yushimito del Valle, Carlos. "N.N." *Bogotá contada*, edited by Antonio García Ángel, IDARTES/Libro al Viento, 2013, pp. 16–29.

———. "Los elefantes de Holmberg." *La ciudad contada: Buenos Aires en la mirada de la nueva narrativa hispanoamericana*, edited by Maximiliano

Tomas, Ministerio de Cultura del Gobierno de la Ciudad Autónoma de Buenos Aires, 2012, pp. 59–74.
Zaid, Gariel. *Leer*. Ocean, 2012.
Zanetti, Susana. *Leer en América Latina*. El Otro, El Mismo, 2004.
Zapata López, Fernando. *Las Ferias del Libro: Manual para expositores y visitantes profesionales*. CERLALC/UNESCO, 2012.

Argentine Newsletters Consulted for Chapter 3 (from Buenos Aires unless other city indicated)

Latin American Ephemera Collection, section "Socio economic crisis and political participation in Argentina I, 1995–2005," Princeton University Library

Aguante Palermo Viejo (Asamblea Vecinal Plaza Palermo Viejo)
Alameda (Asamblea Parque Avellaneda)
Almagro en Asamblea (Asamblea de Almagro)
Asambleas: Periódico Mensual de la Asamblea Popular de Liniers
Boletín Asamblea Caballito Gastón Riva
Boletín Asamblea de la Plaza Estación Coghlan
Boletín Asamblea de Vecinos Autoconvocados de Villa Urquiza
Boletín Asamblea Popular Belgrano-Nuñez
Boletín Asamblea Popular Boedo y San Cristóbal (La Plata)
Boletín Asamblea Popular Cid Campeador
Boletín Asamblea Popular de Caballito Parque Rivadavia
Boletín de la Asamblea Barrio Hipódromo (La Plata)
Boletín de la Asamblea Plaza 10 de Mayo, Balvanera
Boletín de la Asamblea Popular Florida Puente Saavedra
Boletín de la Asamblea Vecinos de Constitución
La Cacerola (Vecinos Autoconvocados de Córdoba y M. Bravo)
La Cacerola de Cornelio (Parque Saavedra, La Plata)
La Cacerola de Zapiola (Colegiales)
La Cacerola Parlanchina (Asamblea Vecinal de Agronomía-Parque Chas-Villa Ortuzar)
Carta abierta (Asamblea Vecinal de Boedo)
Claraboya (Biblioteca Popular Cornelio Saavedra)
Congreso (Asamblea Popular de Ayacucho y Rivadavia)
El Fortín (Asamblea Popular de San Andrés Norte)
En la Plaza (Asamblea de Vecinos Autoconvocados de Villa del Parque)
Plaza Tomada
Prensa Asamblea Popular Villa Pueyrredón
"Proyecto de Ley de Comunas de Participación Directa" (Project for the Neighborhood Law of Direct Participation)
Proyecto Mono del Sur (Associatión Vecinos Autoconvocados de Barracas)
El Puente: Encontrando Palabras (Parque Lezama Sur)

Index

Abbate, Florencia, 122–124, 140, 145, 250n1
Acosta, Abraham, 239–140n4
Acree, William, 8
Alarcón, Daniel, 243n10, 254n15
Álvarez Zapata, Didier, 12, 20
Amapola Cartonera. *See under* cartonera publishers
Anderson, Benedict, 26, 45
Archivo Provincial de la Memoria, 35, 193–202, 195f, 197f, 199f, 224–225, 224f, 226, 231
Argüelles, Juan Domingo, 14, 16–17, 36
Aylwin, Patricio, 89

Bachelet, Michelle, 90, 234
Barilaro, Javier, 127, 154
Bartra, Roger, 25, 29, 30
Berni, Antonio, 227, 228, 237
Betancourt Pulecio, Ingrid, 50
Biblioteca de José Vasconcelos, 10, 13, 18
Biblioteca de Santiago, 15–16, 31, 150, 240–241n12
Biblioteca Luis Ángel Arango, 15, 49–51
Bilbija, Ksenija, 154, 160–161, 164, 193, 196, 203, 208, 253n5, 260n24
Bishop, Karen, 198, 225
Bogotá, Colombia, 1, 12–13, 15, 20–21, 28, 37, 39, 41, 77, 81–83, 86–92, 94–96, 98–102, 105, 121, 181–186, 229–230, 232–234, 240n10; as World Book Capital, 46–64, 47f, 54f, 62f, 63f
book fairs, 18–21, 37, 48, 66–68, 67f, 79–82, 191, 209, 231
Borges, Jorge Luis, 39, 64, 69, 72, 75–76, 115, 209
Borja, Jordi, 25, 104–105
Brodsky, Marcelo, 191–192, 192f, 225f, 226
Brukman Factory, 134f, 135
Buenos Aires, Argentina, 9, 12, 19–20, 24–25, 38–39, 40f, 41, 45–46, 121, 123–124, 127–130, 133, 136–137, 141, 146, 150–154, 159–162, 174, 176, 191, 193–194, 196, 202, 209, 211, 221, 223, 228, 230, 242n23, 242nn1–2 (chap. 1), 251n4, 251n7, 251n10; as World Book Capital, 64–83, 68–69f, 71f, 246n4

cacerolazos, 34, 122–123, 125, 125f, 128, 142, 144, 146–147
Cala Buendía, Felipe, 28, 86, 92, 163, 177
Calhoun, Craig, 26, 28
Cárcamo-Huechante, Luis, 32, 119
cartonera publishers: Amapola Cartonera, 35, 152, 155, 179, 181–188, 182f, 183f, 186f; Animita Cartonera, 160–161, 254n13;

cartonera publishers (*continued*)
Dulcinéia Catadora, 35, 152–153, 156–157, 156–157f, 161, 164–173, 167f, 169f, 179–181, 186–187, 189; Eloísa Cartonera, 24, 127, 151–156, 151– 152f, 156f, 159–165, 160f, 165f, 174–178, 175–176f, 186–187; La Propia Cartonera, 158, 161; La Sofia Cartonera, 231–232; Magnolia Cartonera, 232; Quinti Qartunira, 22, 163; Sarita Cartonera, 35, 152, 160–163, 187–188; Yerba Mala Cartonera, 230, 253n17
Casanova, Pascale, 65, 82, 239n3, 245nn23–24
Celis Carbajal, Paloma, 154, 160–161
Centro Latinoamericano de Economia Humana (CLAEH), 43, 45
Centro Regional del Libro en America Latina y el Caribe (CERLALC), 12, 17, 18–20, 94, 120
CERLALC. *See* Centro Regional del Libro en America Latina y el Caribe
Cerruti, Isabel, 204, 206, 208–210, 222, 230
Certeau, Michel de, 29–31, 93, 114, 214
Chartier, Roger, 236
CLACSO. *See* Consejo Latinoamericano de Ciencias Sociales
CLAEH. *See* Centro Latinoamericano de Economia Humana
Comisión Nacional de Bibliotecas Populares (CONABIP), 15, 135–136
CONABIP. *See* Comisión Nacional de Bibliotecas Populares
Consejo Latinoamericano de Ciencias Sociales (CLACSO), 25
cordel literature, 10–11, 11f
Cortázar, Julio, 61, 70, 75–76, 96, 114–115, 179, 226
crónicas, 49, 51–52, 75, 77–78, 99–100, 110

Cuban book fair, 19–20; and literacy campaign, 21–22
Cucurto, Washington, 127, 154, 159, 174, 176–178, 186–190, 253n6, 256n26, 256nn29–31
Cultura Ciudadana, 28, 92
cultural management (gestión cultural), 13, 30, 33, 42–45, 232–233

Darrigrandi, Claudia, 2–3
Degiovanni, Fernando, 288
Delgado, Josefina, 66, 68, 71, 77, 80–81
dictatorship: in Argentina, 12, 29, 35, 122, 129–130, 191–194, 196, 200, 202, 206, 209, 211, 218–219, 230, 235; in Chile, 16, 86–87, 89, 93, 119. *See also* postdictatorship
Draper, Susana, 206, 208, 223
Dulcinéia Catadora. *See under* cartonera publishers

Eloísa Cartonera. *See under* cartonera publishers
Epplin, Craig, 154, 158, 160, 174, 178
Escuela Superior de Mecánica Armada (ESMA), 198, 258n9
ESMA. *See* Escuela Superior de Mecánica Armada
Esmois, Manuel, 44–45

favelas, 170, 172
Feinman, José Pablo, 140
Freire, Paolo, 59, 244n19
Fuguet, Alberto, 32, 105

Galeano, Eduardo, 132, 141, 152n18
García Ángel, Antonio, 75–76, 101, 230
García Canclini, Néstor, 25, 27, 43–44
García Márquez, Gabriel, 49, 76, 96
Garzón, Luis Eduardo, 46, 48, 94, 101
Gente y Cuentos. *See* People and Stories/Gente y Cuentos

Girondo, Oliverio, 70–72, 76, 84–85, 246nn2–3, 249n2
González Uribe, Guillermo, 56
Gordon-Burroughs, Jessica, 89
Gorelik, Adrián, 127
Greene F., Ricardo, 109, 249n31
Grieta, La, 35, 193, 211–221, 223, 225–226, 234–236, 259–260n19, 260n20. *See also* Libros que Muerden
Griffin, Jane, 107, 117, 249n29

Habermas, Jürgen, 26–29
Hardt, Michael, and Antonio Negri, 229, 233, 236, 260n2
Harvey, David, 7, 30
Havana, Cuba, 19
Heffes, Gisela, 154–155, 168
Henkin, David, 4
Hernández, Paola, 206, 223, 258n8

Instituto Espacio para la Memoria, 196, 203, 209, 258n7, 259n13

Jelin, Elizabeth, 196

Kirchner, Néstor and Cristina Fernández de, 46, 65–66, 146, 208, 234, 243n4, 259n14

Labbé, Carlos, 93, 108–109, 247n14, 250n33
Lago, Ricardo, 89–91
Laguna, Fernanda, 154. *See also* Rosetti, Dalia
Langland, Victoria, 196
Lefebvre, Henri, 29
lettered city, the, 2, 7, 13, 26, 33, 41–42, 46, 53, 64, 76, 82, 88, 121, 229, 233
libraries, 5, 9, 12–17, 21, 33, 39, 48, 53, 59, 62, 66, 104, 121–122, 135–136, 139–140, 146, 222, 225, 235, 237, 258n9; of banned books, 192–194, 226, 258n9
Libro al Viento, 1, 33–34, 46, 50, 62, 83, 85, 87, 93, 94–105, 95f, 97f,

103f, 119–120, 229–230, 237, 248n18
Libros que Muerden, 210–211, 213–215, 217–220, 217f, 220f, 226
literacy campaigns, 2, 9, 21–22, 33, 42–46, 76, 81–82, 121
Lombardi, Hernán, 64, 70, 73

Macri, Mauricio, 46, 64, 66, 69, 208–209, 234, 259n14
Martinell, Alfons, 42, 233
Masiello, Francine, 32, 184, 187
Medellín, Colombia, 5, 15, 247–248n16
Melicchio, Pablo, 77–80
memory centers, 1, 28, 35, 193, 196–210, 195f, 197f, 199f, 204f, 205f, 207f, 210f, 223, 226, 229, 232, 257–258n6, 258n7
Metrobus (Buenos Aires), 70, 85, 88
Mexico City, Mexico, 9, 10f, 13, 16, 20, 25, 44, 85, 88, 94, 242n23, 246n1, 247n6, 247n15, 248n18, 249n26, 250n40, 253–254n11
Minera Escondida, 105, 107, 118
Minujín, Marta, 39, 40f, 64, 68, 257n2
Mires Ortiz, Alfredo, 22–23
Mockus, Antanas, 28, 90, 92
Morena Rojas, Samuel, 46, 48
Mothers of the Plaza de Mayo, 130f, 224, 260n25
murals, 5–6, 55, 128–130, 176, 194–195, 201, 203, 237
Museo del Libro y de la Lengua, 194, 195f

Nel Gómez, Pedro, 4–5, 6f
neoliberalism, 2, 19, 24, 28, 31, 32, 36, 42, 85–87, 92, 107, 119, 124, 125, 127, 135, 161, 177, 233–234
New Literacy Studies, 3, 96, 239n4

Olimpo Center, 35, 193–194, 196, 198, 202–210, 204f, 205f, 207f, 210f, 218, 222–223, 225–226, 230, 258n7, 259nn11–13
Ossa, Carlos, 31, 37

Paraderos Paralibros Paraparques, 51, 243n12
Para Leer de Boleto en el Metro, 94, 249n26
Paredes Castro, Julio, 96–99, 104–105
Parrochia Beguin, Juan, 89, 247n10
Payne, Leigh, 193, 196, 203, 208, 253n5, 260n24
Peñalosa, Enrique, 90–92, 234
People and Stories/Gente y Cuentos, 23, 59–60, 60f, 77, 244nn16–17, 244n20
Pesclevi, Gabriela, 212–216, 219–221, 226–227, 234–236, 259–260n19, 260n1 (concl.)
Petit, Michele, 227, 238, 261n3
Pinochet, Augusto, 86–90, 92
Plagio, 105–107, 118
Poblete, Juan, 8, 239n2, 240n8
postdictatorship, 32, 43, 87, 200, 212, 247n10, 247n14. *See also* dictatorship

Quiroga, José, 19, 241n16, 241n19

Rama, Ángel, 7, 26–27, 240n6
Retomo la Palabra, 23
Reyes, Alfonso, 38, 242n26
Richard, Nelly, 31, 37, 192, 200
River Plate, 9, 177
Roda Fornaguera, Ana, 46, 55, 94, 96–97, 104, 248n17
Rosa, Lúcia, 156f, 164–168, 170, 173
Rosa, Marcos, 173
Rosetti, Dalia, 253n. *See also* Laguna, Fernanda
Rozza, Virginia, 201–202, 224, 159n10

Sábato, Ernesto, 70, 76
Sáiz, Paloma, 20, 241n17
Sánchez, Mery Yolanda, 21
Santiago, Chile, 19, 33–34, 62, 85, 86, 88–92, 108, 110, 116, 118–121, 160
Santiago en 100 Palabras, 1, 28, 33–34, 37–38, 84–85, 87, 93, 105–121, 105–106f

São Paulo, Brazil, 11, 150, 164–166, 179, 187
Sarita Cartonera. *See under* cartonera publishers
Sarmiento, Domingo Faustino, 9, 15, 135
Schwartz, Jorge, 84–85
Schwartz, Marcy, 13, 246n32, 250n35, 254n15, 260n23
Scorer, James, 127, 168, 251n4, 254n19, 254n21
Senn, Martha, 39, 47–48, 62, 63
Street, Brian, 3

Téllez, Armando Silva, 31, 37
Tönnies, Ferdinand, 25
Transantiago (Santiago), 34, 88, 90–93, 107, 112, 247n12
TransMilenio (Bogotá), 34, 49, 57, 62, 63, 88–92, 94–95, 97, 98, 100, 102, 104, 247nn6–7, 247n9

UNESCO (United Nations Educational Scientific and Cultural Organization), 1, 5, 16, 20, 39, 41, 45, 47–48, 53, 62, 64–67, 81–82, 95, 242n2, 250n41
Uribe, Álvaro, 25, 45–46

Valenzuela, Luisa, 140, 252n17
Vargas Luna, Jaime, 158, 162, 188, 190
Vasconcelos, José, 9
Vélez, Jean-Paul, 91, 247n9
Viu, Antonia, 2–3

Warner, Michael, 27, 30–31, 242n25
Weintraub, Jeff, 27, 42
Williams, Raymond, 44
Wolfe, Alan, 27–28
World Book Capitals, 1, 20, 39, 41–55, 64–76, 80–83, 96, 230, 232–233, 242n2, 246n4. *See also* Bogotá; Buenos Aires

Zaid, Gabriel, 229
Zanetti, Susana, 4, 265n32

www.ingramcontent.com/pod-product-compliance
Lightning Source LLC
Jackson TN
JSHW020314120426
100741JS00003B/17